The Ethnic Handbook

A Guide to the Cultures and Traditions of Chicago's Diverse Communities

Edited by Cynthia Linton

An Illinois Ethnic Coalition Publication

ISBN 0-9658445-0-1 (An Illinois Ethnic Coalition Publication)
Library of Congress Catalog Card Number: 96-079780

Published by
The Illinois Ethnic Coalition
55 East Monroe Street, Suite 2930
Chicago, IL 60603
(312) 368-1155

Printed by
The Business Press
Schiller Park, Illinois

Other publications available from the Illinois Ethnic Coalition:
    The Directory of Chicago Ethnic Organizations
    The Guide to Ethnic Media for Chicago

Table of Contents

Foreword

About two years ago, the Illinois Ethnic Coalition decided to create an Ethnic Handbook, to further our mission of improving intergroup cooperation and understanding across racial and ethnic lines. With a 26-year history, IEC had gained a unique appreciation of the city's ethnic landscape and we wanted to share our experience with the public. The dozens of inquiries IEC was receiving each month revealed a hunger for such information.

IEC did not produce the Ethnic Handbook to focus on differences, although we think it is important to understand them. We were more interested in exploring the histories and attitudes that shape how Chicagoans view themselves in terms of ethnicity and race, two of the most vexing issues we face as a society.

This book was a collaboration in the truest sense. We could not and did not do it alone. Dozens of the city's most respected scholars and ethnic experts were asked to write ethnic community profiles. We especially sought authors for those groups with significant numbers, that had an ethnic presence in the city and were not yet completely assimilated. Despite hectic schedules, scholars and community leaders agreed that this kind of resource was a timely and necessary project. With their help, we ultimately profiled 33 ethnic groups, about one-third of the total represented in the Chicago area.

Although the pages share a common format, we wanted to let each author's distinct voice shine through. What we're sharing is the personalized accounts of the histories and traditions of the ethnic groups. For readers who want to continue the learning process, the authors have helped us provide a reading list at the end of the book.

The abundant facts and figures in the Handbook are complemented by personal essays written by nine Chicagoans of various ethnic backgrounds — people who could tell us why ethnic and racial identity mean something to them. Their stories put a human face on the data.

Cynthia Linton, our project director and chief editor, coordinated and saw the Handbook through from start to finish. As the former executive editor of Lerner Newspapers and now an adjunct professor at Northwestern University's Medill School of Journalism, she has a keen sense of how to interpret often complex information to a broad audience. She convinced us to keep the book simple and easy to use. Her vision, skill and professionalism held this project together and kept it moving.

For underwriting support we turned to AT&T. Recognized as a corporate leader in the global economy and in promoting a diverse workplace, the organization did not disappoint us. Without AT&T's generous help, the book might still be in the idea stage. Additional funding followed.

IEC did not intend to publish the definitive analysis of ethnicity, an academic treatise, or a "how to" on diversity. Quite simply, we wanted to put out a useful resource that would also be a catalyst to broaden understanding. With eyes on the past, present and future, we invite you to join us in our efforts to improve Chicago's intergroup climate as we approach the new century just ahead.

The Illinois Ethnic Coalition
December, 1996

Marcia Lazar, President
Joseph McCord, Executive Vice President
Ross Masao Harano, Immediate Past President

Officers:
Jae Choi, Alexander Domanskis,
Louise Año Nuevo Kerr, Christine Przybyla Long

In loving memory of David G. Roth, whose spirit lives on in these pages

Acknowledgments

The Illinois Ethnic Coalition is especially grateful to AT&T for providing the initial, and majority, funding for this project. Their recognition of the need for such a book and, in particular, Alison Pikus' and Dorothy Foster's enthusiastic support enabled IEC to get this long-planned project off the ground. Additional funding came from the Polk Brothers Foundation, Playboy Foundation and City of Chicago Department of Cultural Affairs. We sincerely thank them all.

The Handbook, of course, would not have been possible without the hard work of the ethnic scholars and experts who shared their considerable knowledge with us by writing the 33 chapters of the book. They all put in many conscientious hours of research and writing. Because of them, each section of this book is packed with valuable, insightful information that only an expert with an inside view could have provided. And the essayists who shared their deep feelings about their ethnicity added a personal touch to enrich this publication.

For the maps, we thank Phillip Beverly, a doctoral candidate at the University of Illinois at Chicago and assistant professor at Chicago State University. He was generously assisted on the city maps by Michelle Rymes, director of research, and Duane Davy, both at the City of Chicago Department of Planning and Development; and on the Cook County maps, by Peter Haas at the Center for Neighborhood Technology. Charlene Ceci of Northern Illinois University's Center for Governmental Studies analyzed Census figures to give us what demographic information was available for our ethnic groups in the six-county area. Rakhi Chaudhuri, a student intern from Northwestern's Medill School of Journalism, contributed research and editing. Jessica Lazar, another Medill student, helped with the initial work of finding the scholars, and we thank Medill for her time. Members of the IEC board of directors who read the individual chapters offered many valuable suggestions, as did a number of other scholars and friends. The Chicago Chapter of the American Jewish Committee offered much in-kind support. Our thanks to Paul Woolner of Flair Communications Agency for his technical rescue. Finally, *muchas gracias* to Matthew Holzman, art production manager at Flair, for supervising design and layout of the book.

Introduction
by Jeryl Levin

"A large pot constructed out of wood and crepe paper stood in the center of the auditorium stage and the graduates entered the "Melting Pot" decked out in the apparel of the old country and came out the other side dressed resplendently in identical American clothes..."[1]

This graduation ritual was common in some public schools 60 or 70 years ago. Today's younger people growing up in the age of multiculturalism may find this ceremony — and the melting pot ideology it symbolizes — absurd and demeaning. Others may see it as symbolizing a more secure and confident past, a time when commonality and not difference was celebrated. When we knew what it meant to be "American."

Demographers report that by the year 2020, the United States will be the most broadly multicultural nation on the planet. There will be no dominant majority. (Chicago is already like that.) News of this demographic shift regularly makes newspaper headlines. Powerful stuff, it is greeted either with alarm by those who envision us becoming a nation of ethnic tribes, or with a sense of relief by those Americans who sense they have always been seen as outsiders in a "white" nation.

Every wave of immigration brings people different from the ones already here. Yesterday's Europeans: the Irish, Italians, Greeks, Jews, Poles and so on, were not always considered homogenous white folks. Many of them were once thought to be "unassimilable," like the Africans who were brought here in chains, the Native peoples already on this land, and those repatriated and excluded from citizenship. Intermarriage between ethnic and racial groups was shunned or outright forbidden. Over time, the notion of who belonged would gradually expand somewhat to accommodate the reality of who was actually here ... and it continues to expand, as we wrestle with defining who "we" are as a nation.

There is, I think, an ideological war and a good deal of confusion going on as the United States confronts its ethnic and racial diversity. On one side of the debate sit those who seem genuinely afraid that the nation is going to hell in a handbasket; that "minorities" are taking over and rewriting a sancrosanct history that, for the most part, has always had white men as its heroes. On the other side sit the ardent multiculturalists, those who see America as a country divided between "white male" oppressors and beleaguered "people of color" and women. These extremes react to each other in the public and academic realms, and the media react to them.

The majority of us, however, are someplace in the middle, trying to figure this whole thing out. We are aware in varying degrees that ethnicity has been and still is a necessary organizing principle of American life and that, like it or not, ethnicity and race do mean something here. If they were insignificant, we could banish the racial classifications of the Census tomorrow. At the same time, many of us are also smart enough to know that ethnocentrism does not bode well for the future of any country.

Is assimilation a good thing, and if it is, into what should we assimilate? Is a nation of hyphenated Americans in danger of becoming a nation of hostile tribes?

I suppose the answer in large part depends on whether you see the glass half-empty or half-full. I think something very important and essential to understanding American life is reflected in the hyphens. I know many people who think of themselves as 100% American, but want to add an adjective before the noun because it more fully explains who they are. They do not see the hyphens as a sign of tribalism but as an affirmation of a shared identity, a punctuation that complements and connects rather than negates and separates. The hyphens represent the myriad stories encompassed in the American experience.

They reflect the reality that while we are all Americans, there are among us important differences in how we got here, how others see us, and the obstacles endured and overcome. There is also disagreement about who is entitled to tell the story and determine its heroes. Every nation has to have its narrative and someone's got to write it. I think we are watching it expand — perhaps too quickly for some and not fast enough for others.

As for "ethnocentrism," I have learned that most ethnic groups did not develop nic awareness" or "ethnic pride" in a vacuum; rather the nativism, bigotry or outright racism they encountered fostered a heightened sense of ethnic identity and self-protection. I recall reading one study of early immigrants, which remarked that allegiance to one's homeland was far more pronounced once the immigrants had come here than it was back home.

Even if all ethnic groups desired to walk through that magic door, which promises to conform them, their distinctiveness would be perpetuated by a society that, despite its color-blind creed, has a history of closing the door when confronted by ethnic, racial or religious "others." The story of the American experience is as much about trying to keep the "other" out as it is about accommodation and acceptance.

For many Americans, it is important — even critical — to remember the legacy of the struggles and aspirations of their people; to retain pieces of their unique histories in a country whose most potent metaphor is the melting pot. The stories of those who have yet to "melt" provide the impetus for this Handbook and the basis of our work. After generations in the mainstream, many hold onto and celebrate pieces of their heritage.

As we enter the new millenium, we hope the Illinois Ethnic Coalition's **Ethnic Handbook: A Guide to the Cultures and Traditions of Chicago's Diverse Communities** will help expand and enrich who we are as a city and a nation.

We hope that educators will use the material in this book to widen their students' understanding of Chicago's diversity; that journalists will use it as a resource to better cover communities that constitute their "beats" and their audience; that foundations, given a mandate to ensure diversity in their grantmaking, will see the broad range of groups far more complex than the conventional racial classifications. And we hope that as corporate America moves toward the truly global economy and enjoys a more diverse workforce than ever before, it will find our information a valuable asset in that journey.

Jeryl Levin is Executive Director of the Illinois Ethnic Coalition.

[1] See Krickus, Richard. *Pursuing the American Dream: White Ethnics and the New Populism*, NY: Doubleday, 1975

Editor's Note

This book contains both 1990 Census and ethnic community population estimates. There usually is considerable divergence between the two and neither is completly reliable. The true figure is probably somewhere in between.

The 1990 Census is seven years old and it relied on people filling out forms, something many new immigrants did not do. One Ethiopian American told us he was the only person he knew who filled out a form. There is an officially acknowledged undercount of Hispanics and African Americans in Chicago and many agree Asian Americans are undercounted too.

For many groups that have been here several generations, the numbers depend on whether people indicated ancestry on the Census form.

Because Census figures are the only hard numbers we have, we've made good use of them. Based on Census tract data, we have provided Chicago maps, with the neighborhoods numbered (see key in Appendix 1), and Cook County maps. These will help readers see the population distribution for each group. The maps show single or first ancestry, but not second reported ancestry.

Some ethnicities are not broken out by Census tract, however, so for eight groups we do not have maps and must rely on community estimates and anecdotal information.

For purposes of this book, the metropolitan area covers six counties (Cook, Lake, DuPage, Kane, Will and McHenry) and includes the city of Chicago in the Cook County number.

C.C.L.

African Americans

City population:
1,076,099 (1990 Census)
1,200,000 (1996 community estimate)

Metro area population:
1,408,048 (1990 Census)
1,500,000 (1996 community estimate)

Foreign-born:
About 1.3% in city and 1.5% for metro

Note: These figures do not include people who checked both black and Hispanic on the Census form.

Demographics:

In Chicago African Americans make up about 40% of the population. Most are concentrated on the South Side, from 26th Street to 131st Street and from Ashland Avenue to Lake Michigan; on the West Side from Garfield Park to the city limits, between Lake Street and Cermak Road; and in a relatively compact settlement on the near North Side, west of Halsted and south of Division Street. These three areas are contiguous and form the condition that caused population experts to call Chicago "the most racially segregated city in the United States." In these areas there is a considerable amount of education and affluence and a tremendous amount of poverty. There are African Americans, Africans and Afro-Caribbeans throughout the city, including the far North Side, but an estimated 90-95% live in these three areas. No other ancestry group is so segregated. African Americans also are found in growing numbers in many south, west and southwest suburbs, such as Maywood, Oak Park, Harvey, Dolton, Country Club Hills, Flossmoor, Olympia Fields, Robbins and Ford Heights, and in north suburban Evanston and North Chicago. Early moves to the suburbs in most cases were met with stiff resistance. That is no longer true.

According to the 1990 Census, the median household income of metro-area African Americans is about $23,000. For Chicago, it is $19,500. In the city some 122,000 own their homes. Nearly 63% of those over the age of 25 have a high school diploma and 37% have at least some college, with 10% getting a bachelor's degree or higher. About 20% of those in the labor force are in professional or managerial positions. One-third of African Americans in Chicago live at or below the poverty line. Many of that segment are children under 18 in single-parent households. An estimated 5% of African Americans nationwide are in interracial marriages, with the percent growing and about twice as many men as women marrying people of other races.

Historical background:

The first permanent settler in Chicago was a black man from Haiti by the name of Jean-Baptiste Pointe DuSable, who was a trader here in 1774. He later moved, but blacks have lived in the area since that time and have formed a small but important part of the population since 1840.

One-third of African Americans in Chicago live at or below the poverty line.

Migrants came from the South for basically the same reason millions left Europe before WWI: better economic conditions.

Most of the movement is to the suburbs, because of the relaxation of housing restrictions, better schools, safer streets and the growth of suburban jobs.

The African American family was undermined in large part by the abandonment of the inner city and disappearance of unskilled and semi-skilled jobs since the '60s.

• The first Great Migration had its strongest momentum during and immediately after WWI, with the population growing from 44,000 in 1910 to 277,000 by 1940. Migrants came from the South for basically the same reason millions left Europe before WWI: better economic conditions. Many saw opportunities, including an adequate education, denied them in the South. They also left because of the Jim Crow system of discrimination, fleeing political and economic repression and physical terrorism. What they found in Chicago was less than they hoped for but better than they left. They found racial prejudice, segregation, and discrimination in housing, jobs and social conditions; but they also found political freedom and economic opportunities they never dreamed of in the South, and took full advantage of both. The sudden mass arrival of African Americans created new tensions and problems for the old residents and recently arrived immigrants from Europe. The competition for jobs, housing and recreation space intensified. It was during that time that the Chicago race riot of 1919 broke out, when whites at the 35th Street Beach stoned black swimmers because they had crossed an imaginary line. The riots lasted four days, leaving 38 dead, 520 injured and thousands of homes damaged.

Blacks were confined to the "Black Belt," stretching from 26th Street to 47th Street and from the Rock Island Railroad tracks to Cottage Grove Avenue, concentrated at 81,000 per square mile compared with 19,000 for the rest of the city. Their work generally was in menial jobs in the Stockyards, where they could make 10 times what they had made picking cotton, and in the steel mills of South Chicago, International Harvester and small businesses inside the Black Belt. Later that area was to take on the names of "Bronzeville" and "Black Metropolis." Bronzeville was a self-supporting community, distinguished by notable accomplishments in both business and politics. Thriving businesses included Robert S. Abbott's *Chicago Defender,* Jesse Binga's first state-chartered African American bank in the U.S. and Anthony Overton's cosmetics business. By the mid-1920s, Chicago was the black business capital of the country. In politics, three congressmen — Oscar DePriest, Arthur Mitchell and William Dawson — were elected before Harlem ever elected Adam Clayton Powell. There was fun, friendship and joyful noise all over the ghettos of the South and West Sides. But it was much too crowded for human health, so there was pressure to move beyond its confines and constant, sometimes violent, resistance from those on the outside who wanted to confine this population.

• The second Great Migration came with the U.S. entry into WWII. Hundreds of thousands of blacks and poor whites left the cotton and tobacco fields of the South for better-paying jobs in the war industry. Chicago's black population skyrocketed to near one-half million in 1950. A Chicago Renaissance occurred on the South Side from about 1945-60 that included the South Side Community Arts Center, the writings of people like Margaret Walker, Margaret Burroughs and Gwendolyn Brooks, gospel music and urban blues, the Johnson Publishing empire, and the founding of DuSable Museum.

• Starting in the 1970s, schools began to deteriorate, tension increased and white flight to the suburbs accelerated. Industry and business left the city, claiming they needed more trained, disciplined, skilled workers. The result for Chicago in the final decades of the 20th century was an erosion of both the industrial base and the middle-class population, leaving an increasingly unskilled, poor black and Hispanic population to forage for themselves. The increase in disappointment, frustration, anger, poverty, violence and crime seemed to be the natural outcome of these historical economic, social and cultural changes.

Current migration patterns:

The migration from the South has all but stopped. The reason is economic — the vast industrial base that once attracted migrants to Chicago no longer exists. Relatively few African Americans are returning to the South, mainly retirees. Most of the movement is to the suburbs, because of relaxed housing restrictions, better schools, safer streets and growth of suburban jobs.

Religion:

Most are Christians of various denominations, such as Episcopal and Methodist or a combination of the two (African Methodist Episcopal, Christian Methodist Episcopal, AME Zion), and also Baptist, Lutheran and Catholic, as well as increasing numbers of Pentecostals and Jehovah's Wtinesses. There also are growing numbers of traditional Muslims, in addition to those in the Nation of Islam. Churches have played a major role in African American issues, from the vigilance committees of the 1850s that protected runaway slaves to the religious groups that spearheaded the Civil Rights Movement. Many churches have provided food, housing, health care and other social services to the community.

Important traditions:

Religion and extended family are traditionally very important among African Americans. Births and deaths are celebrated, expressing a reverence for life. New babies are cherished, and at funerals friends and family celebrate the life of those who have passed on. For the substantial number in the middle class, there tend to be stable two-parent families who pass along to their children traditions of religion, education, honesty, fidelity and careful spending habits. But for many others, a lack of job opportunities and poverty have had a devastating effect on the African American community and the family. Marriage, in contrast to the past, is at a low ebb. For those who do marry, separation and divorce are frequent, and one-parent families are the norm (also a growing trend in the population at large). Teen pregnancies are high, in part because abortion is not acceptable. For large areas of the city, the infusion of drugs and guns in disproportionate amounts have created an aura of insecurity and instability to all the institutions and traditions of a formerly stable community. In the early days, the entire African American community was like a family. That community support has deteriorated. The relationship between family and economics is strong. The African American family was undermined in large part by the abandonment of the inner city and disappearance of unskilled and semi-skilled jobs since the '60s. Conditions today make it difficult for many families to pass down traditional values to their children.

Holidays and special events:

Birthdays, Easter, Thanksgiving, Mother's Day, Christmas and now **Kwaanza** are important times for celebration. Kwaanza, the festival of the harvest (of life) is the coming together of the community to celebrate life and enjoy the fruits of life. A new holiday, Kwaanza is born out of the African tradition and occurs around the same time as Christmas and Chanukah, but is not a religious holiday. **Dr. Martin Luther King Jr.'s Birthday** (Jan. 15) is celebrated with special programs and at City Hall. It is a state and school holiday (celebrated on the closest Monday). **Black History Month** (February) is also an occasion when schools, churches and other institutions plan special programming. **Juneteenth** (in June) marks the signing of the Emancipation Proclamation. And the traditional **Bud Billiken Parade** (second Saturday in August), celebrates the mythical figure who protects children. It was started by the *Chicago Defender* to honor its newsboys.

Foods for special occasions:

During holidays and celebrations, the preparation and eating of food is important. Aside from the usual turkey, ham, chicken, greens, roots, herbs, barbecue and drink at Thanksgiving and Christmas, many families indulge in a dish called chitterlings (chittlins), which derives from plantation days in the South when blacks had to make do with the leavings of the master's meals. Such dishes were prepared with great care and became almost delicacies.

Dietary restrictions:

None for Christians. Muslims avoid pork and alcohol.

Names:

Formerly, most African Americans continued to use their slave names, such as John, Joe, Robert, Walter and Mary, along with nicknames like Tim, Rob, Skeeball, Arch and Slim. Since Malcolm X, many of the younger generations have turned to African and other non-Western names such as Tuisha, Aesha and Hakim. Traditional last names came from plantation owners. Some also have changed their last names to African names.

Major issues for community:

Almost without dissent, Chicago's African Americans are united on issues of racism and the denial of equal access to decent affordable housing, jobs, quality education and neighborhood safety. Crime and violence are probably the top issues, followed closely by the need for adequate employment and decent housing, the poor state of the Chicago Public Schools, and the problems of youth in general. The exodus of jobs to the suburbs has made access to employment a serious issue. There is inadequate transportation to get to where the jobs are. And the jobs themselves have changed, with more in the white-collar and service sector, requiring computer skills. Two other issues hotly debated in the community are the threatened elimination of affirmative action and how much assimilation is too much.

Political participation:

This depends on the issues, the candidates and the section of the city involved. In some places interest is very low; the middle class tends to be more active. In the campaign and election of the late Mayor Harold Washington, almost every man, woman and child was involved in one way or another. He was elected only because this was so. After his death, candidates have not seemed to reflect the needs and concerns of the community, especially the poorer and younger members. Political interest has lagged. For many there is a growing distrust of government and a sentiment of "What difference does it make?" Since Franklin Roosevelt was president, African Americans have voted overwhelmingly for Democrats (before that they were loyal to Abraham Lincoln's Republican party). But nowadays turnout is very low, even among registered voters.

Links to homeland:

African Americans have a relationship with the African continent through business, tourism, the arts, folklore and politics. There are strong ties to South Africa, where they long advocated an end to apartheid. Events there, as well as in other African and Caribbean nations, are of particular interest. Some have tried to trace their roots, a difficult task because their ancestors were brought here in chains many generations ago.

Myths & misconceptions:

Myth: Blacks are genetically inferior to whites.

Fact: This myth began as a justification for slavery and, later, for discrimination. The recent book, *The Bell Curve,* has brought it up again, at a time efforts are afoot to scrap affirmative action. Most of the scientific community gives it no credence. Intelligence is a combination of genetics and environment. Many African Americans, caught in a cycle of poverty and poor education, fare poorly on standardized tests, which in themselves are culturally biased. The myth ignores the many blacks who have excelled intellectually, as academics, writers, scientists, doctors, lawyers, politicians and community leaders.

Myth: Blacks are inherently more criminal, more violent.

Fact: It is true a greater proportion of blacks than whites end up in prison, but that is largely a function of the neighborhoods they grow up in. The social disorganization of the past 30 years, with its increased single-parent households, has contributed to this problem. Poverty, not race, is the major factor in predicting violent crime. In addition, an anti-black bias in arrests, prosecutions and sentencing has been acknowledged by many in the criminal justice system. It should be noted that blacks are most often the victims of crime.

Myth: Blacks are oversensitive on the issue of race.

Fact: There is hypersensitivity among some blacks and it can create problems in relationships with others. It is important to keep in mind that only through vigilance and direct action has there been civil rights progress. It didn't just happen. Most Americans don't understand the symbolism of slavery and that the history of struggle is part of the self-definition of African Americans.

—By Timuel Black, Professor Emeritus of City Colleges of Chicago

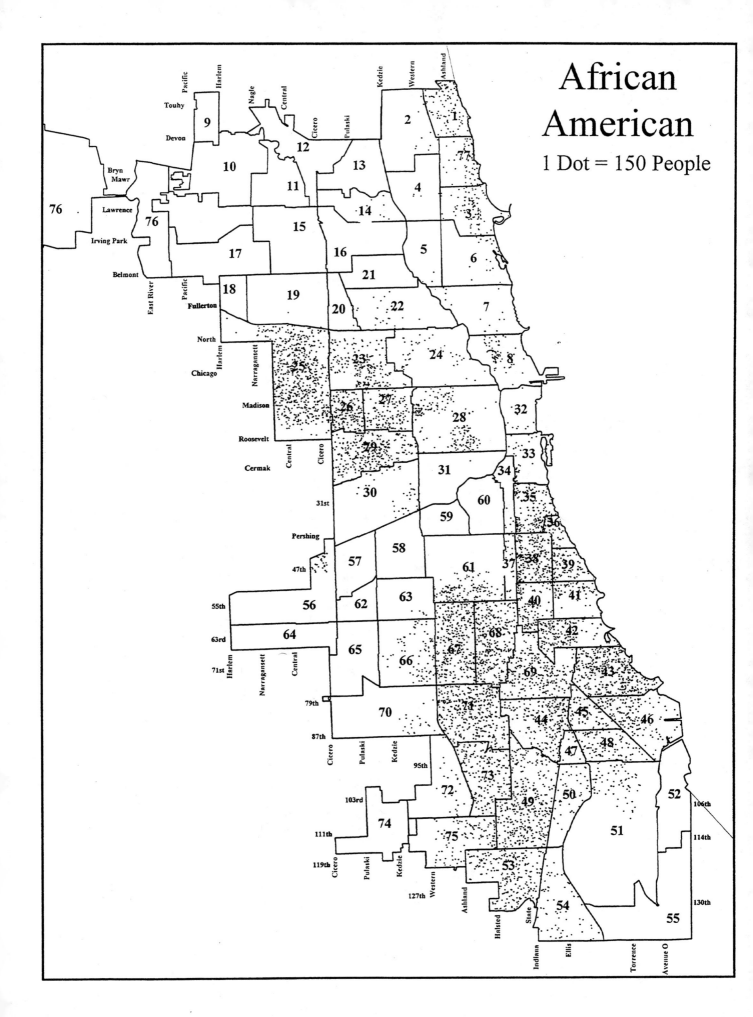

African American

1 Dot = 150 People

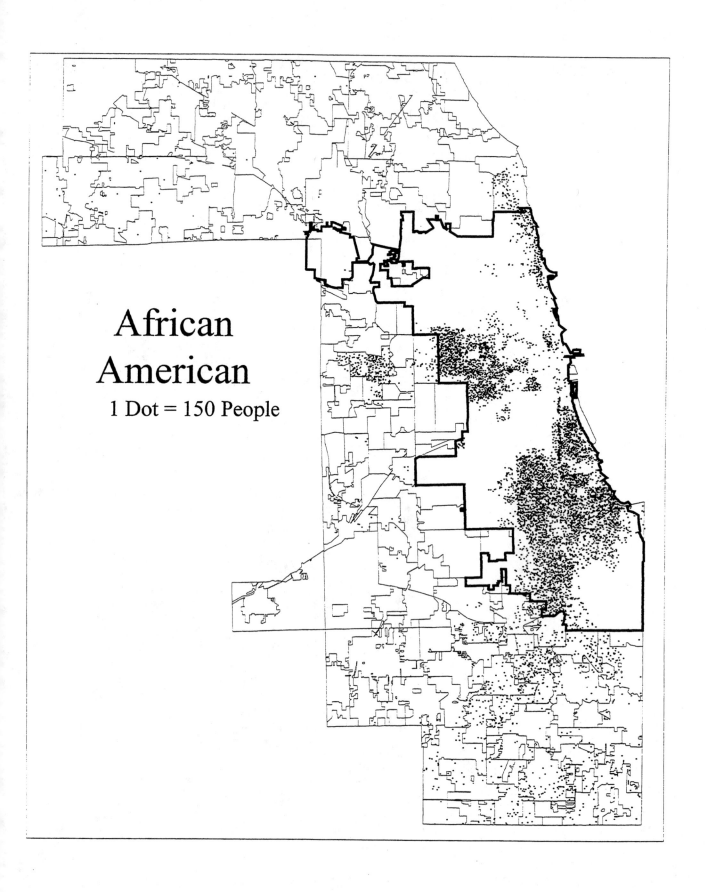

African
American

1 Dot = 150 People

HALF EMPTY OR HALF FULL?

By Derrick K. Baker

After more than three decades of calling Chicago home (save four years in Iowa at college), I've become totally enamored with, and publicly proud of, the nation's third largest city. It is gorgeous, historic, vibrant, cultural, diverse and wealthy. If you're going to reside in one of the major cities, Chicago is a good choice.

I've also reached the point where living in the Windy City finds me both excited and depressed, optimistic and pessimistic, successful and stonewalled, clearheaded and confused, lauded and ignored, open-minded and opinionated, benevolent and selfish. I'm as brave as a lion on the outside, while the timidity of a sheep lurks within. For me, life in the Windy City is akin to looking at glass of water and constantly trying to decide if it's half empty or half full.

Why? Chicago and the 2.8 million who live here can create such confusion, especially if you look like me: a 34-year-old African American man. That's because for my race and gender, this city — like other urban metropolises — can disguise itself as your oyster, but the shell sometimes slams shut as you extend your hand to sample the dish.

Case in point: Several years ago while attending a job fair that featured major corporations and mid-size businesses specifically in search of talented minorities, my resume traveled among almost two dozen corporate recruiters faster than a feather in a windstorm. More than a few of the "suits" openly gushed over my life-on-a-page and lauded my potential. All of which left me naively optimistic. But not a single company offered me a follow-up interview. Most weren't merciful enough to send even the tersest rejection letter.

Or consider the city's bustling yet contradictory night life, which successfully beckons you to Rush Street. But when you're a young African American man barhopping with two white female friends, what you get is an unforgettable lesson in Facism 101, or a humiliating lesson in what happens when you can't produce three picture IDs, when everyone else gets in by flashing a driver's license.

But Chicago also has offered me — a black man with dreams, goals, and a burning desire to see people do the right things at the right time for the right reasons — the opportunity to excel, meet literally thousands of people from all walks of life, and find a certain level of happiness.

And in what some might see as a form of reverse racism, Chicago continues to appeal to me because virtually everywhere I venture, I see African Americans. All shapes, colors and sizes. All socio-economic backgrounds. Married and single. Driving, biking, rollerblading, on public transportation and walking. In Water Tower Place. In the Harold Washington Library. In the express line at Jewel. In the dressing room at Marshall Field's. In the concession-stand line at the Fine Arts Theatre. In nightclubs on the North Side and restaurants on the South Side. Even in Bridgeport.

What's comforting about "seeing yourself" everywhere you go? The same feeling of inner peace and camaraderie that comforts people of any ethnic group who live in a city, village or neighborhood that's populated with a respectable percentage of their own. There always are people to whom you can relate, and to whom you can freely reveal a part of yourself that might be frowned upon or misunderstood by the mainstream.

I find comfort in knowing there are more than a million African Americans in Chicago. It's like putting an ice cube on the sidewalk in July and watching it not melt. Given this city's documented history of institutional and overt racism toward African Americans, we nevertheless have excelled and continue to tangibly contribute to Chicago's march toward the next century.

Consider that Harold Washington, Chicago's first black mayor, quickly gained national prominence after his election. Consider that Michael Jordan "owns" the world.

To be African American in Chicago means being profoundly proud of the beauty, history and tranquility of upscale Beverly, Pill Hill and Chatham, especially when such neighborhoods are in a city whose first settler was one of your own.

Despite the first word in the latest moniker bestowed upon African Americans, my strongest allegiance is to the United States, even with all its warts. The combination of my never having traveled to Africa (though I hope to some day), coupled with my parents' and relatives' never really speaking of our genealogical connection to the Motherland, has made me relatively ignorant of key facts about our ancestors' birthplace. That, of course, is not to disparage the rich, majestic heritage of Africa. It's simply that, like millions of other African Americans born and raised in this country, being reared in the richest, strongest and most industrialized land of opportunity necessarily directs your focus to your own birthplace.

My parents were born and raised in small towns in Mississippi. So were their brothers and sisters, and their parents. I've traveled South by car on Interstates 57 and 55 dozens of times to visit that state, which has fewer people than the city of Chicago. My parents' connections to Mississippi still run deep — as do mine — and I have the utmost respect for Mississippians. But history tells us that hundreds of thousands of African Americans migrated to Chicago, which prompts me to ask, "What were they looking for in the North?" The same employment, economic and cultural opportunities I would have sought. Did my parents find a pot of gold at the end of the rainbow? Sometimes I think yes; on other occasions, no. It depends on when you ask them.

Have I found gold at the end of the rainbow I've been chasing for 3½ decades? My answer also depends on when you ask me. But I do know this: The city of Chicago has shaped the quality and direction of my life as much as have my family and friends.

Derrick K. Baker is a contributing editor for N'DIGO, where he writes a bi-weekly column titled, "The Way I See It."

Assyrian Americans

Chicago population:

8,007 (1990 Census, first ancestry)
587 (Census, second ancestry)
40,000 (1996 community estimate)

Metro area population:

12,500 (U.S. Census, first ancestry)
1,140 (Census, second ancestry)
72,000 (1996 community estimate)

Foreign-born:

NA

Demographics:

The largest concentration of Assyrians in Chicago is in West Rogers Park. There is a smaller group in Albany Park. Others are scattered in other North Side neighborhoods such as Edgewater, East Rogers Park, Budlong Woods, Ravenswood, Andersonville, Peterson Park and Hollywood Park. A growing number live in north and northwest suburbs like Skokie, Morton Grove, Niles, Des Plaines, Itasca, Schaumburg and Arlington Heights, and in Kane and Lake counties. There is virtually no Census breakdown on Assyrians, who come from several different countries. A random sample of the 244 case files for newly arrived Assyrians at the Assyrian Universal Alliance Foundation in Chicago shows that 47% are employed, 10% students, 23% homemakers, 11% retired and 9% unemployed. The impression is that Assyrians work in significant numbers in clerical positions in stores, banks, and offices; and as skilled tradesman, such as mechanics and electricians. Many newcomers work as unskilled and semi-skilled factory employees, in building maintenance, and in hotel jobs. A growing number are computer technicians and programmers, engineers, physicians, accountants and lawyers. Many own small businesses. An unpublished 1991 survey showed at least 289 Assyrian-owed businesses in the Chicago metro area, mostly on the far North Side and in neighboring suburbs. This is probably a low estimate; there may have been twice as many Assyrian small businesses at the time. The most common type of business was video rental shops; 43 were counted, but community members reported 150. Other Assyrian-owned businesses included air-conditioning/heating contractors, auto dealers, auto repair shops and gas stations, beauty salons, convenience grocery stores, fruit markets, painting contractors and restaurants. There also were at least two metal-anodizing plants, two sewing factories and a major parking garage/parking lot chain. Assyrians claim that few live in poverty, because those who are unemployed get support through informal kin networks.

Among Assyrian adults who arrived in Chicago since the 1970s, primarily from Iraq, it is estimated the majority had 6-12 years of education. The majority of middle-aged males received most or part of their education in English; younger males (and females) typically studied very little English before coming here. Some elderly women had no formal education at all. The impression is that most Assyrians here finish high school, and a growing minority are entering college or trade schools. It is widely perceived that the intermarriage rate for the Assyrians who came

Assyrians are an ethnic minority from the Middle East. Their homeland is what is now northern Iraq, southeastern Turkey, northwestern Iran and northeastern Syria.

Assyrians are not Arabs. They have their own language, which is only remotely related to Arabic.

There were an estimated 5,000 Assyrians in Chicago in 1944, more than three times as many as in any other American city.

since the 1970s is still low, 10% or so. Preliminary genealogical research indicates nearly every family that arrived before WWII has intermarried. The estimated number of undocumented Assyrians in Chicago is very small.

Historical background:

Assyrians are an ethnic minority from the Middle East. They speak their own language. Their homeland is located in what is now northern Iraq, southeastern Turkey, northwestern Iran and northeastern Syria, territories that are inhabited largely by Kurds and Azerbaijani Turks. Assyrians here claim a heritage that goes back to the ancient Assyrian Empire (in Mesopotamia). The history of Assyrians in Chicago dates from 1889, when they began to come as theology and medical students.

• In the first decade of the 20th century, a significant number began to settle permanently. By 1909, there were 600 young Assyrian men living in Chicago, and 30 families. Most worked as masons, carpenters, painters, tailors or in other trades. A few were employed in factories, stores, hotels and restaurants.

• During WWI, Assyrians were victims of famine and genocide, which led to a new influx, causing the community to swell to about 2,327, according to a census published in 1924. Males between the ages of 20 and 40 predominated, and they clustered in the Near North neighborhood around Clark and Huron. The later arrivals were generally less educated and worked primarily as cooks, waiters, janitors, hotel men and unskilled factory workers. The majority in these early waves came from villages in northwestern Iran. In the 1930s Assyrians tended to move northward in the city into Lincoln Park, Lake View and Uptown. Small numbers trickled in from Iran, Iraq and Syria through WWII. According to one estimate there were 5,000 Assyrians in Chicago in 1944, more than three times as many as in any other American city.

• Following a Kurdish and Azerbaijani insurrection in northwestern Iran in 1948, another wave of Assyrians entered from that country. Starting in the 1960s, a growing number began arriving from Baghdad, Kirkuk, Basrah and other cities in Iraq.

• In 1975-76, during the Lebanese Civil War, up to 1,000 Assyrians living on the outskirts of Beirut were accepted for resettlement in Chicago. This was the first group of Assyrian newcomers who got government benefits as a refugee-like group. Earlier arrivals were helped by Assyrian aid societies and churches, as well as through family support networks.

• A significantly larger wave came to Chicago from Iraq in the 1970s and '80s, primarily to escape the Iran-Iraq War. According to the Office of Refugee Resettlement, 1,955 Iraqis came to Chicago with refugee status from 1983-94, the vast majority of them Assyrians. This does not include the many Assyrians who came to Chicago from Iraq, Iran, Syria and Lebanon as students or as family-reunification immigrants. The Assyrian Universal Alliance Foundation and Assyrian National Council of Illinois have helped all classifications of Assyrian immigrants, while Catholic Charities and InterChurch Refugee and Immigration Ministries have assisted those classified as refugees to adjust and find jobs.

Current migration patterns:

The movement of Assyrians to the north and northwest continues in Chicago. Assyrians have moved into communities where other Assyrians already live, though they have not settled in the same blocks but scattered throughout those communities. Few Assyrians have returned permanently to their countries of origin. Conditions in Iraq, in particular, are precarious. A number of Assyrians have made visits to relatives in Iraq, Iran, Lebanon and Syria.

Language:

Most Assyrian immigrants in Chicago speak modern Assyrian, sometimes called neo-Syriac, modern Syriac, Surit or neo-Aramaic. It is a Semitic language related to Hebrew and, more distantly, to Arabic. Many dialects can be heard in Chicago, but the majority speak either a relatively standardized urban Iraqi dialect or an equally standardized Iranian one. Since governments in the Middle East generally have discouraged the teaching of modern Assyrian, relatively few can read and write in this language, which has its own unique alphabet. The vast majority of Assyrian immigrants also speak, read and write the language of their country of origin, usually Arabic or Persian.

Religion:

Almost by definition, Assyrians are Christian. Before the influence of Western missionaries, they belonged to either the Church of the East (also known by the misnomer "Nestorian") or the Syrian Orthodox Church (known by the misnomer "Jacobite"). In Chicago, Assyrians belong to various denominations. The largest single one is the Church of the East, with three sizable churches in Chicago and one in Bartlett. Some, who reject certain reforms in the Church of the East, have formed a separate Ancient Church of the East, and have an active congregation in Chicago. Smaller groups of Assyrians belong to the Chaldean Uniate and Syrian Orthodox churches. Some Protestants have separate Assyrian churches, including Presbyterian, Assyrian Evangelical (United Church of Christ), Evangelical Covenant and Pentecostal.

Important traditions:

Modern Assyrian identity is more than an attachment to a Christian heritage. It is also rooted in ties to the homeland, to language and to distinctive cultural traditions. They are a close-knit community and those from one tribe, clan or village feel closely related to people from the same tribe, clan or village. Assyrians have distinctive life-cycle ceremonies, which many families celebrate, regardless of religious affiliation. These include *ma'modita* (baptism), *talibuta* or *shirinligh* (betrothal parties), and large weddings. When a person dies, the funeral is followed by several days when immediate relatives accept visitors to pay their respects, literally "to cure the head" (*basamta d-risha*). On the third, seventh and 40th days of mourning, as well as after one year, there are special gatherings. Assyrians take matters of hospitality very seriously, frequently welcoming guests into their home, and hosting special events and holiday gatherings. The demands of contemporary American life put a strain on the ability of some families to live up to traditional hospitality standards. Assyrians also place great value on extended families (or "houses") maintaining a good reputation (*shimma spay*). This includes high standards of modesty and propriety. Assyrian men and women mix more in public than many other Middle Easterners. The adaptation to American mores has varied dramatically from one family to another. In some families, as with other immigrants, this has caused a generation gap.

Holidays and special events:

Assyrians celebrate the major Christian holidays of **Good Friday**, **Easter** and **Christmas**. They consider Easter the "Big Holiday" (*'ida gura*) and Christmas the "Little Holiday" (*'ida s'ura*). Another major religious holiday is the **Ba'uta d-Ninwayé** or Rogation of the Ninevites (usually in February). This commemorates the prophet Jonah's mission to the people of Nineveh, the capital of Assyria, and usually includes a three-day partial fast. Assyrians continue the tradition of celebrating **Saints' Days**, to commemorate both the birthdays and the death anniversaries of the saints. Many are local saints, so their celebrations are hosted by Assyrian tribes or villages with whom those saints are associated. The commemorations of saints are called *shahras*, and can range from small family reunions to huge outdoor picnics. Another important holiday is **Kha B'Nissan** (April 1), the Assyrian New Year. In recent years it has been marked by a parade down King Sargon Boulevard (Western Avenue), followed by large parties. **Assyrian Martyrs' Day** (Aug. 7), which was first instituted to mark the 1933 massacre of Assyrians by the Iraqi army, now commemorates the martyrdom of Assyrians throughout their long history of persecution.

Foods for special occasions:

Dukhrana, a sacrificial meal on shahras and other occasions, consists of distributing the meat of a sacrificial lamb. Another popular Assyrian dish for special occasions is *harisa* (wheat cooked with chicken, lamb or mutton, whipped and served with melted butter). It also can be baked, with ground coriander seeds. *Girdu* is rice baked in yogurt or sour milk and served hot with melted butter on the top. *Dolma* is vine leaves, zucchini, eggplant, tomatoes or bell-pepper stuffed with chopped vegetables and ground or diced meat.

Dietary restrictions:

Assyrians traditionally refrain from eating meat and/or dairy products on Wednesdays and Fridays, as well as during Advent, the 25 days before Christmas, and Lent, the 50 days preceding Easter.

Names:

A large number of Assyrians have biblical names, taken from both the Old and New Testaments. Common ones include: Oraham (Abraham), Yako (Jacob), Yosip (Joseph), Astar (Esther), Rabka (Rebecca) and Maryam (Mary). Names of ancient Assyrian gods, goddesses, kings and queens also are common. Male names include Ashor, Sargon and Sankheru. Female names include Atorina, Ninwé and Shamiram. A few have ancient Persian names such as Diryawash (Darius) and Kurosh (Cyrus) for boys and Narjis for girls. Some boys are named after Christian saints in the Syriac tradition, such as Aprim, Narsay and Zaya. Some compound names from the Syriac tradition are also used, such as Odisho (servant of Jesus) and Sorisho (hope of Jesus). Nowadays, many Assyrians, especially girls, have non-biblical Western names, such as Linda, Diana, Janet and Louisa. In Iraq it was not unusual for Assyrians to name boys after the last names of British officers, such as Wilson and Johnson — or less commonly, girls after cities or countries their sojourning fathers visited, like Berlin and Argentina. It was usual for Assyrians to have a given name, followed by that of their father and grandfather. Clan names, usually preceded by *bet* (house of), were generally suppressed by the Iraqi government, but have been resurrected by some Assyrians in Chicago. Many go by informal nicknames.

Major issues for community:

Many Assyrians are worried about melting into American society and losing their distinctive culture. Assyrian nationalism is very strong in the Chicago community. Assyrians have rallied around leaders who are working for some form of cultural or political self-determination in northern Iraq.

Political participation:

Because the majority are newcomers, relatively few Assyrians vote, though a growing number have become active in politics in both the Democratic and Republican parties. John Nimrod (Republican) was a long-time state senator from Glenview and Adam Benjamin (Democrat) a long-time U.S. congressman from Gary, IN. Many Assyrians, whether they vote or not, follow international affairs closely.

Links to homeland:

The majority of Assyrians, who left their homeland under duress, have not maintained their original citizenship. Many, however, say they want to return if political and economic conditions improve. As time goes on, the desire to return usually dims. Many send money to relatives taking refuge in Jordan, Turkey, Russia, Greece and other countries of temporary asylum. Organized charities, such as the Assyrian Aid Society of America, have raised money to help support these refugees. Such charities have been able to provide some emergency medical relief and money to build schools and other institutions in northern Iraq. The Persian Gulf War mobilized many Assyrians who feared for the safety and welfare of their relatives in Iraq. Some have contacted federal officials about the fate of Assyrians in northern Iraq and in countries of temporary asylum. Assyrians maintain close contacts with Assyrians dispersed all over the world, through magazines newspapers, faxes, videotapes, cable television and the Internet.

Myths & misconceptions:

Myth: Assyrians are Arabs or Syrians. (Thus, they are the victims of the same prejudices and ethnic slurs that bedevil Arabs).

Fact: Assyrians are not Arabs. They have their own language, which is only remotely related to Arabic. Most Assyrians who have come to Chicago from Arab countries had been resettled as refugees in those countries after WWI. Although some Syrians are ethnic Assyrians, most Syrians are Arabs.

By Daniel Wolk, a Doctoral Candidate in anthropology at the University of Chicago; also contributing: Homer Ashurian, Executive Director of Assyrian Universal Alliance Foundation

Cambodian Americans

Chicago population:

1,572 (1990 Census)
5,000 (1996 community estimate)

Metro area population:

2,405 (1990 Census)
8,500 (1996 community estimate)

Foreign-born:

78% of city, 79% of metro

Demographics:

In the city of Chicago, the median household income for Cambodian Americans reported in the 1990 Census was $12,342, much lower than other ethnic groups. In Chicago 58% of Cambodians live below the poverty line. For people over the age of 25, those without a high-school diploma outnumber those with college degrees about 13:1. In the city, 37% do not speak English well or at all. Less than 2% are in professional or managerial jobs, while 8% are in technical sales and administrative positions; 9% in service occupations; 2% in crafts; 12% in manufacturer or laborer jobs. In the six-county metropolitan area, median household income rises substantially to $27,708. For people over the age of 25, those without a high school diploma outnumber those with a college degree 6:1; 41% live below the poverty line; 32% speak English "not well" or not at all; 3% are in managerial or professional positions; while 9% are in sales or administrative jobs, 9% in service occupations; 6% in crafts; and 12% are manufacturers or laborers. (Ed. note: Because the sample was so small, these statistics are not very reliable. Also, it is widely believed many Cambodians did not fill out the Census form, so those who did may not be representative.) Cambodian Americans living in the suburbs seem to be primarily in Cook, DuPage and Kane counties. Because Cambodians (also known as Khmer) could come here legally as refugees, the estimated number of undocumented is virtually zero.

Historical background:

Cambodians began coming to Chicago in 1975 as refugees from war-torn Cambodia. The communist Khmer Rouge ruled Cambodia from April 1975 to January 1979. During this period, as many as 3 million (out of 7.5 million) Cambodians were killed and many others were forced into work camps in the countryside. Border conflicts resulted in the invasion of Cambodia by the Vietnamese communist government, which then helped installed a Cambodian regime trained in Hanoi. The indiscriminate killings of innocent people during the Khmer Rouge era and subsequent armed conflicts between the Khmer Rouge and new regime forced many Cambodians to flee to Thailand and seek asylum in third countries. Continued fighting and burning of rice reserves led to famine and starvation in 1979-80.

When Cambodians resettled in America, the youth adopted the new culture, which caused conflicts at home.

The language barrier is difficult to overcome because many adults are illiterate in their own language.

This community suffers greatly from the loss of family members, caused by the vicious killing in their home country.

• Although Cambodian refugees have been resettled to the United States for two decades, the largest numbers came from 1980-85. Most settled in California. Only 4% came to Illinois, with about half of those settling in Chicago in neighborhoods like Uptown and Albany Park, where housing was inexpensive and agencies were available to help with resettlement. Uptown, especially, seemed an ideal port of entry for these reasons. Agencies helping to resettle the refugees included Travelers & Immigrants Aid, Lutheran Child & Family Services, Catholic Charities, World Relief and Jewish Family & Community Service. The Cambodian Association, a community self-help effort in Uptown, was founded in 1976 to provide translation services and help the refugees carry on their traditions. In 1980 it got funding to provide social services such as employment and counseling, to help newly arrived Cambodians become self-sufficient. The first wave of Cambodians resettled in Chicago were better educated than the later immigrants, who tended to come from rural areas. Most of the refugees came here in late 1979 and early 1980. Immigration of Cambodians slowed in 1985. Coming from rural areas, many of the refugees were not literate and had difficulty adjusting to life in urban America.

Current migration patterns:
Only a few Cambodians are now arriving in Chicago, mostly through family-reunification. Some city dwellers who have gotten good jobs and could afford it have moved northwest to such suburbs as Skokie and Niles for better schools. A few have moved to Lowell, Mass., where there is a substantial Cambodian population.

Language:
Cambodian, also known as Khmer. People speak various dialects, which differ from one another mostly in pronunciation.

Religion:
Theravada Buddhism. More than 80% are Buddhists. The rest include Muslims, Christians and Hindus.

Important traditions:
Cambodians teach their children to value traditional clothes, dance, food and weddings, as well as ways of talking, acting and respecting one another. The young should listen to older people, such as older brothers and sisters, grandparents, aunts and uncles. Young people should not look at an older person's eyes when talking to them. Likewise, older people should take care of the younger ones. Cambodian parents expect their children to listen to them and respect them. Talking back to parents and other older people is bad. Students should listen to the teacher. Parents depend completely on teachers to teach their children everything. Parents listen to the teacher more than their children do. Cambodian parents don't allow their children to have boyfriends or girlfriends at a young age. Males and females aren't allowed to touch unless they are married. Marriage is arranged by parents. Children must be good in order to maintain the family's reputation. When Cambodians resettled in America, the youth adopted the new culture, which caused conflicts at home. Their parents still wanted them to behave with traditional Cambodian values, but the children no longer accepted these values as relevant to their lives. Parents, themselves, are having problems adjusting to the new culture, which makes them want to hold on to their traditional culture even more.

Holidays and special events:
Cambodian New Year is celebrated in April, for three days. *Maha Sangkran Day* (April 14) is the last day of the old year. *Vana Bat Day* (April 15) divides the old year from the new. And *Loeung Sak Day* (April 16) is when the new year begins. In Cambodian villages some celebrated for as long as a month. Before the New Year, Cambodians clean and decorate the house and set the table with flowers, fruit, incense and candles to wait for the new guardian angel. The next day, Cambodians cook, meet with family, bring food and gifts to their parents and food to the temple. At the temple, monks pray to the dead and bless everyone for the year. People offer food to the monks. Then they eat together and bathe their parents. After that everyone washes the Buddha statue and asks for blessings for the year to come. Finally, friends and family throw water at one

another for best wishes, and build sand or rice dunes to symbolize prosperity in the coming year. **Bon Phchum Bend** (the Ancestor Festival) comes in September, for 15 days. Cambodians believe when people die they are reincarnated, and that those who committed bad deeds in their last life became ghosts. These spirits wait for food and blessings from friends and relatives, offered to them through monks. The first 14 days of this festival, *Kaun Bend,* people divide into 14 groups and each brings food to the temple one day. The 15th day, *Phchum Bend,* is when everyone comes to the temple and eats together. The monks pray for forgiveness for the sins of the departed and offer good will and food to the wandering spirits who might come to receive them. **Visakh Boja** celebrates the birth, enlightenment and death of Buddha. It is celebrated in May because all these events occurred on the full moon in *Visakh* (May). Buddhists offer food to the monks in the morning and incense and flowers in the afternoon. At night they go to the temple to hear sermons and the chanting of *Buddhappawatti.*

Food for special occasions:

On *Bon Phchum Bend* families prepare food to offer to ancestors. *Num ansom* (cylinder cake), *non kaom* (sweet, coconut, sticky rice cake), *samlaw misuor* (noodle soup) and sticky rice balls are put in banana leaves so the spirits will be able to carry them on their journey to places they will have new lives.

Names:

Cambodians give their children names that rhyme with the names of family members. Surnames come first in Cambodia, but most Cambodian Americans have switched the order of first and last names, to follow the custom here. Most of the names have meanings, like Bopha (flower).

Major issues for community:

Because they are mostly from a rural background, with little or no education, Cambodians in Chicago have found it difficult to get well-paying jobs. The language barrier is difficult to overcome because many adults were illiterate when they arrived, unable to read and write in even their own language. This community suffers greatly from the loss of family members, caused by the vicious killing in their home country. Many families are headed by widows and often there is little adult supervision. Adults who themselves are struggling to survive, often are unable to give their children direction. The result has been a severe generation gap, causing some youths to join gangs as a support system. Because of its small size, the community has difficulty getting funding and attention to help solve its problems.

Political participation:

Few Cambodian Americans vote and there is no political clout. Cambodians Americans report few crimes because they don't trust police, who they think don't understand their culture and way of life. Only a few community leaders are involved in government activities.

Links to homeland:

About 30-40% of adult Cambodians have become U.S. citizens. Only about 2% maintain Cambodian citizenship. However, many have returned to Cambodia to visit relatives or friends or the country itself. A few have returned there to live and work. Many send money home to help families and friends.

Myths & misconceptions:

Myth: All Asians are doing well in school and business.
Fact: Some small groups of Asians, like Cambodians, are still struggling to survive.

Etc.:

Some Cambodians who settled in the Uptown area are now buying houses in the suburbs and in other neighborhoods. Many Cambodian children have graduated from college and gotten jobs.

At the same time, there are Cambodian children who drop out of school. Many Cambodian Americans suffer from mental illness because they have gone through such traumatic experiences, having worked in slave-like conditions under communism, often without enough to eat, being physically abused and witnessing the killing of family members. These experiences were followed by life in refugee camps where they were confined to a small space with limited food. On top of that, adjustment to America has been difficult because the language and culture are so completely different.

— By Borita Khim, a teacher at Stockton Elementary School and Kompha Seth, Executive Director of the Cambodian Association of Illinois

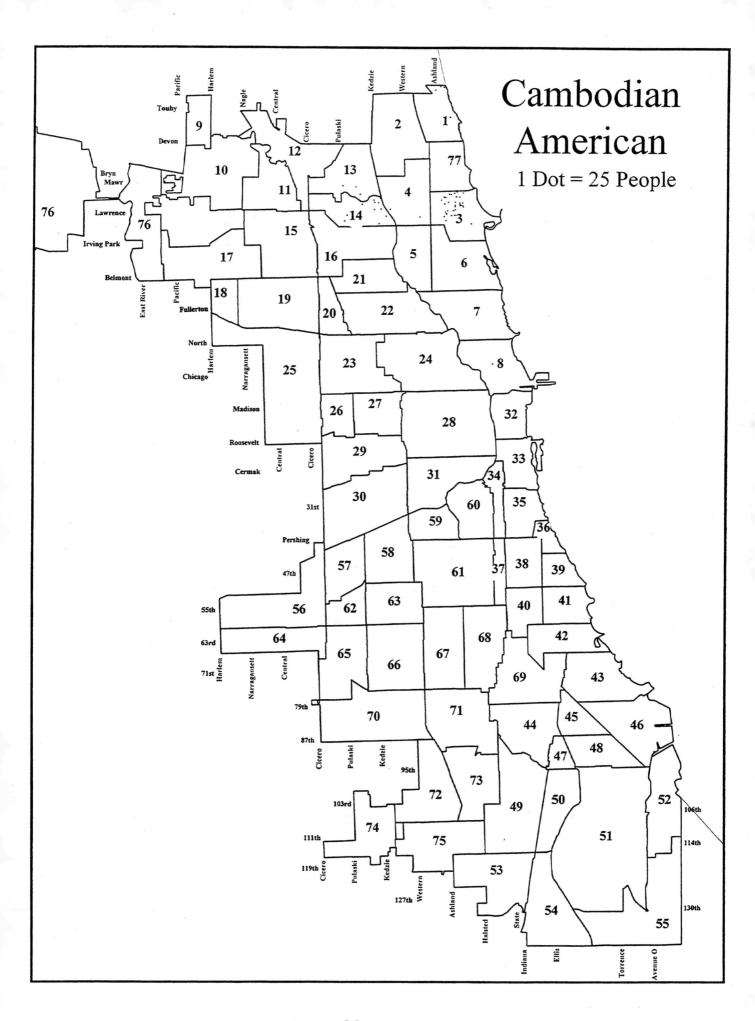

Cambodian
American

1 Dot = 25 People

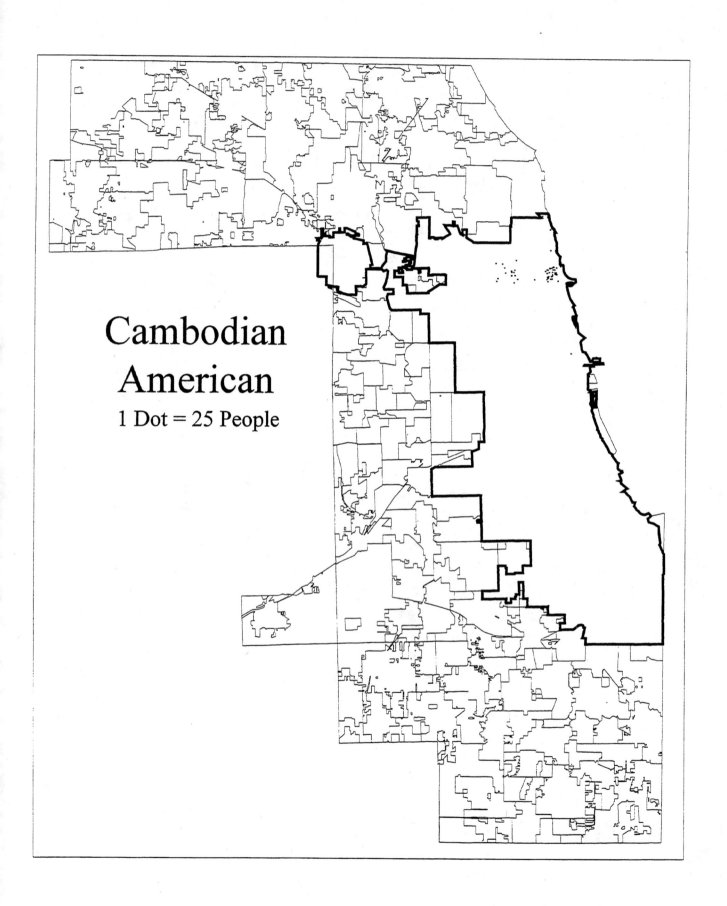

Cambodian
American

1 Dot = 25 People

Chinese Americans

Chicago population:

23,233 (1990 Census)
30,000-35,000 (1996 community estimate)

Metro area population:

42,511 (1990 Census)
50,000-75,000 (1996 community estimate)

Foreign-born:

76% in Chicago, 71% in metro area

Demographics:

The nearly 50,000 Chinese Americans in the state make Illinois the fifth largest state for this community. In the metro area, the distribution of Chinese Americans is almost evenly split between Chicago and the suburbs. Chinese Americans are geographically dispersed throughout the city with one exception. The South Chinatown area — bounded unofficially by the south branch of the Chicago River and Cermak on the north, the Dan Ryan on the east, 35th Avenue on the south, and Halsted on the west — encompasses an Asian (mostly Chinese) population of about 8,800. About one-third of the Chinese American population in the city resides around Chinatown. Ethnic Chinese, largely from Southeast Asian countries, also live on the North Side of Chicago, with business districts around Argyle and Broadway. In northern Cook County, suburbs like Skokie, Lincolnwood and Morton Grove have the highest percentages of Chinese. In DuPage County, Oak Brook, Glendale Heights and Naperville have large numbers. Nearly one-quarter of Chinese in the metro area do not speak English well. Suburban areas attract mostly middle-class married couples, while Chicago's Chinese enclaves also include the elderly without families, singles, and refugees (66% of Chinatown's residents are married couples). In the city, Chinese who didn't finish high school outnumber those with college degrees. In the entire metro area, however, there are almost twice as many college graduates as there are people without a high school diploma. Those in DuPage, Cook and Lake County suburbs are overwhelmingly college graduates and many have advanced degrees. The median family income in Chicago is $23,723. For the whole metro area it is $33,522. In Chicago 22% of the Chinese live in poverty. Statewide, 15% of Chinese American women and 12% of the men marry outside their ethnic group. For U.S.-born Chinese Americans, 64% of the women and 71% of the men marry out. Estimates on undocumented Chinese in the Chicago area range from 5,000 to 20,000.

Historical background:

There were four distinct periods of Chinese immigration to the U.S. mainland: free immigration from 1849-82; exclusion from 1882-1943; limited entry from 1943-65; and revived entry from 1965 to the present. Chinese immigrants came to California in the late 1840s to work in the large gold-mining operations. For the next two decades, Chinese laborers arrived

The median family income for Chinese in Chicago is $23,723. For the metro area it is $33,522.

The Exclusion Act kept Chinese laborers from entering the U.S., and those already here were denied citizenship.

The rise of the Chinese laundry reflected the growth of the Chinese immigrant community in Chicago and its limited occupational opportunities.

By the mid-1970s, immigrants started arriving from mainland China, adding to the majority of Chinese from Taiwan, Hong Kong and Southeast Asia.

on the West Coast by the tens of thousands. They were recruited to fill labor needs in agriculture, small industries and railroads, but by the late 1870s conditions had changed. With a major recession in California, an anti-Chinese movement erupted. By 1882, the first exclusion law targeting a specific group was enacted. The Exclusion Act prohibited Chinese laborers from entering the U.S., and those already here were denied citizenship and civil liberties. Given this chilly climate on the West Coast, cities like Chicago beckoned.

• The first Chinatown was established in the 1880s near Clark and Van Buren. In 1872, as the city recovered from the Great Chicago Fire, the first Chinese laundry opened at 167 W. Madison. Two years later there were 18 such laundries. While several other occupations were open to Chinese, including restaurant ownership and railroad jobs, the rise of the Chicago Chinese laundry reflected the growth of the Chinese immigrant community and its limited occupation opportunities. During the 1870s, most of the laundries were concentrated on South Clark Street. By 1884, they totaled more than 200 and could be found in almost every neighborhood. Downtown Chinatown fulfilled business and social needs. Unlike other American Chinatowns, it was not a residential enclave. This lack of traditional community and family life was fueled by two factors. First, few Chinese women were allowed to enter the U.S. (In Chicago, in 1910, there were 65 women and 1,713 men. This severe imbalance would not change until after WWII.) Second, with hard lessons learned from their West Coast experience, most Chinese chose not to live in Chinatown, preferring to "dilute" themselves, scattering around town and living behind their storefront businesses. Chinatown instead hosted several grocery stores, two Tong organizations, family associations, and a Chinese Baptist Mission. The majority of the early Chicago Chinese pioneers were Toishan-speaking men, from an impoverished area in Canton province. Most of them were sojourners — intending not to settle here, but to work a few years, accumulate wealth and retire well in China. They were willing to work long hours, in any menial labor, as long as they could save and send money back to China to support their families.

• By about 1910, higher rents and internal factionalism in the original Chinatown led the leaders to expand to a second Chinatown, around Wentworth and Cermak, which provided low-rent storefronts and apartments. The Loop Chinatown remained until 1975, when it was razed to prepare for the Metropolitan Correctional Center. During the 1920s and '30s, Chicago's Chinese Americans continued to participate mainly in laundry or restaurant-related businesses. Again, this was due not to a natural proclivity (Chinese are not engaged in such occupations in China), but because of economic and structural barriers. Even for the second generation, who had requisite language skills for employment outside the ethnic enclave, job opportunities outside of Chinatown or the ethnic economy were severely restricted.

• With the end of WWII and the 1949 establishment of the People's Republic of China, many Chinese immigrants and students no longer thought of returning to China. The exclusion laws against Chinese had been repealed in 1943, reunifying many Chinese American families. An influx of new immigrants arrived in the 1950s, mainly Mandarin-speaking professionals displaced by the 1949 Revolution in China. Many of them settled outside of the central city and in the suburbs. New Cantonese-speaking immigrants and refugees from China and Hong Kong tended to live around Chinatown, joining the growing second-generation community in renovating and expanding the South Side Chinatown.

• By the mid-1970s, another major immigration occurred, as China and America renewed relations and the 1965 Immigration Act allowed annual quotas of 20,000 per country. Immigrants arrived from mainland China, adding to the majority of Chinese from Taiwan, Hong Kong and Southeast Asia. Accompanying this growth spurt, a second Chinatown developed on the North Side, around Argyle and Broadway, with the arrival of ethnic Chinese refugees and immigrants from Southeast Asia. While this new Chinatown is also known as Little Saigon or Asian Village, Chinese dialects are easily heard and Chinese Americans are well-represented among shoppers, business owners, residents, nonprofits groups and other community participants.

Current migration patterns:

Nearly 10,000 immigrants came to the Chicago area from China, Taiwan and Hong Kong from 1990-94. With current immigration policies favoring professionals, the self-supporting or those reuniting with family members, it is expected many of them will bypass inner-city enclaves and settle on the North and Northwest Sides and in suburban areas. The most likely candidates for out-migration are highly skilled professionals facing blocked mobility or the "glass ceiling" in corporate America, who may see better opportunities back in the newly industrialized Asian countries, including Taiwan.

Languages:

Cantonese, Toishanese, Mandarin, Teochiu, Fukienese, Taiwanese, etc.

Religion:

Buddhism, Christianity, Ancestral Worship, Taoism, Confucianism (a philosophy). These are not necessarily mutually exclusive. Many in South Side Chinatown are Christians. The largest church there, the Chinese Union Christian Church, has services in three languages or dialects.

Important traditions:

Family harmony and filial piety emphasize the interdependence of family members and respect for authority accorded the older generation. The younger generation should yield to the guidelines and preferences of their parents. Those traditions are problematic for some Chinese American families, where second-generation members adhere to the American value of placing the individual first and to the American need to assert oneself and demand one's rights, particularly after they reach 18. Marriage traditions vary with religious practices and levels of acculturation. When babies are born, there is a one-month-old celebration, a family and community event heralding a healthy future for the child. When people die, the preference is for full-body burial in a local cemetery. Older Chinese still would like to be buried in their ancestral family home or, if they die before returning to China, have their bones sent back to the native village for burial. Many Chinese Americans maintain practices related to ancestral worship in the home or at public occasions by burning incense, paper money and candles, and providing food or other necessities for the afterlife on alter tables at home or at gravesites.

Holiday and special events:

Lunar New Year (varies with the lunar calendar, usually late January to mid-February) is the most important holiday. It is celebrated by parades in both Chinatowns, family banquets, eating special foods, and dissemination of "red" envelopes from the older generation to children or unmarried adults. For all ages, occupations and regional groups, the New Year ranks as the premier celebration. By New Year's Day, debtors are supposed to settle their accounts. Everyone, especially children, tries to wear new clothes. Households are not supposed to cook on New Year's Day because it can bring bad luck. Traditional households begin New Year's preparation about a month earlier. On New Year's Day, they don't clean house, light fires or pour water. Fragrant candles are lit, and in their newest finery, people entertain guests. Mahjong is a popular pastime among the women, with the more devout going to temples. Children and their fathers might go out to a public celebration or movie. Businesses shut down for several days. *August Moon Festival* celebrates the harvest and full moon of the eighth lunar month. It is celebrated by sharing moon cakes with friends and families. On *special birthdays*, at age 70 or 80, children honor their parents by hosting banquets to acknowledge their family lineage. *Chingming/Ghost Festival* (usually April) marks the coming of spring and honors those who have passed away. People visit gravesites, bringing special foods, and graves are traditionally swept, pruned and maintained.

Foods for special occasions:

At New Year's Chinese traditionally eat *chiaotse* (meat and vegetable dumplings); whole chickens, ducks and pigs in soy sauce; glutinous rice flour dumplings; *neinkao* (steamed cake made from glutinous rice flour and brown sugar); fresh whole fish; pig's knuckles; and finally, tangerines and oranges, which symbolize good luck and may be given as gifts. At the month-old baby anniversary, hard-boiled eggs, dyed red, are given away. On special birthdays fresh noodles are served long and uncut (the longer the noodles, the longer the life), as are pastry peaches symbolizing longevity. For August Moon, relatives and friends exchange moon cakes filled with black bean paste, fruits with meats and nuts, yellow bean paste or crushed lotus seeds and nuts, surrounding a center of salted cooked duck's egg. For Chingming/Ghost Festival, cold dumplings, cooked red lotus root, whole chickens, barbecued pork, rice wine and other special foods are arranged at gravesites, then sometimes eaten by relatives.

Dietary restrictions:

Devout Buddhists are vegetarians.

Names:

In traditional or first-generation families, same-sex siblings receive a common name selected according to its meaning and/or possible homonyms (e.g. for sisters, a popular name would be "Mei" meaning beautiful; hence, they might be named Mei Li and Mei Ling). Most Chinese Americans who were born here have Western first names, though they may also be given a Chinese name to be used by family and close friends. That name may be revealed at the one-month anniversary. Studies show the most popular practice for Chinese Americans is for infants to have two Western given names. There are only 100 Chinese surnames. Common ones are Chan, Moy, Liu, Ong and Wong. Early immigrants often joined name societies, which were very powerful. After the 1960s, when many more Chinese began arriving, people tended to join societies based on region or dialect instead.

Major issues for community:

Issues of common concern include: future policies of the People's Republic of China and how they will affect Hong Kong and Taiwan in particular; how to build community and Chinese identity among Asia-born and American-born Chinese in the U.S.; reunification of families and U.S. immigration policies. Beyond that, issues vary by circumstance and class. For recent inner-city immigrants, the primary issues are economic survival and maintaining their families. Those from disadvantaged backgrounds have concerns similar to other residents of impoverished neighborhoods — street crime, jobs and security of their families. For ethnic Chinese from privileged or professional backgrounds, issues include the glass ceiling; certification in their profession; retention of ethnic pride and heritage, especially in white-dominated neighborhoods; upward mobility; political empowerment; and civil rights.

Political participation:

While there has been little research, local politicians and the politically connected say there is limited active participation among first-generation Chinese immigrants. The overwhelming perception is that they are focused on survival and acculturation. If anything, they are more involved in homeland issues. Research shows Asian Americans in general have the highest naturalization rates, but extremely low voter-registration rates. That seems to change over time as they become more acculturated. The lack of political clout in the Chinese American community was particularly evident during the last congressional remap. Both Democrats and Republicans were eager to maintain three strong African American districts and to create the strongest possible Latino district. Chinatown was used to help form the Latino district. Similarly, Chinatown was split down the middle by the new City Council map into the 11th Ward and 25th Ward, maintaining a white 11th Ward.

Links to homeland:

If they have immediate family there, Chinese Americans probably visit as often as possible, and some parents here send their children back to Asia for the summer. Financial support, especially for parents and the elderly, is common and part of the tradition of filial piety. Business with the homeland and Asia-based enterprises has been evident.

Myths & misconceptions:

Myth: Chinese American families are rich.
Fact: Their higher median income usually reflects more workers per household than whites or blacks, and more hours at work.
Myth: Chinese are only good at numbers and computers, possessing a special gene for math.
Fact: More Chinese Americans are pursuing careers in the arts, literature, business, health care and other fields.

— By Dr. Yvonne Lau, Director of Asian and Asian American Studies at Loyola University

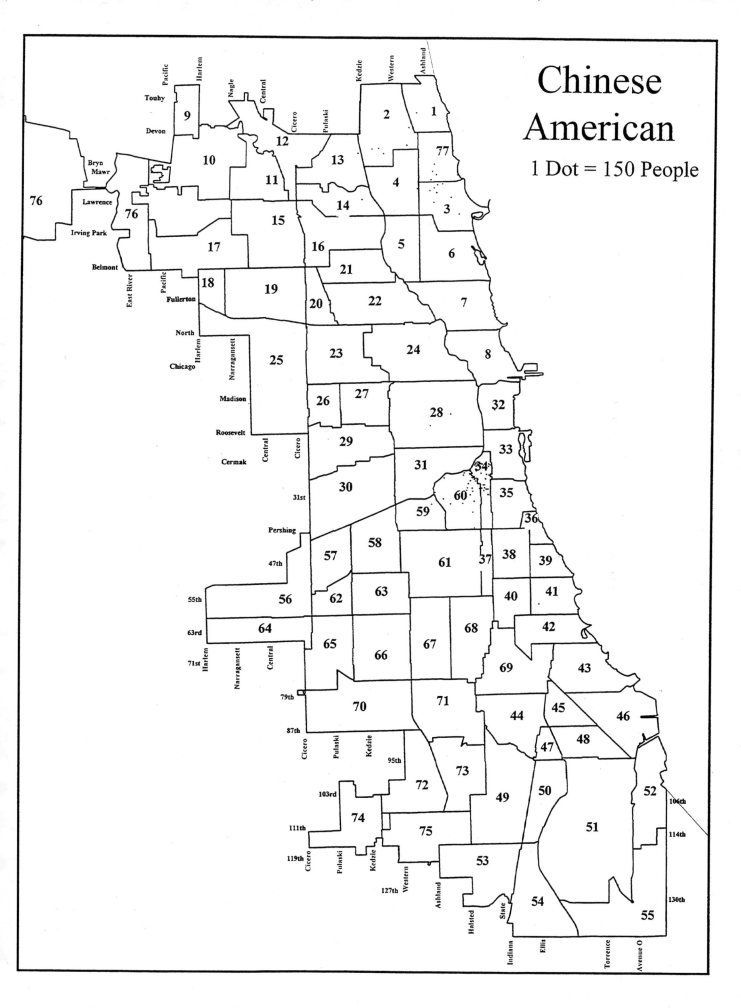

Chinese American

1 Dot = 150 People

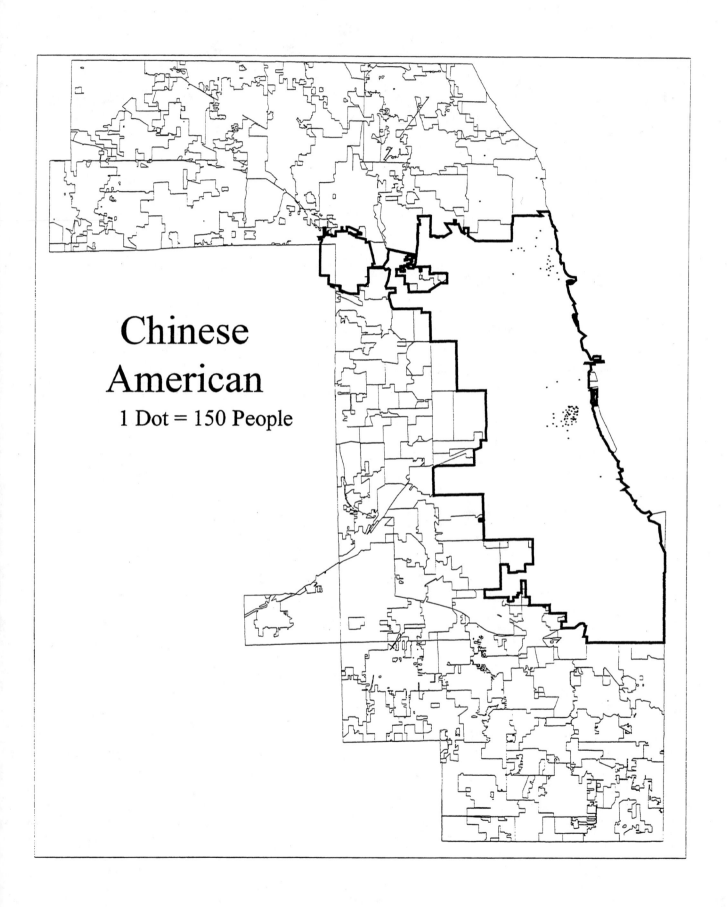

Chinese
American

1 Dot = 150 People

Croatian Americans

Chicago population:
8,357 (1990 Census, first ancestry)
2,969 (Census, second ancestry)
130,000 (1996 community estimate)

Metro area population:
31,939 (1990 Census, first ancestry)
14,855 (Census, second ancestry)
190,000 (1996 community estimate)

Foreign-born:
NA

Demographics:
There is virtually no Census breakdown for Croatians and the issue is further confused by use of the category "Yugoslavian." Traditional Croatian neighborhoods on Chicago's South Side essentially no longer exist. Many Croatians have relocated to the suburbs, especially to the north and northwest, where they like to construct their own homes with ample space for growing fruit and vegetable gardens.

Historical background:
Starting in the 1600s, Croatian ships traveled with some regularity from Dubrovnik and other Croatian ports to trading centers in North and Spanish America. Those traveling on these ships were not just sailors but also missionaries, merchants, craftsmen and adventurers.
• The first well-known Croat in the Chicago area arrived in the late 1830s. This was Fr. Josip Kundek, the first Vicar General of the Vincennese Diocese, which at that time comprised the entire state of Indiana and most of Illinois. Fr. Kundek was instrumental in establishing several cities and the St. Meinrad Abbey in Indiana (1854). His missionary work took him as far as the Chicago area, then a wild and trackless land with only a small settlement around Fort Dearborn.
• Some Croatian settlers were in Chicago by 1860, but the great surge of Croatian immigrants came to Lake Michigan's shores in the 1880s. The first Croatian-language newspaper, *Hrvastska Zora* (Croatian Dawn), was published on Aug. 4, 1892, by Janko Kovačević who came to America in 1890. Only two months later, on Oct. 21, Nikola Polić began a second Croatian newspaper, entitled *Chicago*.
• Between 1880 and 1914 up to 600,000 Croatians immigrated to America. Finding themselves without any socio-economic security here, they started organizing their own fraternal associations in Chicago in 1892. (Croatian Federal Union is the largest Croatian organization outside Croatia, with a current membership of nearly 90,000 and assets of $150 million.) At the beginning of the 20th century, there were some 20,000 Croats in Chicago, according to the city's Croatian newspapers. The massive immigration continued, so the number of Croatians in metropolitan Chicago could have been as great as 70,000 by the late 1920s. The Quota Law of 1921 greatly restricted further immigration. When WWI and the forced inclusion of Croatia, Bosnia and Herzegovina into the dictorial Yugoslav Kingdom had extinguished all hopes of

Traditional Croatian neighborhoods on Chicago's South Side essentially no longer exist.

When the forced inclusion of Croatia into the Yugoslav Kingdom extinguished all hopes of returning to the homeland, they started bringing wives and children here.

American Croatians celebrate their freedom from communism and from Yugoslavia on Croatian Independence Day (May 30).

Croatian immigrants returning to their homeland, they started bringing wives and children here and permanently establishing their families in America. Many children were born here as well. A case study of the Croatian Ethnic Institute indicated that between 1914 and 1925 a total of 1,644 children were baptized in Sacred Heart Croatian Parish in South Chicago and 1,860 at St. Jerome's Church.

• Beginning in 1900, Croatians established Croatian Catholic parishes in areas where they already lived in large numbers; and new immigrants were most likely to settle where the parishes were. Thus were established: the "Western Colony" around Holy Trinity Church, 1850 S. Throop St., the "Dalmatian Colony" around St. Jerome's Church (2823 S. Princeton Ave.), the "Southern Colony" around Sacred Heart Church (2846 E. 96th St.), "Sixtieth Street" settlement near Assumption of B.V.M. Croatian Church (6001 S. Marshfield Ave.) and the "Žumberak Colony" around the Croatian Byzantine Catholic Church (3048 S. Central Park). The Croatian-language parishes not only addressed the faith, language and solidarity among Croats, but also were catalysts for adapting to the new homeland, spreading American patriotism through the parish schools and many parish societies. This was particularly expressed when America needed it most — during the two World Wars. From one parish alone, for example (Sacred Heart in South Chicago), 707 men and women served in WWII, 21 of whom gave their lives for America.

• WWII and the subsequent occupation of Croatia, Bosnia and Herzegovina by communist Yugoslavia was a terrible shock to American Croats. Practically everyone lost family members or friends in the war. During and immediately after the war, some 250,000 Croatians succeeded in escaping to other Western countries. Those who escaped often waited years in refugee camps until they were accepted overseas. Another 405,000 Croatians left or were driven out during the 45-year reign of Yugoslav communism from 1945-90. An estimated 20,000 came to the greater Chicago area. Among them were a considerable number with university degrees and training in medicine, electrical engineering, toolmaking, architecture, manufacturing, and all fields of the humanities. The Croatian parishes, and especially the Croatian Franciscan Monastery in Chicago (4851 S. Drexel Blvd.), invested enormous efforts caring for the new immigrants, obtaining employment for them and introducing them to the American way of life.

Current migration patterns:

The outbreak of the war against Croatia and Bosnia and Herzegovina in 1991-92 created millions of refugees and displaced persons. In December 1992, Croatia was caring for 663,000 displaced persons and refugees, mostly Muslims and Croats. Hundreds of thousands of others were accepted by Germany, Austria, Switzerland, Hungary and other European countries, and relatively few by the U.S. Newcomers from Croatia and Bosnia and Herzegovina during the 1990s thus far probably total about 1,000 in Chicago, mostly displaced families and young individuals.

Language:

The Croatian language is written with the Latin alphabet. For the most part, third and later generations of Croatian Americans do not speak Croatian, though in recent years adults in these groups have shown a growing interest in learning the language. The second generation for the most part speaks both Croatian and their native English.

Religion:

More than 95% of Croatians came to the United States as Roman Catholics.

Important traditions:

Family values and religious education are strong traditions among Croatians. Baptism, confirmation, first communion, and marriage are the central family celebrations, often attended by many relatives and friends. Namesdays or the feast days of the personal patron saints also are celebrated. American Croats gather in large numbers in their churches for prayers and Masses for the deceased. Few Croatians enter marriage outside the Church and divorce is relatively uncommon.

Holidays and special events:

Christmas, Easter, the *Assumption of Mary*, and *New Year's Day* are celebrated as major religious, family and community feasts. In addition to American national holidays, American Croatians celebrate their freedom from communism and from Yugoslavia in 1990 on **Croatian Independence Day** (May 30). Each year on **Assumption Day** (Aug. 15), Chicago Croatians enjoy a large traditional celebration and procession through the streets at St. Jerome's Church, 2823 S. Princeton Ave.

Foods for special occasions:

Coming from a country that is at once Central European, Adriatic-Mediterranean, and Pannonian, American Croatians brought with them to America a very diverse and rich culinary tradition. The Croatian diet is build around fresh fruits and vegetables; thick, rich soups; ragouts and stews; sausage and sour cabbage; a variety of meat- and rice-stuffed vegetables; and a selection of grilled meats and fish. No Christmas celebration would be complete without *pečenka* (a whole roast piglet) and no Easter without *peceno janje* (a young lamb roasted over live coals and served with green onions and homemade whole wheat brown bread). The blessing of food at Easter is a tradition Croatian Americans value highly. On Holy Saturday they prepare and bring to church baskets containing homemade bread, *pisanice* (decorated eggs), onions, ham and various pastries. The women compete to make the nicest cloths, with embroidery and needlepoint, to cover the baskets. Before the *Paschal* (Easter) meal, people must first taste some of the blessed food. Croatian culinary creativity is best expressed in pastries and sweets, as they have been enamored with breads and pastries for centuries. Among the most distinctive pastries are *savijača* (various fillings in layers of flaky pastry), *torta* (baked in layers, filled with creams and glazes), puff pastries, *pita* (a crumbly shortcake filled with fruits, almonds, walnuts, meat, cheese, potatoes or vegetables), *pokladnice* (light round yeast cakes filled with jam, fried and served warm), *orehnmjača* and *makovnjača*. The latter two are the famous Croatian coffee-cake rolls filled with walnuts or poppy seeds, favorites for dessert or with coffee.

Dietary restrictions:

Except for days of religious fasting, there are no dietary restrictions.

Names:

First names are most often saints' names from the Church calendar, or are taken from original national documents of the Croatian Kingdom from the seventh through the 10th centuries. Common Croatian national names are Tomislav, Jelena, Branimir, Ljubomir and Zvonimir, while the saints' names commonly given include Ivan, Ante, Marija, Ana and Josip. Family names often are derived from the name of a paternal or maternal ancestor, formed by adding a suffix to the first name: Tomislavić, Ivanić, Marijić, Josipović. (The suffix "ić" is only one of some 430 possible variants and "ć" is pronounced like the "t" in "future").

Major issues for community:

The Census Bureau method of presenting the Croatian language as Serbo-Croatian, and Croatian ancestry as Yugoslavian, are experienced by the American Croats as injustice and injury, especially after Yugoslavia waged war in 1991-95 against Croatia and Bosnia and Herzegovina and millions of people experienced the horrors of "ethnic cleansing."

Political participation:

Politics among Croatian Americans has always been a two-way street: Croatians have strong feeling about their homeland, yet this has neither prevented them from becoming U.S. citizens nor kept them from voting or serving in the U.S. armed forces. Tens of thousands served in both World Wars, and hundreds were killed in action. A long list of American Croatians have been awarded Presidential citations, victory medals and ribbons with multiple battle stars; and at least four have won the Congressional Medal of Honor. Croatian Americans, whether they are Democrats or Republicans, are most likely to support the American government that has a good relationship with Croatia. Public opinion about America in Croatia seems to be directly influenced by the American Croats. A survey in Croatia conducted in 1994 by the U.S. Information Agency showed opinion of the U.S. in Croatia is exceedingly positive, more so than anywhere else in the region, including Western Europe.

Links to homeland:

American Croatians, along with those in their native homeland, welcomed the renewal of Croatia's independence and democracy in 1990 with great enthusiasm. Yugoslavia — both the royal and the communist — was for Croatians a state in which their human and civil rights were suppressed: freedom of thought, speech and the press, the right to their language and national identity. Croatians generally didn't feel Yugoslavia was their country. For these reasons, receiving U.S. citizenship and a passport, especially for Croatians who fled from Yugoslavia, was a great experience because by their own choice they were able to be citizens of an independent and free nation for the first time. Following the re-establishment of a free and independent Croatia, many American Croats wanted to have Croatian citizenship as well, so that they could feel comfortable in both homelands. During the war against Croatia and Bosnia and Herzegovina (1991-95), all the Croatian parishes, fraternal organizations and societies in the U.S. collected and sent humanitarian and financial aid in abundance. American Croatians fully support the initiative and leading role of the U.S. in the peace process in Croatia and Bosnia and Herzegovina, especially the Washington and Dayton agreements, and they anticipate even stronger involvement by the U.S. in rebuilding those countries and enabling the people driven out to return to their homes.

Myths & misconceptions:

Myth: Croatia is a Balkan country.

Fact: Croatia does not form part of the Balkans, either from a geopolitical or historical viewpoint. Croatia is a Central European and Mediterranean country. From the seventh century on, it has been in cultural, economic, religious and political unity with this part of Europe (except while under the Yugoslav regime). In 1918, against the will of the Croatian people, it was forced into Yugoslavia, a Balkan state. In 1991, 94% of its citizens voted not to be part of Yugoslavia.

Myth: The war in Croatia from 1991-95, was a "civil war."

Fact: A deliberate, unprovoked attack by one country or group on another is aggression. The war waged by Serbia and Montenegro (Yugoslavia) against Croatia in 1991 has been identified and condemned by the European Community, United Nations and many others. The term "civil war," launched by Belgrade, has been part of the war strategy to cover up ethnic cleansing, genocide and occupation.

— By Ljubo Krasić, Director of the Croatian Ethnic Institute in Chicago

Cuban Americans

Chicago population:
10,478 (1990 Census)
10,000-11,000 (1996 community estimate)

Metro area population:
16,910 (1990 Census)
16,000-17,000 (1996 community estimate)

Foreign-born:
69% in the city, 67% in metro area

Note: If community estimates seem low, it is because some Cubans have left the area.

Demographics:

In the Chicago metropolitan area most Cubans live in Cook County (14,437), but they can be found in other counties as well: DuPage (1,286), Kane (264), Lake (539), McHenry (99) and Will (185). Cubans are among the most assimilated Hispanics and live all over the metropolitan area. They do not form clusters or Latino neighborhoods as is the case with some other ethnic groups. The largest concentrations of Cubans in the city are in Logan Square (1,294), Edgewater (914), Albany Park (684) and Irving Park (657). An estimated 6,866 Cubans live in the suburbs. Popular suburbs for Cubans have been Skokie, Oak Park, Stone Park, Melrose Park and Maywood. The 1990 Census counted 497 Cubans in Skokie and 476 in Melrose Park. Median family income in the metropolitan area is $32,703, higher than other Hispanic groups. Three-quarters of Cubans between 18 and 24 years of age are high school graduates (or higher), while 19% of Cubans 25 years and over hold bachelor's degrees (or higher); 14% live below the poverty level. While 25% of those who work are laborers, 23% have managerial jobs. It is believed that Cubans (especially second-generation and those living outside the Miami metropolitan area) tend to out-marry at a higher rate than other Hispanics. In the metro area, 19% speak English poorly or not at all.

Historical background:

Most Cubans came to Chicago after 1959, in the aftermath of Fidel Castro's successful revolution. In 1960 there were fewer than 2,500 Cubans in Chicago. From 1959-73 an estimated 20,000 came to the area. Fleeing as political refugees, they came to Chicago lured by job opportunities, financial aid and resettlement programs provided by the U.S. government, local churches and other private agencies.
 • The first wave (1960-62) included many professionals, such as doctors, dentists, lawyers, accountants and teachers. The first Cubans tended to live together in the same neighborhoods, mostly in Edgewater, Uptown and Logan Square.
 • The second wave (1966-73) coincided with the "freedom flights," that let Cubans reunite with their families in the United States. Because of stiffer exit regulations in Cuba, another hiatus in direct immigration

Cubans are among the most assimilated Hispanics and live all over the metropolitan area.

The first wave (1960-62) included many professionals, such as doctors, dentists, lawyers, accountants and teachers.

Since 1994, U.S. laws have not considered Cubans political refugees, so the last wave may get fewer benefits.

Cubans speak Spanish with a marked Caribbean accent.

occurred from 1973-80. But during this period, many Cubans came here from third countries, especially Spain.

>   • In 1980 a third wave was composed mostly of those who came in the Mariel boatlift. Some had relatives in Chicago, some did not. Many in this and the next wave were single men in their 20s.

>   • The fourth, and last, wave are those coming from Guantanamo, often with help from Catholic Charities. Since 1980, Cubans who have come to Chicago tended to be less educated and younger than those who arrived earlier. As a whole, they have not adapted as well or as quickly as those who came in the '60s or '70s. But there are many success stories among these late-comers. The new arrivals tend to live on the North Side, especially in Logan Square. As they become more assimilated, Cubans move to the suburbs.

Current migration patterns:

From 1990-94, about 350 Cubans arrived legally in the Chicago area. Some are *balseros* (boat people) who were picked by the U.S. Coast Guard and later transferred to Guantanamo or Panama. It is expected that between 1,000 and 2,000 will have settled in the Chicago area by the end of 1996. Lately, because of stiffer immigration guidelines (in both Cuba and the United States), some undocumented Cubans are known to be coming to Chicago from Mexico, Central America and other Spanish-speaking countries, but as with any illegal flow, numbers are difficult to obtain. There also is some outmigration. Many Cubans, including retirees, have left Chicago for the Miami area, where they owned real estate before they left Chicago. Since 1994 U.S. laws have not considered Cubans political refugees, and so the last wave may get fewer benefits.

Language:

Cubans speak Spanish with a marked Caribbean accent. Many second-generation Cubans speak Spanglish (a mixture of English and Spanish). Many older Cubans incorporate Anglicisms into their everyday language as well.

Religion:

Cuban Americans in Chicago are predominantly Roman Catholic, but some are Baptist, Methodist, Assembly of God or Pentecostal. A sizable number of Cubans are Jehovah's Witnesses, and many others practice *Santeria,* a mix of African religion and Roman Catholicism.

Important traditions:

Many older Cubans in Chicago celebrate their saint names, act as chaperones for their daughters, and encourage unmarried children of both sexes to live at home. They celebrate girls coming of age at 15, not as elaborately as Mexican Americans but with close family and friends. Older Cuban men like to play dominoes and women play Bingo and Lotto.

Holidays and special events:

Many Cubans in Chicago celebrate the **Birth of Jose Marti**, patriot in the Spanish Civil War and leader in exile who was killed when he returned to Cuba, on Jan. 28 by attending civic events. They observe the **Feast of Our Lady of Charity**, patroness of Cuba, Sept. 8 by attending a Mass at St. Ita's Church, where the main celebrant is usually a Cuban priest from Miami. The **Birth of the Cuban Republic** is observed May 20. Most Cubans celebrate Catholic religious holidays such as **Christmas** and **New Year**. In Chicago Cuban American children generally receive their Christmas toys Dec. 25. The tradition back in Cuba is to get gifts Jan. 6, the Feast of Epiphany. Most Cuban Americans in Chicago celebrate American traditions and holidays such as Thanksgiving and July 4. Cubans who practice Santeria celebrate the feasts of **St. Barbara** (Dec. 4) and **St. Lazarus** (Dec. 17), two Catholic saints who are worshipped as *orishas* (African deities).

Foods for special occasions:

On *Nochebuena* (Christmas Eve) and on special occasions such as marriages, baptisms, celebrations for 15-year-old girls and national holidays, many Cubans celebrate with native dishes.

These may include, but are not limited to, *lechon asado* (pork roast), *moros y cirstianos* (rice mixed with beans), *ropa vieja* (shredded beef), *boliche* (pot roast) or *pollo asado* (roast chicken). Popular staples are *platanos fritos* (fried plantains), and the native roots *malanga* and *yucca*. For dessert they serve *flan* (custard), *arroz con leche* (rice pudding), or *natilla* (egg pudding), and Espresso coffee.

Names:

Cubans, like most Hispanics, have two surnames and many have hyphenated last names. Married women keep their maiden name and add to it their husband's last name. Common names for males are José, Juan, Luis, Carlos, Manuel, Alberto and Julio. Popular women's names are María, Carmen, Lourdes, Josefa, Caridad, Mercedes, Barbara and Teresa. It is common for men to have two first names, like Juan Carlos, and women also, as in Ana María.

Major issues for community:

Cubans rally around the issues of human rights, the U.S. embargo of Cuba and the Island political system. Many Chicago Cubans pay attention to other issues, such as unemployment, discrimination, housing, political empowerment, education and health care.

Political participation:

Cuban activists have lobbied Illinois politicians to help enact embargo laws and other regulations that would shorten the Castro regime. Most popular political and civic organizations have been — and in many cases still are — local chapters of national Cuban American organizations such as the Cuban American National Foundation, *La Junta Patriótica Cubana* and *Cuba Independiente y Democratica*. Most Cubans vote in local elections and some prominent residents have been appointed to governmental commissions and boards. Professionals with the most political influence in the city include doctors, lawyers, teachers and those in media and marketing. Many Cubans are leery of government programs because they failed to serve their needs back home.

Links to homeland:

Most Cubans have become American citizens and relatively few — no more than 20% —would return to Cuba should the political climate change there. Many have gone back to visit family. They also send them money, medicine and clothes regularly. Cuban Americans in Chicago communicate with their families in Cuba by telephone rather than by mail, as there is no direct mail between Cuba and the United States.

Myths & misconceptions:

Myth: Cubans are zealous anti-communists, vote Republican and espouse right-wing policies.

Fact: Most Cuban Americans are not irrational or fanatic and, like most people, they show common sense. Their political activism is a result of having lived under a one-man, one-party rule rather than embracing right-wing policies. All Cubans do not vote Republican.

Myth: Most Cubans are middle class, rich or business-minded.

Fact: 14% of Cuban families in 1990 lived below poverty level and about one-quarter of those who work hold laborer or factory jobs.

Myth: Most Cubans are white or light-skinned.

Fact: More than 50% of Cubans are black or mixed-raced. In the United States the rate is about 20%.

Myth: Cuban families are tightly knit. Divorce is rare.

Fact: Cuban families suffer from one of the highest divorce rates among Hispanics.

Etc.:

Many Cubans are emotionally charged and talk loudly and fast, sometimes interrupting others in conversation. They are very friendly, expressing affection by eye contact, touching and hugs. They tend to show appreciation, not by saying *gracias* (thank you), but with a smile or a pat on the back. This is part of their Spanish character, derived from southern Spain.

— By Dr. Jorge Rodriguez-Florido, Professor of Spanish at Chicago State University

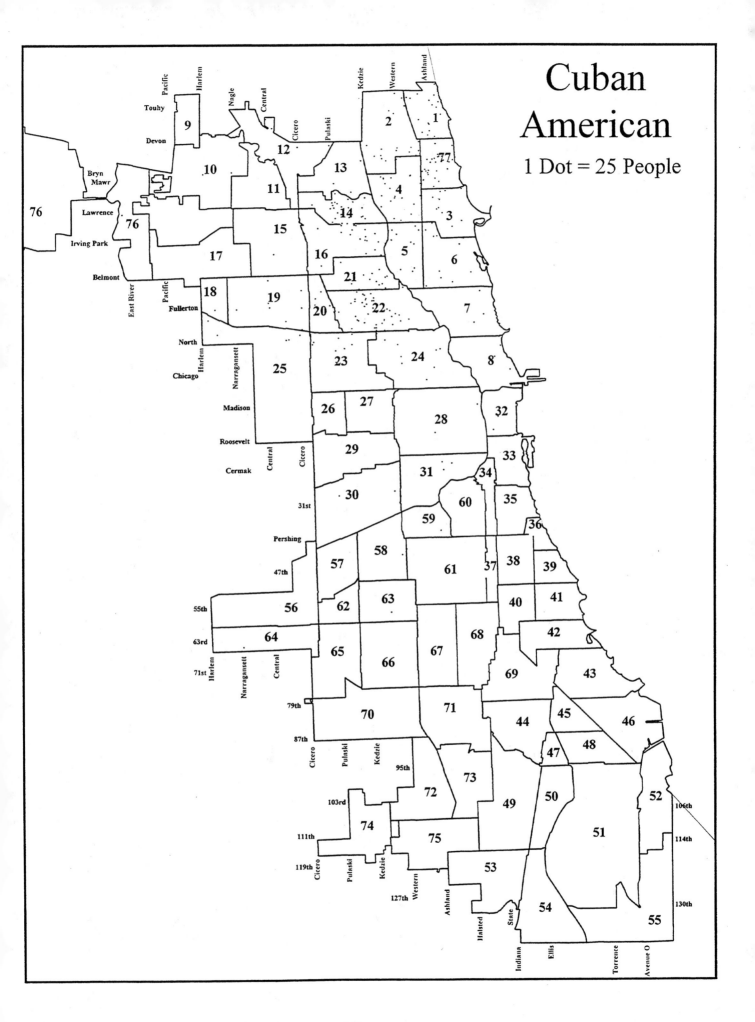

Cuban
American

1 Dot = 25 People

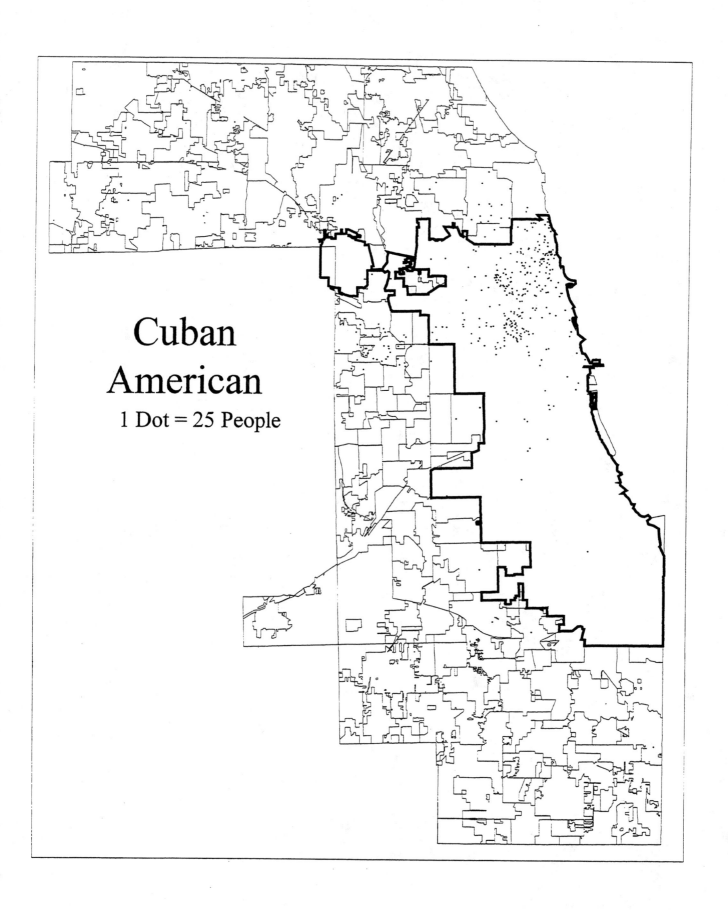

Cuban
American

1 Dot = 25 People

Czech Americans

Chicago population:

8,872 (1990 Census, first ancestry)
7,173 (Census, second ancestry)
21,000 (1996 community estimate)

Metro area population:

67,239 (1990 Census, first ancestry)
46,834 (Census, second ancestry)
100,000 (1996 community estimate)

Foreign-born:

NA

Note: In addition to those who reported Czech ancestry in Chicago, 2,527 listed Czechoslovakian as first ancestry. In the entire metro area, 16,022 listed Czechoslovakian as first ancestry. It is impossible to tell how many of these should be considered Czechs and how many Slovaks, a distinction that becomes more important with the breakup of the country into the Czech and Slovak Republics.

Demographics:

The overwhelming majority of Czech Americans now live in the suburbs. Though people of Czech ancestry are quite spread out, some favorite suburbs include North Riverside and Stickney, where they are the largest ethnic group, and Brookfield, Forest View and Highwood, where they are second. In the city, many live on the Southwest Side in places like Garfield Ridge, West Elsdon, West Lawn, Gage Park, Ashburn and South Lawndale. Others are scattered on the North and Northwest Sides. There is little Census breakdown for Czechs and the issue is complicated by those claiming Czechoslovakian ancestry. Also, some from the earlier generations think of themselves as Bohemians, rather than Czechs or Czechoslovakians. It is estimated there are few undocumented Czechs, though some who came to study or visit may have overstayed visas.

Historical background:

Immigration of the Czech people to the U.S. dates back to 1640. The 1730s brought the Moravian brethren, a religious community.

• Hundreds of thousands came to America in the later decades of the 19th century and the early 20th century. Both of these large migrations brought Czech people to Illinois. Manufacturing and other jobs attracted them to the Chicago area. Mass immigration occurred because of political persecution in the Austrian Empire and the revolutionary events of 1848. Settlers were concentrated in the manufacturing belt of the East and Midwest states. Mines, steel mills, factories, business, railroads, farming and construction were large draws for the immigrant population. Many who came at that time were farmers or laborers. The early settlers in Chicago lived around Pulaski and Foster, site of the Bohemian National Cemetery, founded in 1877.

A significant number entered the banking and savings-and-loan field, which for this very thrift-oriented people proved a successful venture.

There has been a definite westward pattern, generally staying between Roosevelt Road and 39th Street.

This is a culture that is private about its politics because history has shown it can be dangerous to be on the wrong side.

Political concerns include a widespread belief that the current government in the homeland is not as devoid of communists as they would like us to think.

• Other major immigration waves followed, because of political persecution and events in 1938 (Nazi invasion), 1948 (communist government) and 1968 (Soviet invasion). These political refugees often were highly educated professionals, though many had to take work other than their education dictated. Many Czechs were entrepreneurial and opened businesses such as mortuaries, retail shops, contracting firms and restaurants. Although various other immigrant groups tended to associate only with their own counterparts, many did business with those of Czech heritage. Fraternal, religious, social and cultural organizations were formed over the years, some splitting onto multiple groups, others merging to form larger, stronger groups. By the 1930s and '40s, the Czech settlements were more concentrated in Pilsen and what is now known as Little Village. The 1950s and '60s moved the Czech concentration farther out into areas such as Cicero, Berwyn, Riverside and North Riverside. LaGrange Park, Westchester, Downers Grove and Hinsdale soon followed. There has been a definite westward pattern, generally staying between Roosevelt and 39th Street. Last year the Bohemian Home for the Aged, now known as Tabor Hills, moved from the city to the west end of Naperville, an area increasingly central to the Czech population.

Current migration patterns:

The Velvet Revolution that ended communism in 1989 brought some limited immigration. In many cases this represented the migration of family members who had been left behind. Current immigration is very sparse, mostly because Czechs now have the freedom to come and go.

Religion:

Moravians, from the eastern half of the Czech lands, are predominantly Catholic. Czechs also may be Protestant (Hussites) or rationalists, who often use the term "Freethinkers." In the case of the latter group, fraternal organizations such as CSA Fraternal Life or Masonic orders often filled the sociological role of a church community.

Language:

Czech. Several Saturday language schools for children still function in the area, about four of them Freethinkers and one Catholic. At least two groups offer adult language education.

Important traditions:

In addition to retaining language, important traditions include music, physical fitness, dance and folklore. The *Sokol* gymnastics organizations operate several local units in the Chicago area, with the national organization headquartered in Berwyn. They provide gymnastic and calisthenic training for members, from toddlers to senior citizens. In addition, several folk dance groups meet regularly and perform for many events throughout the year. There is a Czechoslovak Heritage Museum in Oak Brook, which features hundreds of artifacts, folk costumes both life-size and on dolls, a library, and archives of thousands of volumes.

Holidays and special events:

St. Joseph Day (March 19) is a celebration for all people named Joseph (a fairly common name among Czechs) that is similar to a birthday. The celebration of such days is a widespread custom, and because certain names often recur in a family, it can become a significant family event. *Lidice* (June 10) commemorates the annihilation of a small Czech town in 1942 by the Nazis, seeking revenge for the murder of Reinhard Hydrich, Hitler's top operative in Czechoslovakia. All the men were shot, and women and children were sent to concentration camps where most of them died. The town itself was leveled and Hitler tried to wipe the name Lidice from the face of the earth. Instead towns all over the world changed their names to Lidice. Commemorative ceremonies are conducted at a monument in Crest Hill (near Joliet), where a service is held each year on the Saturday closest to June 10. *St. Wenceslaus (Svaty Vaclav),* on Sept. 28, is the feast of the patron saint of the Czech people. He is the same one heralded in the Christmas Carol. *Czechoslovak Independence Day* (Oct. 28) celebrates the founding of the Czechoslovak Republic in 1918. In addition, festivals held annually include *Czechoslovak Day Festival* (the last Sunday in July); *Moravian Day* (the fourth weekend in September); the *Houby (Mushroom) Festival* (the weekend preceding Columbus Day); and *Moravian Folk Fest* (the first Saturday in November).

Foods for special occasions:

Vanocka (a sweet-egg bread twist with raisins and almonds slivers) is traditionally prepared for Christmas, but also is popular in local bakeries year 'round. *Bochanek* is a round Easter version of the same. The top is usually cut in a cross to symbolize the crucifixion. *Svickova* (a marinated beef dish, with a heavy sour-cream gravy made from the vegetables and marinade used in cooking) is a festival meal, and served with dumplings. Carp is the traditional fish served on Christmas Eve. It was acquired live and allowed to swim in a tub at home to "clean it out." *Kuba* (a mushroom-garlic-barley casserole) also is prepared for Christmas Eve. Roast goose or duck is the traditional Christmas Day dinner, served with sauerkraut or cabbage and dumplings. Lentils are the good luck food for New Year's Day. The round shape resembles coins and therefore they are expected to bring prosperity.

Names:

Given names are often passed from generation to generation. Common male names include Anthony, Frank, George, John, Joseph, Petr, (Peter), Vaclav (James), Vladimir and Zdenek. Common female names include Anna, Emily, Jarmila (Geraldine or Jerri), Jirina (Georgina), Marie, Mildred, Vera, Vlasta (Patricia) and Zdenka. Surnames often end in "in," "ak," "ek" "ik," "a," or "ky," but not exclusively.

Major issues for community:

This is a proud community, seldom resorting to any welfare or even unemployment benefits. They are savers and take pride in ownership. Any perceived denial of ownership rights, such as not having power over whom to sell to, is very serious.

Political participation:

The culture is private about its politics because history has shown it can be dangerous to be on the wrong side. Czechs are civic-minded in that they become citizens at the earliest opportunity; and they vote, but do not like to be polled or asked about their politics. There is no strong voting bloc because of the privacy of their beliefs. The people are not stereotypically either Democrats or Republicans, although both parties could count a large following among Czechs. The date and reason for their immigration plays a large part in their individual politics. Refugees from communism tend to be more conservative and Republican. The offspring of turn-of-the-century immigrants who came here for jobs are more likely to be Democrats. Few run for public office unless they are several generations removed from immigration.

Links to homeland:

Only those whose immediate families remain in the old country tend to retain original citizenship for the convenience of travel. Until recently, a visa was required from the Czech government and some feared it would be denied if they gave up Czech citizenship. Rarely do Czechs return to the homeland permanently, because there are better economic opportunities here. A few, however, have chosen to retire there because their U.S. pension dollar goes further. This phenomenon is more common now that the communists are not in power. Visits to the homeland are more common since the "Velvet Revolution" of 1989; previously, many who had fled communism feared returning under that government. Immigrants who came earlier and second- and third-generation Czechs traveled there frequently even during communism. Money was sent home more when the oppressive government allowed no free enterprise. Political concerns include a widespread belief that the current government is not as devoid of communists as they would like us to think. Many of the same people are in power now as under communism, and therefore many Czech emigres are less jubilant over the new freedom than might be expected. Many Czech American organizations have been encouraged by the Czech Embassy to help lobby for the acceptance of the Czech Republic into NATO. Most Czech Americans think this is a good cause and believe that because of its economic development, the Czech Republic is an excellent prospect. Current help for the homeland tends to be in the form of economic and educational opportunities, and Western business training. Some charitable programs were undertaken in the early '90s to provide textbooks, medical and computer equipment.

Myths & misconceptions:

Myth: Czech people are cheap.

Fact: They are very industrious, thrifty and good savers. They are protective of the assets they accumulate and don't spend frivolously.

Myth: Czech people are foolhardy.

Fact: They manage to generate humor in their darkest times, and used that to survive. They are not fighters and, at the heart of Europe, they have been conquered or ruled by almost everyone. They have survived such rule by making fun of their oppressors.

— By Vera A. Wilt, President of the Czechoslovak American Congress and CSA Fraternal Life

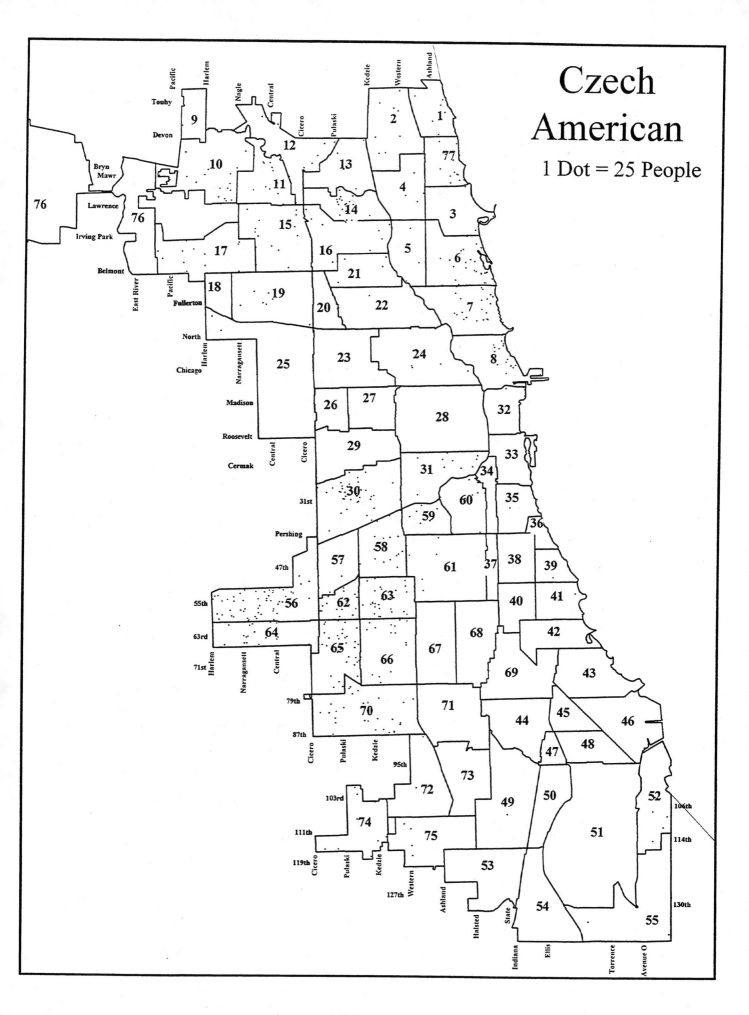

Czech American

1 Dot = 25 People

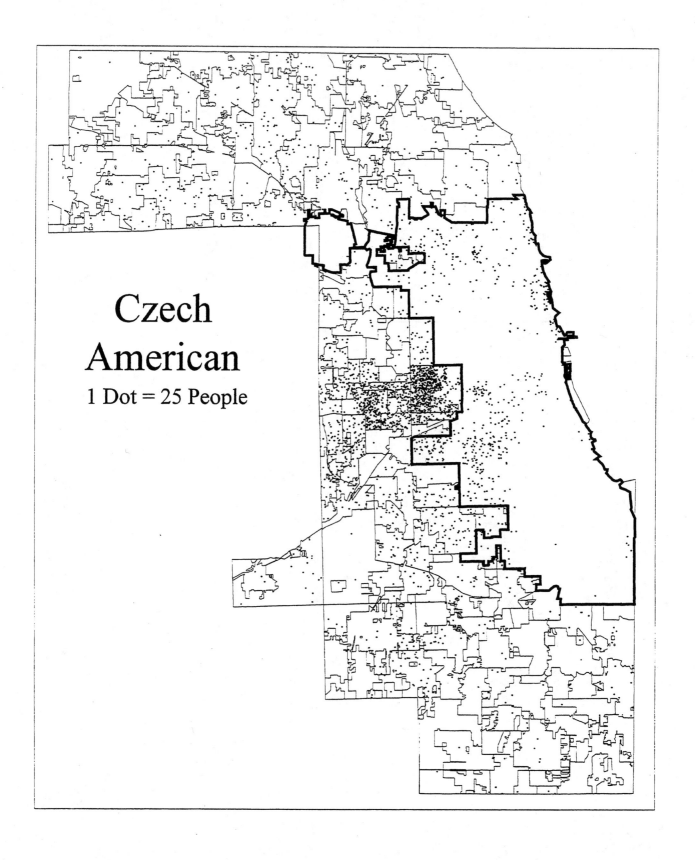

Czech
American

1 Dot = 25 People

Ethiopian Americans

Chicago population:
515 (1990 Census)
3,500 (1996 community estimate)

Metro area population:
849 (1990 Census)
4,000 (1996 community estimate)

Foreign-born:
Overwhelming majority

Demographics:
Census data on Ethiopians is very sparse and unreliable. Community leaders say few filled out the forms and many came after 1990. Because the sample is so small it is difficult to extrapolate Census figures to the Ethiopian population as a whole. Estimates based on information from the Department of Health and Human Services, Ethiopian Community Development Council and other sources suggest about 90 percent of Ethiopians in the metropolitan area live in Chicago, with the biggest concentration in Uptown, Edgewater and East Rogers Park. The rest live all over the suburbs, with the largest clusters in Elgin and Wheaton. It is estimated that at least 10% have college degrees, 40% some level of college education, and 30% high school diplomas. An estimated 15% live in poverty. While 15% may be in professional jobs, an estimated 85% are doing menial jobs. As many as 40% of the people work and go to school at the same time. Intermarriage is insignificant in the Ethiopian community in the Chicago area. At least 95% speak English well. An estimated 60-80 individuals in the metropolitan area are undocumented.

Historical background:
The Ethiopian population in Chicago before 1980 consisted mainly of students. Because of civil war raging at that time in Ethiopia, 70-80 refugees arrived in Chicago in 1980, mainly from the Sudan and Dijibuti refugee camps. Nationally, about 8-10% of these refugees had a college education and most (75-85%) had a high school education; almost all (95%) were young adults in their 20s. Those who came to Chicago lived in Uptown and Edgewater when they first arrived. Many Ethiopians who were here earlier accepted the refugees with open arms and helped make their adjustment easier. Most refugees were young people who lacked transferable skills. And, because of language and cultural barriers, most had menial jobs with no future: washing dishes, keeping house, busing tables. The 1980 Refugee Act set the ground rules for resettlement of refugees, providing financial, material and educational assistance, including job training. Resettlement agencies helped with cultural adjustment, English as a Second Language, and job training and placement. Refugees also got cash and medical assistance from the federal government through the state. From 1980-92 an estimated 2,000 Ethiopian refugees came to Chicago. From 1985-92 the demographic characteristic of the refugees coming changed from urban to rural and

About half the Ethiopian population here probably came after 1990.

Some Ethiopians migrate out of Chicago to Wheaton, where Ethiopians still live as a community.

Although Christians and Muslims are almost equal in number in Ethiopia, the Muslim Ethiopian population in Chicago is less than 10% because most came from the North.

from highly educated to less educated.

Current migration patterns:

Since 1992, resettlement of Ethiopian refugees has stopped because of the end of the civil war. The number of people coming to Chicago as legal immigrants (through family reunification, the diversity visa lottery, or as visitors and students changing their status to political asylees) is increasing. About half the Ethiopian population here probably came after 1990 through these immigration avenues. Some came legally but overstayed, and some might not have been granted political asylum so they have undetermined status. The outmigration is balanced by immigration from other cities and states. The number returning home is very insignificant (maybe 5-10 people have returned to Ethiopia since 1991). Those coming since 1991, either as refugees or immigrants, tend to be from urban areas, with at least a high school education. Some Ethiopians migrate out of Chicago to Wheaton, where Ethiopians still live as a community.

Language:

More than 70 languages are spoken in Ethiopia. Most of the refugees, however, speak one or more of the three major languages: Amharic, Tigrigna or Oromigna.

Religion:

Although Christians and Muslims are almost equal in number in Ethiopia, the Muslim Ethiopian population is less than 10% in Chicago because most came from Northern Ethiopia.

Important traditions:

Extended family relationships, parental control of children, and younger members of the family accepting the authority of elders are traditions dearly held. It is important for children to help their parents in the home without being asked. Children have problems accepting these traditions because of peer influence and the different social values and expectations of the mainstream society. There is intergenerational conflict, with children on one side and parents on the other. Parents want to discipline their children but their way of disciplining may conflict with the law. There is tension in many families, particularly those with teenagers. Parents seem to be nervous and totally unprepared to handle the situation.

Holidays and special events:

The **Adwa Victory** (March 2) is celebrated each year with a strong sense of patriotism and nationalism. The battle of Adwa was fought between Ethiopia and Italy on March 2, 1896, at Adwa in Tigray, in Northern Ethiopia. At this battle the modern colonial army of Italy was decisively defeated by the Ethiopian peasant army lead by Emperor Minilik II. The outcome of the battle of Adwa shocked the world and gave birth to black and other oppressed peoples' movements around the world against colonialism. The Adwa Centennial was celebrated by Ethiopians and other Africans and people of African descent around the world, including in Chicago. In Ethiopia it was celebrated with memorial prayers, rallies and patriotic songs that reinforced the need to maintain independence. The **Ethiopian New Year** falls on Sept. 11 of the Western calendar, except following Ethiopian leap year, when it falls on Sept. 12. The New Year celebration starts with lighting or burning of *chibo* (candlewood) on New Year's Eve, which continues into an overnight party. On New Year's Day people stay home and prepare food. In the afternoon, they start the festivities with homemade foods and homemade drinks. It is an eating and partying holiday. The **Ethiopian Christmas** is celebrated Jan. 7 of the Western calendar, as in other Eastern Orthodox churches. Christmas is celebrated by playing a mass hockey-like game, baking breads, and drinking homemade beer called *tella*. The game is the major aspect of the celebration. *Gena* is an all-men's game, played by children and adults of all ages. **Epiphany** is one of the most colorful and highly spirited holidays. It is a celebration in commemoration of the baptism of Christ, celebrated Jan. 19 in the Western calendar. On the eve of Epiphany, all churches take the arc (a wooden tablet) to a fountain or riverside, accompanied by a huge crowd singing and dancing. The priest and clergy put on their colorful church dresses and slowly accompany the chief priest, who carries the arc on his head. They spend the night near the fountain or riverside. Then, about noon, after prayers and rituals, they proceed back to each church. On Epiphany, women put on their best dresses and the saying goes, "If people do not wear their best dresses on Epiphany, having a dress is of no value." **Eid-ul-Fittir** is celebrated by Muslims at the end of the fasting month of Ramadan. All family members put on newly purchased or clean clothes and go to the mosque for morning holiday prayer. Then they go back home and have lunch with the family. Later in the day, mainly children go around the neighborhood to visit family members and relatives, who give them cash to spend as they wish.

Foods for special occasions:

These include spicy chicken stew with *doro wat* (boiled eggs), *kitfo* (tartar with spices and hot pepper), *injera* (pancake-like bread made of a tiny grain called *teff), dulet* (a kind of steak tartar consisting of liver, stomach and lung as well as brisket that is hot and spicy, sometimes with a small drop of bile for taste), *tella* (home-brewed beer), *tej* (honey wine brewed at home), *katicala* (a home-distilled 80% proof alcoholic beverage), and *kurt* (raw meat, mainly brisket, served with hot spicy pepper).

Dietary restrictions:

In the Ethiopian Orthodox, Muslim and Jewish religions, pork is not edible. Shellfish also is restricted by the three major religions practiced in Ethiopia. During Lent or any fasting season, Ethiopian Christians do not eat meat, dairy products and poultry; they eat cereals and vegetables.

Names:

Most Ethiopian names have a meaning that reflects the circumstances around the time of birth. If someone is born immediately after a close family member dies they call her/him Masresha, which means "compensation." Names usually express the environment and family mood and wishes during the birth of a child. People also are named after a grandfather or mother or friend who has passed away. Other names are simply biblical and koranic. In Christian tradition religious names like Gebre Michael, Gebre Yohannes and Gebre Mariam are common. *"Gebre"* means servant; Gebre Michael is servant of St. Michael. Except in very few cases, male and female names are made distinct by adding a suffix to the root word of the name. For example *"worq"* is a root word that means "gold." Adding *"neh"* makes it male and adding *"nesh"* makes it female.

Major issues for community:

Access to economic-development opportunity, cultural maintenance, and opportunities for cultural expression are the major issues of concern in the community.

Political participation:

The Ethiopian community in Chicago is relatively new and small. It was only about 15 years ago that Ethiopian refugees started to arrive. The bulk of the Ethiopian population here have less than eight years of residency. And the majority of Ethiopians until recently considered being here as temporary. They thought of going back home when the conditions that caused their flight changed. Because of these factors, participation in political and civic life of the mainstream society was almost non-existent. Now the need to participate is evolving. With a feeling of belongingness, political and civic participation follow. There is an increased interest in participation and pursuing the American Dream.

Links to homeland:

Even though the trend is to become naturalized citizens, many maintain their Ethiopian citizenship. Since 1991 no less than 30% of Ethiopians have gone back to Ethiopia for visits but almost all have returned here. Nearly all Ethiopians here maintain contact with relatives there. Some family members in Ethiopia absolutely depend on money they receive from relatives in the United States. The majority of Ethiopians here oppose the current Ethiopian government's policies of politicizing ethnicity. Many opposition groups lobby the U.S. government to withdraw its support for the Ethiopian regime. The U.S. is one of the strongest supporters of the current Ethiopian government, which was installed in 1991 with all-around support from the U.S. and other Western powers. The Chicago Ethiopian community has been active with the famine situation in Ethiopia for the past 10 years, raising money to support relief efforts of agencies like UNICEF, World Vision, Oxfam, Save the Children and the Ethiopian Red Cross. Some Ethiopians here do business with Ethiopia and some have small investments there. The community stays informed about developments in Ethiopia through popular magazines, mostly published in the United States.

Myth & misconceptions:

Myth: Ethiopia is a Christian "island" in an ocean of Islam.

Fact: Ethiopia adopted Christianity as a state religion in the fourth century A.D. However, starting in the eighth century, the Ethiopian population has been converting to Islam. Now Muslims constitute nearly half of the Ethiopian population.

Myth: Ethiopians are Semitic.

Fact: Because of the great ancient Ethiopian civilization, and the resistance by Ethiopians to colonialism, Europeans, in order to deny blacks any civilized life, wanted to explain the achievement of this great people in terms of their racial affiliation. They labeled Ethiopians as Semitic or Caucasian (see *New York Times*, March 1896, immediately following the victory of Adwa 100 years ago). Major Ethiopian ethnic groups, such as Amhara and Tigre, speak Semitic languages. But that does not make them Semitic. Ethiopians are a black, Cushite stock of people with various sub-categories of black groups.

Myth: All Ethiopians are famine victims.

Fact: The 1984-85 famine and subsequent ones have affected a significant portion of Ethiopia's population. Periodic draught and continuous civil war have left the majority of people poor. But all Ethiopian people have not been affected by the famine. In one-third of the country there has been no famine, and it remains green.

Etc.:

Many Ethiopians consider it impolite to look people in the eye when they talk with them. This is quite often misinterpreted as weakness or a lack of self-confidence. Ethiopians of the same sex hold hands and kiss each other on the cheek. Roommates of the same sex may sleep in the same bed. Some misinterpret these behaviors as homosexual. They are not. Calling someone with a finger pointed upward is very offensive for Ethiopians. They use a hand with all the fingers pointed down and move them toward the chest to call someone by gesture.

— *By Dr. Erku Yimer, Executive Director of the Ethiopian Community Association*

Filipino Americans

Chicago population:
29,309 (1990 Census)
1996 community estimate: NA

Metro area population:
63,182 (1990 Census)
1996 community estimate: NA

Foreign-born:
77% in the city, 72% in metro area

Demographics:
In Chicago, Filipinos tend to live on the North and Northwest Sides. There are concentrations in Albany Park and North Park, though in general they are scattered throughout the metropolitan area. Suburbs with the largest numbers are Skokie (2,445), Glendale Heights (1,278), North Chicago (1,061), Morton Grove (998) and Bolingbrook (794). Most Filipinos live in Cook County (48,355) but there are 8,694 in DuPage and 4,053 in Lake County, according to the 1990 Census. In Chicago, 10% do not have a high school diploma, while 56% have a bachelor's degree or higher; 27% do not speak English very well; and 31% are in professional or managerial jobs while 2.6% have laborer jobs. Median family income is higher than for most other groups. In Chicago it is $40,327, in the metro area $48,200. Less than 3% in the metro area fall below the poverty line.

Historical background:
• Following American acquisition of the Philippines in 1898, young male Filipinos began coming to the Chicago area as students, first as government-scholarship (*pensionado*) or family-supported students and later as self-supporting students who expected to combine attending classes with employment. Brothers, cousins and townmates followed, creating enclaves on the Near West and Near North Sides. In 1920, the U.S. Census counted 154 Filipinos in Chicago; and in 1940, 1,740. Unofficial estimates put Filipino numbers at approximately 5,000 during the 1930s. Prior to WWII, the typical Filipino in Chicago was a high school graduate with some college who found work in the service sector — several hundred with the Pullman Co. — or with the U.S. Post Office. In 1940, among those over the age of 20, Filipinos (men) outnumbered Filipinas (women) 21:1. Ninety percent of marriages were interracial, with most wives American-born daughters of European immigrants.
• Until the mid-1930s, Filipinos were classified as "nationals" and permitted unrestricted entry into the United States, but were not eligible for citizenship. The Tydings-McDuffie Act of 1934 promised the Philippines independence after 10 years and limited Filipino immigration to 50 per year. After independence, Filipinos were to be totally barred from entering the United States. In 1946, largely in recognition of their valor during WWII, Filipinos in the U.S. became eligible for naturalized citizenship and the annual quota was raised symbolically from 50 to 100. Between 1952-65, however, most Filipinos came as non-quota immi-

Median family income is high: $40,000 in Chicago and $48,000 in the metro area.

Filipinos were permitted unrestricted entry to the U.S. until the mid-1930s, but they were ineligible for citizenship until 1946.

Filipinos currently are the fourth largest group immigrating to the Chicago area, after Mexicans, Poles and Indians.

grants under the family-reunification provisions of the McCarran-Walter Act of 1952.

   • After passage of the Immigration Act of 1965, Filipino immigration surged. Occupational-preference provisions enabled many professionals, especially nurses and doctors, to qualify for entry. Over time, however, family reunification became a more significant factor, permitting the chain immigration of extended family units. By 1970, the Filipino population in the Chicago area was 9,497, with more women than men. By 1980, it reached 41,283 for the metro area.

Current migration patterns:
Filipinos currently are the fourth largest group immigrating to the Chicago area (after Mexicans, Poles and Indians). From 1990-94, about 2,500 came each year, totaling 12,370, according to the INS.

Language:
Coming from an archipelago of more than 7,000 islands, eight major languages and up to an estsimated 121 dialects, Filipino immigrants are commonly multilingual. Depending on their level of education, they typically learn Tagalog — the language of Manila and nearby provinces, which has been designated the Philippine national language and renamed Pilipino — as well as English, which was used in school above the second grade for many years. They also speak the dialect of the locale where they were raised. The eight major languages are Tagalog, Cebuano, Hiligaynon, Ilocano, Bicol, Samareño, Pampango and Pangasinan.

Religion:
Catholics make up about 80% of the Filipino American population. There also are some Protestants and Muslims.

Important traditions:
In their immediate and extended families, Filipinos in the U.S. continue to prize the close family ties, strong family values and religious strength characteristic of Filipino culture. The traditional practice of choosing multiple godparents (*compadrazgo* or ritual co-parenthood) for a baby's baptism, binds real and fictive kin to the baby's family and is typically expected to provide on-going sustenance. Wedding celebrations, debutante balls and anniversary parties bring together family and friends and further serve to demonstrate a family's social status.

Holidays and special events:
Rizal Day (Dec. 30) celebrates the memory of Dr. Jose P. Rizal (1861-96), a surgeon, novelist, sculptor, poet and linguist who focused national and international attention on Spanish misrule and became the Philippines' national hero. He was executed in Manila by a Spanish firing squad Dec. 30, 1896, at the onset of the movement for Philippine independence. In Chicago, Rizal Day was commemorated as early as 1905 at the University of Chicago. By the 1930s, festivities were typically co-sponsored by provincial and work-related clubs and included a banquet, "queen" contest and dance at a downtown hotel. Organizational rivalry sometimes produced two or three celebrations in a single year. Today, the tradition continues with celebrations in the city and suburbs. *Philippine Week* events are celebrated before, on and after June 12, to commemorate that date, in 1898, when the Philippines won their independence from Spain. (Because the Philippines became a U.S. colony following the Spanish-American War, actual independence was not won until July 4, 1946.) Activities include drama, talent shows, a parade, a picnic, sports, art exhibits, receptions and a grand dinner ball. Religious celebrations are prominent in the annual calendar of festivities. The *Christmas* season begins on Dec. 16 with a series of pre-dawn Masses (*Misa de Gallo* or *Simbang Gabi*). After the final Mass at midnight Christmas Eve (*Misa de Aquinaldo*), families gather for a joyous midnight supper (*noche buena*), the year's most important dinner. The Lenten ceremony (*Salubong*) is followed by *Easter Sunday,* when statues of the Blessed Virgin, wearing a black shroud of mourning, and of the Risen Christ are carried in a procession. *Flores de Mayo* is a month-long celebration in May dedicated to the Blessed Virgin, whose crowning has been an annual event in Chicago since the 1940s. *Santacruzan*, the rite commemorating the discovery of the true cross, is re-enacted as a religious procession in May with beauty queens dressed as biblical characters. In addition, new immigrants typically celebrate the feast of

the patron saint of their town of origin.

Foods for special occasions:

Filipino dishes reflect the historical presence of Malay, Islamic, Chinese, Spanish, Mexican and American influences. One of the oldest is *kinilaw* (fish cooked lightly in vinegar). Traditional main courses include *lechon* (a whole pig roasted over charcoal and hot stones and served with a tangy liver sauce), which was prepared in the pre-Spanish era after the harvest or hunt; *adobo* (a pork, chicken and/or seafood stew cooked in vinegar), which is popularly regarded as the Filipino national dish; *pancit* (noodles cooked with meat and vegetables); *pinakbet* (boiled vegetables and pork seasoned with *bagoong*, a fermented shrimp or fish paste); *kare-kare* (oxtails stewed in peanut sauce); and *kalderetta* (goat stew). Most dishes are eaten with rice. *Lumpia* resembles the Chinese egg roll; "fresh" lumpia, the Chinese spring roll. *Paella Valenciana* (a melange of meats and seafood), served on special occasions, and *leche flan*, (an egg-custard dessert made in a caramel-lined pan) are Spanish in origin. *Bibingka* (a sweet, sticky rice cake made with coconut milk) and *halo-halo* (a sundae made with sweet beans and strips of sweetened coconut in syrup) are also popular desserts at Filipino American parties. *Lambanog*, (a coconut wine) and *basi* (a fermented rice wine) are now served as after-dinner liqueurs.

Names:

While some Filipino family names can be considered indigenous — for example, Bacdayan and Macapagel — others derive from the Chinese, such as Cojuangco, Soliongco and Sylianco, or from the Spanish, as in Gonzales, Alamar and Lopez. The mother's family name usually becomes the child's middle name. A Filipino first name is often the name of the saint celebrated on that person's birthday. Sometimes the firstborn son is given his father's first name. Less typically, all sons are named after their father and distinguished by their order of birth, such as Florentino, Florentino II and Florentino III. Or, all children in a family are given first names starting with the same letter or syllable — as in Arturo, Arlinda and Arleen. Nicknames can shorten a name (Pedro becomes "Pido" and Guillermo, "Mo"); or end in "ing" for a daughter or "oy" for a son (e.g. Benigno becomes "Ninoy"). Or, a nickname might represent an element of character or a physical attribute.

Major issues for community:

Like many other Americans, Filipino Americans struggle to cope with the problems caused by separation and divorce, teenage pregnancy, gang affiliation, disinterest in education and multiple wage-earning. Those who hope to be joined in the U.S. by family members still in the Philippines are concerned about proposed legislation that might restrict immigration. Some Filipino Americans have mobilized to win full pay and veterans benefits for the almost 175,000 Philippine Scouts and Philippine Army soldiers who served in the U.S. armed forces in the Pacific during WWII and became eligible for U.S. citizenship in 1990. Locally, Filipino Americans often lament the absence of unity in the community.

Political participation:

Socio-economic position, occupational affiliation, and family tradition typically determine the political party affinity of U.S.-born and naturalized Filipino Americans. Although most would agree that political power can be achieved only through active participation, few Filipino Americans in Chicago have taken this route. No Filipino American has yet held elective office in Chicago.

Links to homeland:

Family ties are reinforced through letters and frequent telephone calls, and by money sent to relatives in the Philippines. When returning home to visit relatives, the *balikbayan* fills large boxes with popular name-brand American goods. Many social clubs are based on the Philippine province of origin. The latest news from the Philippines is an important feature of local Filipino American newspapers.

Etc.:

Individual Filipino Americans are shaped by birth in either the Philippines or the U.S., and by their educational background, economic circumstances, religion, time of arrival in the U.S. and marriage within or outside the group. While some Filipino Americans are involved in organizations that are non-ethnic or Asian American, more belong to clubs and associations identified solely with Filipinos. Many of these groups meet under the umbrella of the Filipino American Council of Chicago (founded in 1948) at the Rizal Center on West Irving Park Road, which has been the center of Filipino American community life in Chicago since 1974.

— By Dr. Barbara Posadas, Associate Professor of History at Northern Illinois University, and Estrella Alamar, President of the Filipino American Historical Society of Chicago; also contributing: Justo Alamar, Willi Buhay and Romeo Munoz

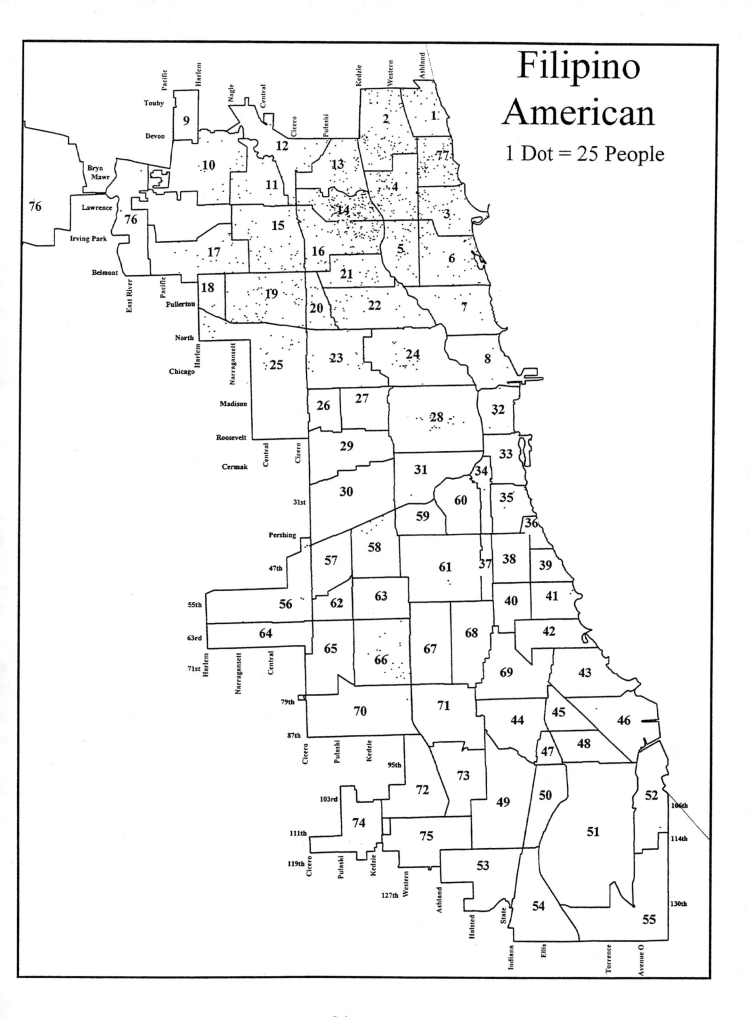

Filipino
American

1 Dot = 25 People

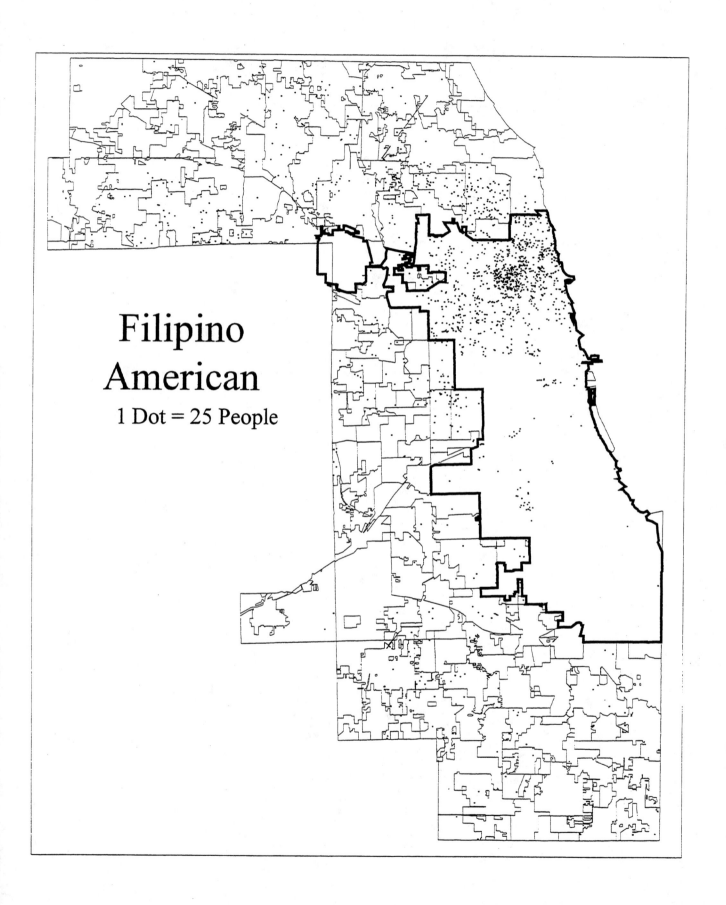

Filipino
American

1 Dot = 25 People

German Americans

Chicago population:

197,236 (1990 Census, first ancestry)
73,098 (Census, second ancestry)
1996 community estimate: About same as Census

Metro area population:

1,210,298 (1990 Census, first ancestry)
420,516 (Census, second ancestry)
1996 community estimate: About same as Census

Foreign-born:

5% of first ancestry in city, 3% in metro area

German Americans are Chicago's largest white ethnic group.

The German American community is especially strong in the suburbs, where 23% report German ancestry.

The words "kindergarten" and "fest" are among many German words adopted by Americans as their own.

After 1865 German was taught in the public schools; WWI ended that.

Demographics:

The 1990 Census shows German Americans remain Chicago's largest white ethnic group. Both city and suburbs maintain many areas where German-descended people represent more than 20% of the population. The city's German American population stood at 7% in 1990. In Chicago, seven neighborhoods have a 20% or greater German population: Beverly, Edison Park, Forest Glen, Jefferson Park, McKinley Park, Montclare and North Center. The German American community is especially strong in the suburbs, where 23% percent report German ancestry. Germans are still the largest ethnic group in roughly 80% percent of the suburbs. In the suburbs, German Americans make up 27% of Arlington Heights, 32% of Lake Zurich, 29% of Palatine and 27% of Des Plaines. There is a similar trend in other northwest suburban communities. While there is no Census breakdown for education and income, it is estimated that most Germans are well-educated, the majority attending college and going on to business or the professions, and there is very little poverty. German Americans have assimilated readily with Italians, Scandinavians, Poles, French and many other European groups.

Historical background:

German immigration to Chicago started in the 1830s, with some immigrants relocating from Pennsylvania. By 1860, there were more than 22,000 Germans in Chicago.

• Large numbers came in 1849 because of political and economic upheaval at home. They worked in the meatpacking plants, helped build the Michigan-Illinois canal, and entered manufacturing and the building trades. Numerous churches were founded in 1846-80, starting with St. Paul's Evangelical Lutheran and St. Peter's Catholic Church in 1846.

• The German population tripled from 1870-1900. There were more than 400,000 by the end of the century, about one-fourth Chicago's population. There was a large community east of the river between Diversey and Devon, much of it clustered around Lincoln Avenue; and smaller settlements were in Hyde Park, South Shore, Humboldt Park and Albany Park. The Orchestral Association, founded in 1891, had a German conductor, Theodor Thomas, and most of its members were German immigrants. Orchestra Hall was built to house that orchestra in 1905. After 1865, German was taught in the public schools. The coming of WWI, however, ended that. After a period of vocal nationalism during the years of American neutrality, German American activities and institutions were dealt a sharp blow when the U.S. entered the war.

• Most organizations active today were founded after the last large-scale immigration, in the 1950s. Prior to WWII the immigration pattern mirrored the political, religious and economic struggles in their homeland. After WWII, in the late '40s and particularly the '50s and early '60s, a large percentage of immigrants were the so-called "displaced persons" who fled from the communists or were expelled from their ancestral homes in Hungary, Romania, the former Yugoslavia and Czechoslovakia, Poland and Russia, where they were a large minority. Immigration often was sponsored by American religious organizations, state agencies and commercial enterprises. In most cases initial jobs and lodgings had to be guaranteed by American sponsors. There was virtually no "illegal" immigration.

Current migration patterns:

Current immigration is relatively small, with maybe a couple hundred coming each year. During the Korean and Vietnam War years immigration of young male Germans to the U.S. declined substantially. Also, rapidly improving economic conditions in Germany contributed to a slowdown in emigration. In the '90s the opportunities in Europe, as well as generous fringe and social benefits, keeps most young Germans at home. For those already here, a greater degree of affluence has led many German Americans to move to the suburbs, and the traditionally German area in Chicago is mainly confined now to Lincoln Square.

Language:

German and, depending on the displaced person's country, they also may speak Hungarian, Romanian, Croatian, Czech or Polish. The German language is spoken mainly by first-generation immigrant families, less by second and later generations.

Religion:

Predominantly Catholic and Lutheran. Also, many American Jews came from Germany.

Important traditions:

Many German customs have become American customs over the generations — such as kindergarten and the Christmas tree. Music is important, with waltzes, operettas and classical music coming from composers that include Mozart, Bach and Hayden. *Saengers* (singers) societies continue today, with one of the largest having more than 4,000 members across America. There are many Germanic fraternal organizations, some centering on music, others on sports (such as soccer), karnevals and other cultural interests. The word "fest" is one of many German words adopted by Americans as their own.

Holidays and special events:

The **Steuben Parade** (a Saturday in September) takes place in downtown Chicago, followed by a weekend Germanfest in the old German neighborhood at Lincoln/Leland/Western, with food, music and entertainment. The parade commemorates General Friedrich von Steuben's achievements during the American Revolution. **German-American Day** (Oct. 6) commemorates the first organized immigration of Germans and is celebrated nationally. Thirteen Mennonite families from Krefield, Germany, landed on that day in 1683 in Philadelphia and founded Germantown, a few miles away. **Karneval** (Nov. 11), **Oktoberfest** and wine festivals are cultural and social events Germans brought with them to America, which have become popular American festivals as well. Main religious holidays for Christians are **Easter** and **Christmas**.

Foods for special occasions:

German cuisine is diversified, depending on region, and often is hearty, because so many worked in the fields and needed a substantial diet. Many dishes have become American favorites, including hamburgers, wieners, bratwurst and cutlets. For festive events like Christmas, roast goose is traditional. On Christmas Eve or Christmas Day, families traditionally enjoy roast goose served with red cabbage and potatoes. Christmas Day is a time to invite friends for traditional German sweets, such as *stollen* (fruit cake), *lebkuchen* (honey cakes) and *pfeffernusse* (spice cookies). *Wienerschnitzel* (veal pounded, seasoned, breaded and deep-fried) and *sauerbraten* (beef marinated in vinegar and spices) are popular dishes, as well as pork shanks with *sauerkraut* and dumplings.

Major issues for community:

Nurturing German American heritage, culture and language; and taking a stand against ethnic bigotry and anti-Germanism.

Political participation:

German Americans take their citizenship seriously. Even though they tend to be politically reticent, they are active voters. Involvement in civic and governmental activities are mainly cultural and educational.

Links to homeland:

German American societies, sister-city arrangements and exchange programs all contribute to maintaining links to the ancestral land. There is considerable travel back to Europe, and the German American National Congress facilitates contacts between German and American businesses.

Myths & misconceptions:

Myth: Germans are either Nazis, mad scientists, cruel or dopey.

Fact: Germans and German Americans have often been the subject of prejudice and stereotyped generalizations, partially based on historical events. In fact, the cultural and economic contributions of Germans and German Americans to the history and prosperity of America are endless and varied. Famous German Americans and German contributions that have become part of America's culture include the Christmas tree, songs like "Silent Night," composers Irving Berlin and Roger Hammerstein, scientific genius Albert Einstein, President Dwight D. Eisenhower, Gen. Norman Schwartzkopf, former Secretary of State Henry Kissinger, Babe Ruth and Marlene Dietrich.

Myth: Germans are authoritarian and militaristic.

Fact: Many Germans left their home country because of religious or political persecution as well as economic hardships. In America they contributed greatly to our nation's struggle for independence, its culture and prosperity. German Americans are proud of their heritage and achievements and live harmoniously with their fellow citizens.

*— By Ernst Ott, National President of the German American National Congress and
Editor-in-chief of the German American Journal*

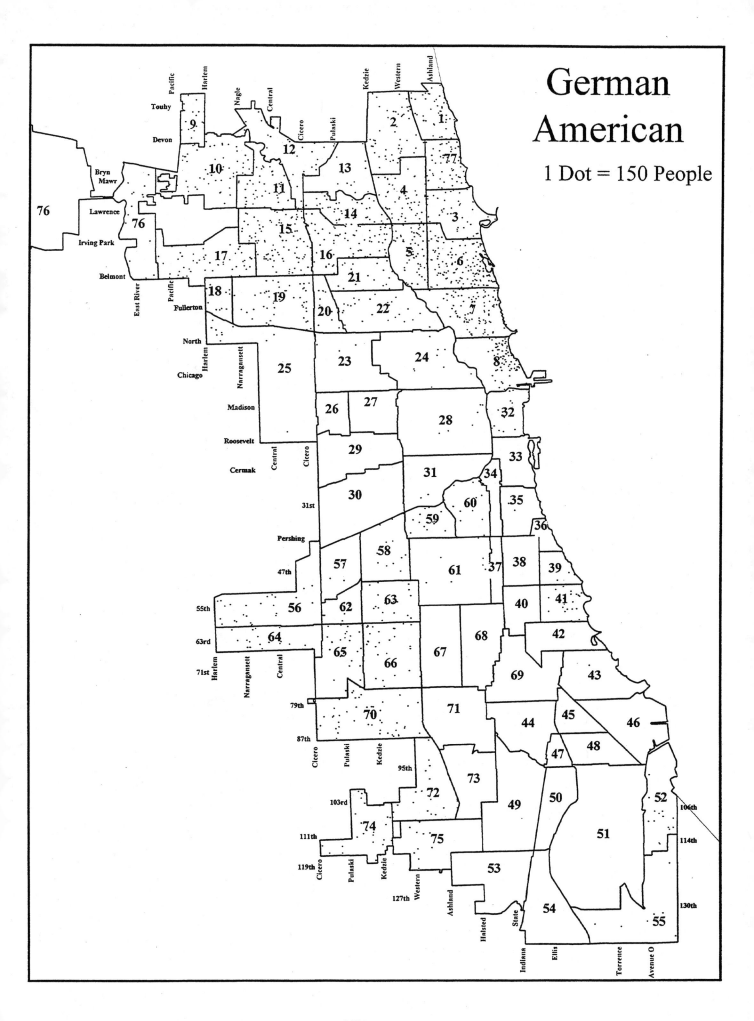

German
American

1 Dot = 150 People

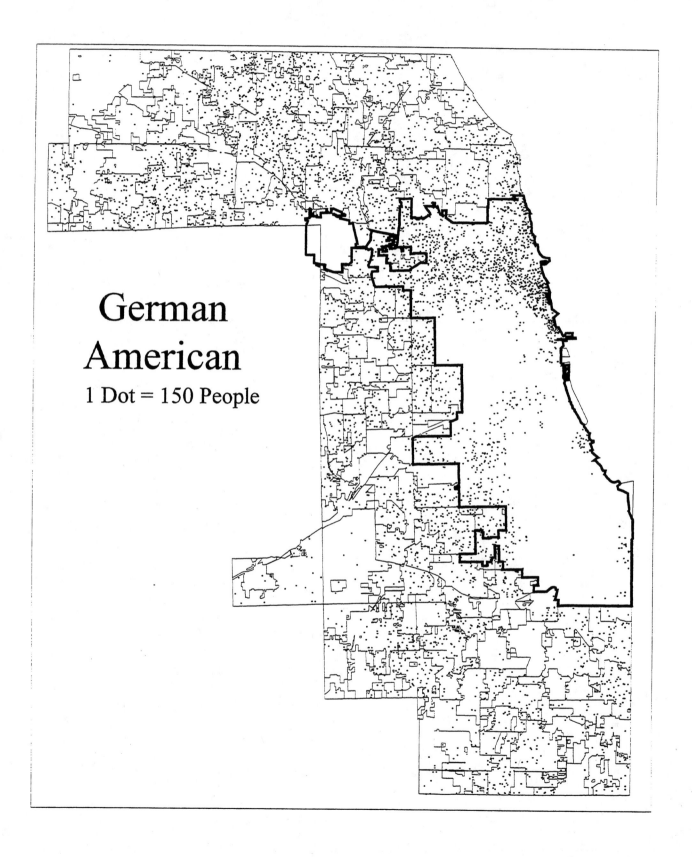

German
American

1 Dot = 150 People

Greek Americans

Chicago population:
21,158 (1990 Census, first ancestry)
2,452 (Census, second ancestry)
60,000 (1996 community estimate)

Metro area population:
71,512 (1990 Census, first ancestry)
4,501 (Census, second ancestry)
90,000-125,000 (1996 community estimate)

Foreign-born:
34% of first ancestry in city, 27% in metro

Demographics:
More than twice as many Greeks live in the suburbs as in Chicago. They traditionally have been concentrated in Chicago neighborhoods, such as Lincoln Square (Greek Town North), Rogers Park and West Rogers Park, Edgewater, Forest Glen and Lake View on the North Side; Woodlawn, Englewood, South Chicago, Hegewisch, Ashburn and Beverly Hills on the South Side; and Austin on the West Side. Today, the largest numbers are found in West Ridge and Lincoln Square. By WWII and thereafter, as Greeks moved up the socio-economic scale, they joined the pattern of affluent Chicagoans moving to the suburbs. The most popular suburbs for Greeks are: Arlington Heights, Berwyn, DesPlaines, Glenview, Morton Grove, Prospect Heights, Oak Lawn, Palos Hills, Park Ridge and Skokie. In 1990 nearly 14,000 Greek Americans live in these 10 suburban communities. Since 1960, the U.S. Census has reported Greeks as having extremely high educational and income levels, as compared with other immigrant groups. The Census revealed that on the national level second-generation Greek American men and women were 70% more likely to have completed college than the native white population, and said Greek Americans enjoy earnings 13.6% higher than the native white average. The relative lack of poverty is attributed by Greek Americans to a strict work ethic. In 1990, just over 2,000 Greeks in Chicago reported they did not speak English well, if at all. For the metro area, that number was 4,818. In the early days of immigration, family size was quite large. Today, the average Greek American family is much smaller and the community is getting smaller, especially because Greek emigration to America has been severely reduced. Given their high educational levels, many are in the professions as doctors, lawyers, educators, politicians, economists, or proprietors of their own businesses. The interfaith marriage rate was 63% in 1993 and steadily increasing, according to the official *1995 Yearbook of the Greek Orthodox Church in America*. There is no evidence of undocumented persons in the Greek community.

Historical background:
   • Greek immigration to Chicago did not begin in earnest until after the Great Chicago Fire of 1871. Realizing that job opportunities were available in rebuilding the city, young Greek men came to Chicago. Prior to this, only occasional Greek seamen arrived by the way of the Mississippi and Illinois rivers, settling in Chicago and intermarrying with

Greek immigration to Chicago began in earnest after the Great Chicago Fire of 1871, when Greek men came to seek jobs rebuilding the city.

Initially, most lived in the central city to be close to their place of work, especially the wholesale market area where they had to procure produce for their food-peddling businesses.

Greek immigrants never intended to stay. About 40 percent of those who came to America returned to Greece.

Greeks are political in nature. They see politics as an honorable tradition.

Irish and Italian women. Their numbers increased rapidly during the first decade of the 20th century. In 1890 there were only 245 people of Greek birth in Chicago; by 1920 the number had risen to 11,546. Greek immigration was primarily a male phenomenon; young boys and men coming to America to escape the extreme poverty in Greece, in the hope of returning with enough money to pay off family debt and provide marriage dowries for their daughters or sisters. It was not until after 1900 that Greek women began to emigrate. Most immigrants to Chicago came from the provinces of Laconia and Arcadia, giving the Greek population of Chicago its Peloponnesian character. The initial illiteracy rate for Greek immigrants was 27%. But because of their strong belief in education, they encouraged schooling for their children, resulting in second and third generations entering the professions. At the turn of the century, Greeks concentrated on the Near West Side, known as the Greek Delta (Halsted, Harrison and Blue Island streets), which emerged as the most prominent and largest Greek Town. There also were settlements on the Near North Side at Clark and Kinzie streets and on the South Side in Woodlawn and Pullman. Initially, most Greek immigrants lived in the central city in order to be close to their place of work, especially to the wholesale market area (Fulton and South Water markets), where they had to procure produce for their food-peddling businesses. For more than a half-century the Delta was the site of the main Greek community of Chicago, attaining a Greek population of more than 30,000, until it was displaced by the University of Illinois Chicago campus in the 1960s.

• By the late 1920s the Greeks were among the foremost restaurant owners, ice cream manufacturers, florists, and fruit, confectionery and vegetable merchants in Chicago. According to the old *Chicago Herald and Examiner*, they operated more than 10,000 stores, 500 of them in the Loop, doing business of over $2 million a day in the 1920s. One-third of the wholesale commission business in Chicago's markets on South Water and Randolph streets, estimated at $250 million annually, was done with Greek American merchants. With passage of the National Quota Act in the 1920s, Greeks immigration to the United States came to virtual standstill.

• After WWII a new wave of immigration to the United States took place, with many coming to Chicago under the Displaced Persons Act. This immigration surge was accelerated with the 1965 repeal of the National Quota Act. As a result, the Chicago area received many new Greek immigrants, making it the largest urban Greek population in the world outside of Greece. (Today New York City has the largest Greek American population.) Greek immigrants never intended to stay. Once enough funds were saved, many returned home. About 40 percent of Greeks who came to America returned to Greece. The devotion for the homeland is reflected by the financial help to their families in Greece, which between 1919-28 averaged $52 million annually. Those who remained formed a stable and well-organized community, participating in the life of the city.

Current migration patterns:
Immigration has all but stopped. There is a minimal amount of repatriation.

Language:
Greek. While most Greek Americans speak English as their native tongue, the vast majority — second- and third-generation offspring — still have a spoken knowledge of Greek.

Religion:
Greek Americans are overwhelmingly Greek Orthodox.

Important traditions:
The highly structured Greek community supports churches, schools and numerous voluntary societies for transmitting its legacy. This shared cultural concern has resulted in the Greek community's continued tradition of family customs, social life, food, holidays, dancing and other shared values as a vibrant characteristic of the Greek populace of Chicago. Family traditions of observing namedays instead of birthdays, and the baptismal custom of naming children after grandparents, continue to be an important part of Greek heritage.

Holidays and special events:
Greek Americans observe ethnic and religious holidays like **Greek Independence Day** (March 25), celebrating independence from the Ottoman Empire in 1821, **Greek Easter**, and major **sum-**

mertime church festivals, the three largest being St. Andrew's, St. Demetrios' and St. Constantine's. Easter is the main holiday. On **New Year's**, gifts are given.

Foods for special occasions:
For Easter, there is lamb, cooked over coal and served with potatoes baked Greek style, a special soup of lamb innards, and red eggs symbolizing the blood of Christ. On occasions such as Easter, *tsoureki* (a sweet bread) is served with the main course. Popular foods include *feta* cheese and *baklava*. (pastry with *filo* dough saturated with honey and nuts). Two special dishs are *pastistio* (a casserole of ground beef and macaroni with special *bechamel* sauce) and *mousaka* (casserole of layered eggplant, ground beef and potatoes, with cheese).

Dietary restrictions:
Fast days for the church are meatless and dairyless.

Major issues for community:
One big issue for Greek Americans is usurpation of the name Macedonia by the former Yugoslav Republic in Skopje. Greeks want to reserve the use of the name because (another) Macedonia has been a Greek province since ancient times. A second issue is the continuing partial occupation of Cyprus by Turkey. Greek Americans object to U.S. aid to Turkey. They feel it is against the interest of the U.S. and NATO because, they say, Turkey uses the aid to buy weapons to use against neighboring countries. Finally, they are concerned about Turkish human rights abuses against Armenians, Kurds and the Ecumenical Patriarchate, world center of the Greek Orthodox Church. Two more issues of current concern are sovereignty over the Aegean Sea and Islands, where Turkey has been violating air and water space, and the human rights of people of Greek ancestry in northern Epirus, an area now in Albania.

Political participation:
Greeks are political in nature. They see politics as an honorable tradition. Forming only 1% of the nation's population, Greeks are over-represented in Congress and among other national and local officials. They have run for many offices, including president of the United States, and serve in many governmental capacities as elected or appointed officials. In Chicago alone, Greek Americans have served in a variety of elected and appointed positions at both the city and state levels. These include state senators and representatives, state director of revenue, superintendent of Chicago's sanitary district, interim superintendent of Chicago Public Schools, state superintendent of public instruction, and currently, CEO of Chicago Public Schools and Cook County commissioner. Greeks in the U.S. initially were Republicans, but after Franklin Roosevelt became president most became Democrats because they liked the New Deal. Now they are split between the two parties, with the preponderance in Chicago probably Democrats. Historically, one newspaper, the *Greek Star*, is Republican, while the other, the *Greek Press*, is Democrat.

Links to homeland:
Links to the homeland are many. Greek Americans enjoy dual citizenship — American and Greek — because Greek law recognizes the children of Greek immigrants born abroad as Greek citizens themselves. Financial remittances of newer immigrants to the homeland remain relatively high. Greek political issues such as Cyprus and Macedonia receive much support from Greek Americans, as does the ongoing conflict with the Ecumenical Patriarchate, world center of the Greek Orthodox faith in Istanbul, Turkey. Several Greek American lobbies coordinating these efforts exist in the nation's capital and only recently, a Greek American from Chicago was elected the first president of a worldwide association of Greeks.

Names:
Many are Christian. Others come from the Bible or Ancient Greece. Common names are George, Constantine (Gus), John, Demetrios (Jim), Helen, Mary and Catherine. Last names tend to end in "s" or (for women) "ou." Many names end in "poulos" which means "son of."

Myths & misconceptions:
Myth: Most Greeks own restaurants.
Fact: Some do, but many others are involved in the professions.

Etc.:
The Greeks of Chicago have maintained their customs and ethnic values while also accommodating to the achievement standards of the larger American society. The "best of two worlds" adaptation may well be the distinguishing mark of Greek American ethnicity.

— By Dr. Andrew T. Kopan, Professor Emeritus in the School of Education, DePaul University, and author of The Greeks in Chicago

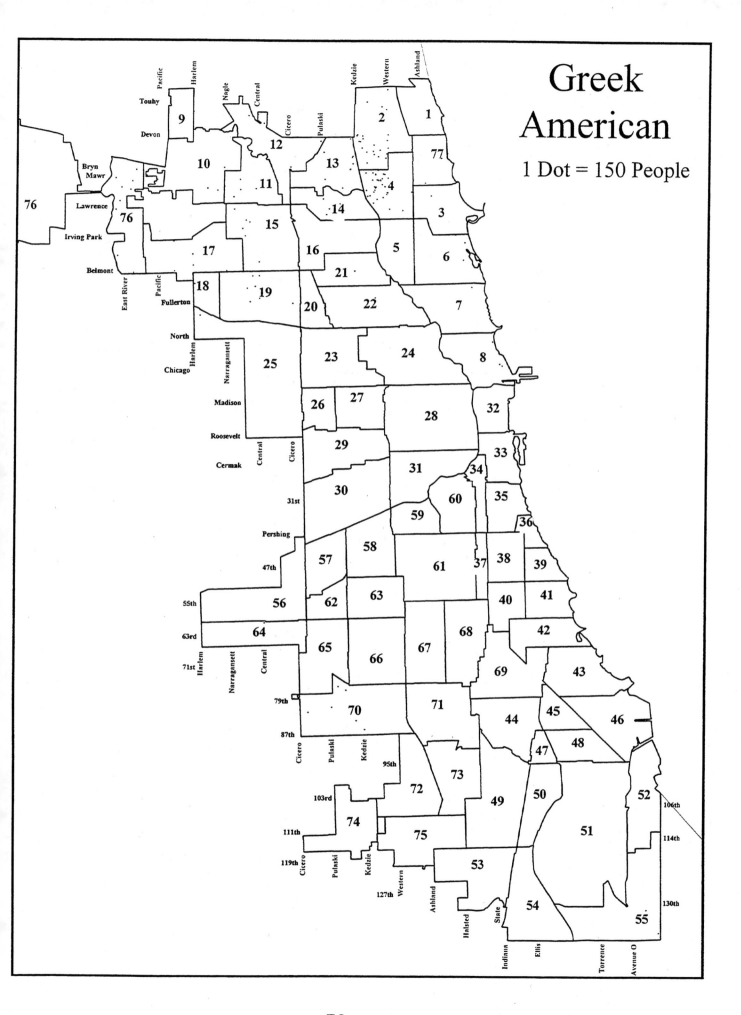

Greek
American

1 Dot = 150 People

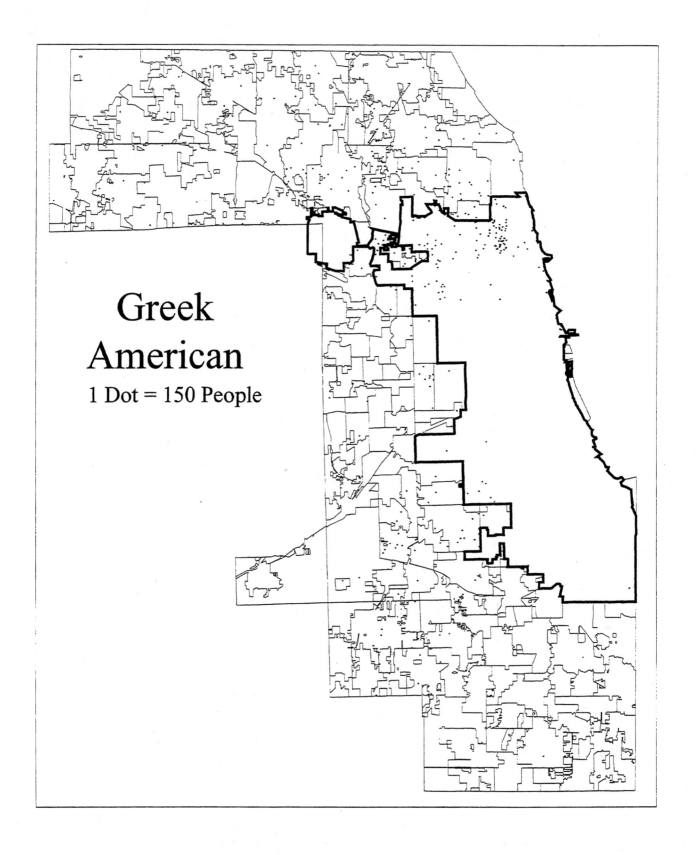

Greek
American
1 Dot = 150 People

Guatemalan Americans

Chicago population:
12,895 (1990 Census)
65,000 (1996 community estimate)

Metro area population:
15,771 (1990 Census)
80,000 (1996 community estimate)

Foreign-born:
77% in city, 75% in metro area

Demographics:

More than 8 in every 10 Guatemalans in the area live in the city, where their median household income is $23,946, according to the 1990 Census. Many live in and around Uptown, where housing is inexpensive and there are agencies to provide services. There also are concentrations in Edgewater, Albany Park and Lincoln Square. Some live in Mexican communities like Pilsen and Little Village. Those without a high school diploma outnumber those with a college degree 10:1 and about 20% live in poverty. Some 28% speak English poorly or not at all; 6% of those who work are in professional or managerial jobs, while about 40% are laborers. Among the foreign-born, 26% have become U.S. citizens. The overwhelming majority, or about 70,000 in the metro area, are undocumented, according to community estimates, making Census data very unreliable. Most of them live in Chicago.

Historical background:

The immigration to Chicago of tens of thousands of Guatemalans over the past several decades has come as a direct result of U.S. policies in Guatemala. Those policies continue to force massive emigration to escape government tyranny, torture and death. During a period of rampant anti-communism in the U.S., a coup d'état supported by the CIA overthrew the democratically elected government of President Jacobo Arbenz Guzman. A central issue was land reform, which was opposed by the American United Fruit Company (UFCO), Guatemala's largest landowner. UFCO, which stood to lose some of its uncultivated property, asked help from then Secretary of State John Foster Dulles and his bother Allen, director of the CIA. When President Arbenz resigned in 1954, he told the Guatemalan people the country was under attack by agents of the U.S. and UFCO. Since then a series of military dictators and presidents elected under military control, have repeatedly tortured and intimidated Guatemalans and maintained a system of exploitation. Conditions that have led hundreds of thousands of Guatemalans to flee to the U.S., Mexico and Europe include: more than 150,000 Guatemalans who have "disappeared," a genocide policy against the Mayans, the destruction of about 450 villages, and the torture of 100,000 by security forces. Because the U.S. government sided with the Guatemalan government, those who fled were not given refugee status.

• Most came here in the 1970s and '80s clandestinely, many with the help of religious organizations under what is known as the

Because the U.S. government sided with the Guatemalan government, those who fled were not given refugee status.

An overwhelming majority, or about 70,000 in the metro area, are undocumented, according to community estimates.

Most came in the '70s and '80s clandestinely, many with the help of religious organizations under the "Sanctuary" movement.

Some Guatemalan children, whose principal language is not Spanish, are put in Spanish-English bilingual tracks here.

"Sanctuary" movement. Because almost all Guatemalans who sought asylum here were rejected, most choose to remain hidden and undocumented rather than risk being sent back to Guatemala. A large number who came through Mexico claim to be Mexicans so that if they are deported they will be sent there. Some live among Mexicans here in Chicago. Because of their undocumented status, many Guatemalans have difficulty finding work at decent wages and are working at jobs below their occupational status in their home country. Some who were school teachers or secretaries are cleaning toilets; some who were accountants are now doing menial jobs. In addition to the middle-class people who came, there are many who were laborers and peasants in Guatemala.

Current migration patterns:

According to the INS, 3,773 Guatemalans immigrated to the Chicago area from 1990-94. Fewer are coming now illegally because of stepped-up border control and some small improvement in the situation at home.

Language:

A total of 23 languages are spoken in Guatemala, the most of any Latin American country. Here, the principal languages are Spanish, Quiche, Cakchiquel, Tzutuhil, Mam, Ixil, Kanjobal, Pocoman, Pochonchi, Achi, Kekchi, Jacalteco and Chuj. This reality has implications for services. For example, Guatemalan children whose principal language is not Spanish are being placed in Spanish-English bilingual tracks.

Religion:

Guatemalans here include Catholics, traditional Protestants and fundamentalist Christians. More important, the old religion based in the Mayan philosophy of life is very much alive and thriving. Mayans believe everything on earth is sacred and that they have to ask permission and give thanks for everything they take from the earth. They believe they don't act just in the present, but that the present, past and future are happening in the same time, but in different dimensions.

Important traditions:

Mayan people, who make up most of the very recent immigrants, have strong traditions and are trying to maintain some of them here. The most important are those that promote group solidarity and strength. Weaving is an important and sacred tradition, by which Mayans told history and religious stories after the Spanish destroyed their religious books. Mayans here are teaching traditional dance and musical instruments to their youth. They celebrate special events with "sweat-lodges," which are traditional ceremonies that give thanks for anything from a birthday to a cured illness. *Meztisos* (mixed-race people), who made up the majority of the earlier immigrants, do not recognize the Indian heritage and have done little to maintain Guatemalan traditions. For the most part, they have adopted the American way of life.

Holidays and special events:

Labor Day is celebrated May 1 instead of in September. Guatemalans try not to work that day and join together to celebrate the labor laws that created the 8-hour day, much different from the longer shifts many of the earlier immigrants had to work. *Mother's Day* (May 10) and *Father's Day* (June 17) are big events for the family, celebrated on the same day every year, not on the nearest Sunday as is the American practice. The *Day of the Revolution* (Oct. 26) commemorates the 10 years of democracy that ended in 1954 and is a time to remember what democracy means. Guatemalans also have an *Independence Day Parade* (Sept.15). *Christmas* and *New Year* are also important times, with some observing eight days of prayer before Christmas.

Foods for special occasions:

A series of nutritious and delicious *tamales* and *cuchitos* are very popular. Corn is a staple and sacred to the Mayans. The tamales are made from corn meal, stuffed with meat and sauces and wrapped in corn or banana leaves. Fruits are important, especially tropical fruits like mangoes, papayas and *zapotes.* There also are many regional foods.

Major issues for community:

Access to health care, education and jobs are major issues; as is justice and punishment to the individuals and institutions that committed and still commit human rights abuses.

Political participation:

Guatemalans in Chicago tend to distrust government, because they have had a succession of military dictators or military governments, all supported by the USA. Another source of distrust is the anti-immigrant campaign launched in this country by important sectors of the political parties.

Links to homeland:

The majority of Guatemalans maintain their original citizenship and are very proud of their nationality. Significant sectors are returning, principally to contribute to the democratization initiated by some progress in the peace process. The principal demand of the democratic sectors both in Guatemala and in Chicago are reflected in the demands presented by the URNG (Guatamalan National Revolutionary Unity) to the government of Guatemala. These demands have produced important accords, dealing with such topics as human rights, resettlement of uprooted populations, acts of violence that have caused suffering in the Guatemalan population, and the rights of the Mayan people. It is important to note that even if accord was reached on human rights, terror and intimidation are an everyday practice, although at this writing it is more of a selective and strategic practice directed at sectors, communities and individuals in a position to enforce these accords.

Myths & misconceptions:

Myth: Guatemalans are here to find a job.
Fact: The majority would not be here except for the civil war. Most fled for their lives.
Myth: Guatemalans aren't able to govern themselves.
Fact: Guatemala would be fine if there hadn't been direct intervention in the country by the U.S. and Europe.

Etc.:

In this population, many were traumatized by torture and war and the disappearance or death of loved ones. It affects them both physically and mentally and has an impact on entire families.

— By Dr. Antonio Martinez, Co-founder and Director of the Marjorie Kovler Center for the Treatment of Survivors of Torture, and Director of the Institute for the Survivors of Human Rights Abuse

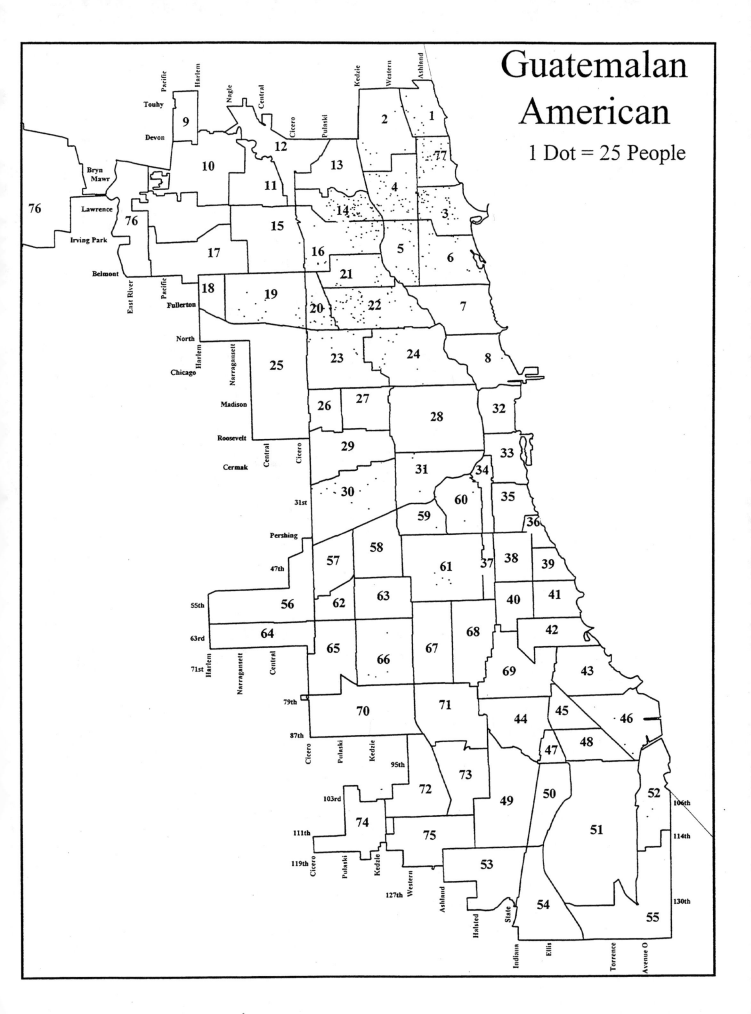

Guatemalan American

1 Dot = 25 People

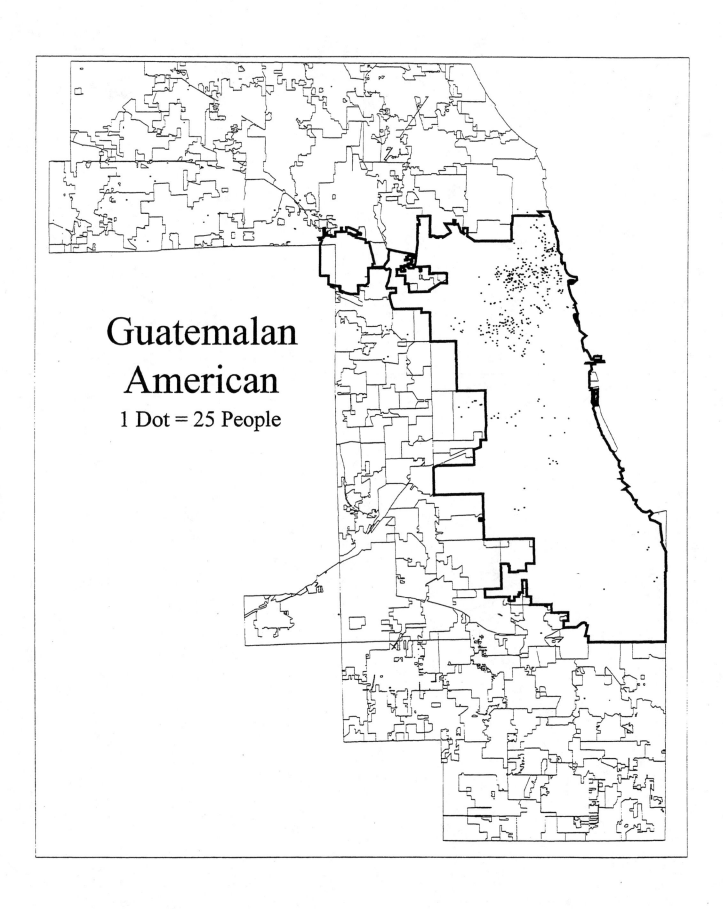

Guatemalan
American

1 Dot = 25 People

Haitian Americans

Chicago population:
2,661 (1990 Census)
1996 community estimate - NA

Metro area population:
4,139 (1990 Census)
10,000-20,000 (Haitian Consulate estimate)
30,000-35,000 (1996 community estimate)

Foreign-born:
75% in city, 71% of metro area

Demographics:
Census information is sketchy. Most Haitians live on the South and far Southwest Sides of the city, according to the Census Many also live on the North Side, especially Rogers Park, and in various suburbs, particularly Evanston, where there is a long-time population, and Skokie. The number of undocumented is difficult to determine because many are just passing through.

Historical background:
Before the Immigration Reform Act of 1965, the Haitian population of Chicago was sparse, though some came to Evanston following WWII. Since 1965, in part because of the family-reunification provision of the new law, the Haitian population has increased.

• Most Haitian immigrants came after the mid-'60s, seeking refuge from the repressive government of Dr. François Duvalier, who held power from 1957 until his death in 1971. Some came as permanent residents, others sought political asylum. Most of the first wave were professionals who came by plane.

• Haitians also left the island in droves during the presidency of Dr. Duvalier's son, Jean-Claude, who succeeded him as president for life until he was forced to relinquish power in 1986. Passage of the Simpson-Mazzoli Act (1986), which extended amnesty to illegal aliens living continuously in the United States since Jan. 1, 1982, and cracked down on employers who knowingly hired illegals, did not deter Haitians from entering the U.S. (and Chicago) illegally. Most of this second surge of refugees were peasants and laborers, and included those known as "boat people."

• A new wave of immigrants left Haiti after the coup d'état that toppled the government of the popularly elected president, Jean-Bertrand Aristide, in 1991. These Haitians came from all rungs of the occupational ladder. Close to 10% were professionals, adding credence to the claim of Haitians that their decision to leave Haiti represents more than an economic exodus. To help ease the adjustment of Haitian immigrants in Chicago, a Haitian Community Center in Rogers Park offers instruction in English, legal advice and a job-placement service. Other organizations have been established to help Haitians adjust to life in Chicago. A Haitian Catholic priest is available to give assistance to Haitians living on the South Side of the city.

Most Haitian immigrants came after the mid-'60s, seeking refuge from the repressive government of Dr. François Duvalier.

Most Haitians are fluent in Kreyol only. French is spoken by a minority, mostly those with a formal education.

Haitian political organizations in Chicago focus mainly on Haiti.

Current migration patterns:

According to the INS, 635 Haitians arrived legally from 1990-94, with the Chicago area as their destination.

Important traditions:

Religious traditions such as baptism and marriage are celebrated here. Haitians maintain their diverse cultural traditions through a number of institutions, including churches, a Masonic Lodge, numerous professional organizations such as the Association of Haitian Medical Doctors, artistic groups, small jazz bands, and athletic clubs like Louverture Soccer Club. The island tradition of both families being involved in a courtship is not reproduced here.

Language:

Most Haitians are fluent in *Kreyol* only. French is spoken by a minority, mostly those with a formal education. Kreyol is not a patois or a dialect as is commonly assumed. It is a bona fide language, derived from West African grammatical and syntactical sources, using French-derived lexicon with important contributions from English, Spanish and other languages, just as English is a Germanic language with much of its vocabulary from Norman French, Latin and Greek sources.

Religion:

Most Haitians are Christians. A large percentage claim Roman Catholicism, but some belong to the Anglican Church and various Protestant denominations. The Afro-Caribbean religion commonly known as *Vodou* has always been an integral part of Haitian life. There are no known Vodou temples in Chicago.

Holidays and special events:

Major holidays observed by Haitians in Chicago are **Independence Day** (Jan. 1), which celebrates independence from France in 1804; **Flag Day** (May 18); and major Catholic religious holidays such as **Ash Wednesday**, **Good Friday**, and **Easter Sunday**. Haitians tend to stay home or visit family members for elaborate dinners and conversation. The Haitian Consulate of Chicago organizes a public Flag Day celebration, usually on the grounds of the DuSable Museum, named after the founder of Chicago, the Haitian Jean-Baptiste Dusable (sic).

Foods for special occasions:

The most popular Haitian dishes are made of rice mixed with kidney beans, rice with a special kind of black mushroom, and plain white rice. Haitians also eat corn, millet, fried green plantains, and *griots* (fried marinated pork served with a very spicy sauce). *Lambi* (conch meat found inside shells) is served grilled or boiled. During special holidays such as Independence Day, Haitians consume an elaborate squash soup. They also tend to eat fish during religious weeks, particularly the week leading to Easter.

Names:

Haitians tend to give at least one "Christian name" to their children. This practice accounts in part for the commonly hyphenated first names of Haitian males and females alike, such as Jean-Baptiste, Jean-Bertrand, Jean-Jacques (Jean, French for John, is the name of one of Christ's Apostles) or Marie-Rose, Marie-Claire, Marie-Michelle (Marie being the name of Christ's mother). This practice, however, is slowly dying. Some Haitians also take the last name of both parents, as in Price-Mars, Bellegarde-Smith and Balan-Gaubert. Many Haitians, particularly but not exclusively from the peasantry, have names that are more meaningful, poetic and intrinsically religious, such as Dieseul (God), Dieula (God is here), Dieuri (God laughs) and Jezula (Jesus is here).

Major issues for community:

Haitians in Chicago are very much concerned about the social, political and economic issues of Haiti. Although many plan to stay in the United States and an increasing number have become naturalized citizens, they keep abreast of the many facets of life in Haiti through Haitian newspapers circulated in the U.S. and radio programming, as well as frequent trips to Haiti and contact with family and friends who remain there.

Political participation:

Haitian political organizations in Chicago focus mainly on Haiti. After the fall of Jean-Claude Duvalier in 1986, Chicago became one of the major bases for Haitian politics. In addition to a proliferation of political organizations, nearly all the prominent political parties of Haiti are represented in Chicago. In 1992, the *Oganizasyon Lavalas* was formed to support the ousted government of Aristide. A radio program run by Aristide supporters began to broadcast in French and Kreyol. While émigré politicians have agitated for the home country, other Haitians have become eager participants in American politics. Many Haitian Americans vote regularly and they tend to vote Democratic. Others continue to express deep mistrust of government, as they did in Haiti. Americans of Haitian descent often are active in Chicago politics.

Links to homeland:

Most Haitians in Chicago maintain strong ties to their homeland. For this reason they tend to retain their citizenship, which for many is a badge of pride. Despite political turmoil and economic hardship in Haiti, many Haitians here express the desire to repatriate. Those who have families in Haiti visit periodically, as their employment condition allows. Most Haitians send money to family members and friends living in Haiti. Some send appliances, clothing, medicine and other practical items through Haitian charitable organizations.

Myths & misconceptions:

Myths: Voodoo is a form of satanic worship.
Fact: Vodou is a religion that includes elements of Christianity.
Myth: Haitians are carriers of AIDS.
Fact: For a time it was commonly believed Haitians were likely AIDS carriers, but the Centers for Disease Control, after an investigation, concluded Haitians were not a high-risk group. Some do have AIDS, but this is not an issue for the group as a whole.

— By William Leslie Balan-Gaubert, Doctoral Candidate and Researcher in the History Department at the University of Chicago

TITUS AND ME

By Natalie Pardo

"You're not from Chicago, are you?" If I'd collected a dollar every time I was asked that question, I'd be a rich Haitian American by now.

Born on American soil in 1963 and a resident of Chicago since 1966, I am happy to report that the assimilation process is still not complete. And my tongue desperately hangs on to an ever-fading French accent.

Although my speech pattern is changing and "Midwesternizing," my appetite sure hasn't met that monochromatic fate. My grandmother Titus' cooking keeps my senses in touch with Haiti. Her kitchen is one of my favorite places in the world. To me, Titus is Haiti.

First of all, her apartment is always hot, hovering at about 85 degrees. And when all four burners are on, the temperature can hit a balmy 90 degrees. Perfect Haitian weather. Then, all the delicious smells of her village, Jeremie, fill the air. There's chicken cooking in an unforgettable sauce of onion, green pepper, garlic and a secret ingredient. On the second burner, a pot of red beans and rice slowly simmers. A third pot holds my sister's favorite dish: *lambis*. The last pot is violently boiling sweet *banane*.

Titus' pantry is a treasure of Haitian delicacies and mysteries, like chicken paté, *bonbon amidon, comparette, akacant,* and her special *pimente*.

Most of the time, I feel like that hyphen in Haitian-American. I am a black woman caught between two worlds: Haiti and the United States. One world I live in every day, and the other I wish I could call home. But that hyphen disappears when I sit at Titus' table, loaded with herbs and light-blue envelopes holding news from the West Indian island.

We communicate with each other in a special way.   Titus, who came to Chicago in 1966 when my parents got married, still speaks Creole and enough English to pay bills and take the bus. She speaks to me in Creole and I respond in English. Mind you, I understand Creole, but it's difficult for me to put the words in the right order.

Feeling my Haitian-ness fading, I decided to take a Basic Creole class at Kennedy-King College. And my study partner is Titus. This class has created a new bond between us. Titus beams with pride as I struggle to speak in Creole. We have a great time teaching each other. You see, Creole just recently became a written language. So Titus is learning to read it, in a Creole Bible I bought her for Christmas, while I'm learning to speak it.

Being with Titus is like being a child again. I'm rediscovering my proud and colorful heritage through her. Now in my 30s, I realize how I took my culture for granted as I was growing up on the South Side and trying to be like the other girls, whose families were from Mississippi and Tennessee. No one in my second-grade class had ever heard of Haiti.

I rarely invited friends over for dinner. A meal at my house was not like dining with the Brady Bunch. Alice, their maid, never served *griot* (spicy fried pork) with black rice and shrimp. I didn't think my classmates would understand having rice at every meal.

I remember the surprise on one friend's face when she arrived at my house. We had just received our first communion and my family was celebrating this important religious event. Baptisms and first communions are major social events in Haiti. At my party, at least 100 people were dancing, eating and drinking into the wee hours of the morning. Her parents couldn't believe all the fanfare over a kid's event, but they stayed and had a great time with the church-going partiers.

I knew then that I lived a different Black life. I played soccer instead of basketball. I wore big, colorful ribbons instead of barrettes. The first and last time I had grits was in college. I didn't have other kinds of soul food, like greens and black-eyed peas, until 1986.

I've always tried to become more American in a "sweet potato pie" kind of way. But I just couldn't cut it. So I always felt like a stranger, a visitor.

I didn't have that sense of home until 1979, when I landed on Haitian soil. The first thing I saw was an old man riding a mule on a dusty road. For the first time in my life, I felt like I belonged and I was home.

I looked Haitian, I walked Haitian, I smiled Haitian. I felt like I fit. Everything was fine until I opened my mouth to speak. My tongue betrayed me. I was again a stranger, a visitor. But Haiti's spirit won't let me go.

When I'm in Miami, I'm seen as a Haitian women. Don't ask me to explain it. I was standing in the airport when a woman frantically spoke to me in Creole. She was looking for the rest of "our" group. But I didn't know her. I responded in French. She apologized and kept searching. That was just a coincidence, I thought. But the next day, as I was walking down the street with my goddaughter, two men told us to stop trying to hide our Haitian-ness and to speak in Creole. In Miami there are a lot of Haitians, but there also are Jamaicans and African Americans. Maybe it was a lucky guess.

Chicago has a relatively small Haitian population, compared with New York and Miami. But people in the diaspora seem to have a sixth sense for picking Haitians out of a crowd. At this year's Taste of Chicago, I was walking through the crowd eating some curried chicken with rice and beans when a man said to me in Creole, "Are you going to eat all of that?" To which I responded in my basic crude Creole, "I'm going to eat the whole thing." Out of all the people at the Taste, what did he see in me that was so Haitian? He disappeared into the massive crowd before I could ask him.

I revisited Haiti in 1991. That island still has a hold on me. Some of my friends describe me as a militant. I take it as a compliment. I believe one of my ancestors was responsible for kicking out the French back in the early 1800s. That victory is a great source of pride for me. If black slaves can free themselves, then I can do anything I put my mind to. I've never been afraid of the "white man," because my people kicked his butt. This knowledge helped me understand that no one can keep you down, no matter the situation.

Haiti is billed as the poorest country in the Western Hemisphere, but that isn't a source of embarrassment for me. In Haiti, I saw the richest people in the world, because they had each other. Haitians are rich with pride, compassion, love and family loyalty. Their work ethic is commendable and inspires me to overcome my daily obstacles.

If it weren't for the lessons I have learned from Titus, who emphasized education, hard work and compassion, I would not be living the American dream — hyphen and all.

Natalie Pardo is a reporter at The Chicago Reporter.

Hungarian Americans

Chicago population:
8,285 (1990 Census, first ancestry)
5,483 (Census, second ancestry)
9,000 (1996 community estimate)

Metro area population:
31,256 (1990 Census, first ancestry)
22,751 (Census, second ancestry)
40,000 (1996 community estimate)

Foreign-born:
22% in city, 16% in metro area

Demographics:

Three-quarters of Hungarian Americans live in the suburbs. The Hungarian population in today's Chicago is quite dispersed. The closely knit ethnic neighborhoods have dissolved and there is a tendency for the Hungarian families to move to the suburbs, including Aurora, Skokie, Niles and Northbrook. In the city, they tend to live on the North Side. About 98% speak English well. There is very little Census breakdown for people of Hungarian ancestry.

Historical background:

In 1870 Chicago had only 159 Hungarian residents, but a dramatic increase was observed after the turn of the century. According to the U.S. Census, the Hungarian population in the Chicago area showed the following increase: 1,841 in 1890; 7,463 in 1900; 37,990 in 1910; 70,209 in 1920. These figures, however, do not always reflect the actual numbers of the ethnic Hungarians (Magyars). Before WWI they sometimes included non-ethnic Hungarians (Germans, Slovaks, Croats, etc.) of the multinational Austro-Hungarian monarchy, and after WWI they excluded those ethnic Hungarians who came from the newly created Yugoslavia, Czechoslovakia, the enlarged Romania and eastern Austria.

• The first Hungarians who came to Chicago were the emigrants of the 1848 Hungarian Revolution against the Hapsburg monarchy. They fled Hungary to escape retribution from the Austrian authorities, and some settled in Chicago around the 1850s. They were the so-called "Forty-niners" or "Kossuth immigrants," mostly educated men, many from the gentry class, and they were given a warm reception. One of the most notable was Julius Kuné. He came to Chicago in 1855, was a member of the Board of Trade, and opened Chicago's first language school. Another, Joseph Pick, taught at the Dearborn Academy. The image of Hungarians as a nation of nobles was established by the revolutionary immigrants.

• That image was undermined by the turn-of-the-century economic immigrants. The so-called Great Economic Immigration was the first large-scale immigration of Hungarians to the United States and to Chicago. These immigrants came solely for economic reasons, and represented the poorest segment of the population. They were the ones to whom the negative adjectives "Hunky" and "Bohemian" were inaccurately given. Although these economic immigrants came from rural areas, most settled in industrial cities and mining areas. In Chicago many worked in

At the end of WWI, Hungary lost two-thirds of its territory, and 3.5 million Hungarians were forced to live outside its new borders as an ethnic minority.

The closely knit ethnic neighborhoods in Chicago have dissolved and there is a tendency for Hungarian families to move to the suburbs.

Most Hungarian Americans marry outside the Hungarian community.

the railroad yards and steel mills, and they settled in great numbers in the industrial areas of the South Side. The largest Hungarian settlement was concentrated around 95th Street and Cottage Grove, and in the Burnside, West Pullman and Roseland neighborhoods. In the larger metro area, East Chicago and Calumet City also had large Hungarian populations.

• The outbreak of WWI in 1914 halted mass migration, while the exclusionary U.S. immigration laws of 1921-24 introduced the quota system, permitting just 1,000 immigrants from Hungary a year. This situation did not change until the Hart-Celler Act of 1965 ended the quotas. At the end of WWI, Hungary lost two-thirds of its territory, and 3.5 million Hungarians were forced to live outside the new borders of Hungary as an ethnic minority. Many felt they could not accommodate themselves to the new circumstances and decided to leave their new country of residence. At the same time, many intellectuals left what remained of Hungary and made their way to Chicago to join relatives and friends. The newly arrived got substantial support from the prewar Hungarian immigrants. Though not all settled in predominantly Hungarian neighborhoods, most participated in ethnic cultural activities.

• After WWII, the pattern of Hungarian immigration to the U.S. changed again. The new immigrants came as political refugees, under the Displaced Persons Acts of 1948 and 1950. Among the displaced persons, 1,000 Hungarian refugees reported Chicago as their residence in 1950. Once more the local Hungarian American communities worked tirelessly to increase the Hungarian quota.

• The communist suppression of the Hungarian Revolution of 1956 made another group of political immigrants seek refuge in the United States. Thousands of the Fifty-Sixers eventually settled in the Chicago area. These political immigrants, together with the intellectual immigrants of the 1930s, diversified the immigrants' social composition and altered the earlier negative image.

• Not even the arrival of the new immigrants, however, could stop the breakdown of the Hungarian neighborhoods and their institutions. Up to the 1950s, Hungarian communities formed cohesive neighborhoods, around 95th and Cottage Grove, and in Burnside, West Pullman, Roseland and South Chicago. The largest settlement was on the South Side around 95th and Cottage Grove. On the North Side, Hungarians settled around the edge of the older German community from North and Wells into Lake View and up Lincoln Avenue. St. Stephen King of Hungary Church was built at 2015 W. Augusta. Hungarian Jews first lived on the Near West Side around Roosevelt Road. When they moved to Edgewater-Uptown on the North Side, they took with them their kosher food shops, coffee houses and stores that sold religious products, as well as their orthodox synagogue, Agudas Achim Congregation, which still stands at 5029 N. Kenmore. Children and grandchildren of immigrants married and moved out from the Hungarian neighborhoods into Hegewisch on the South Side and to the south suburbs, especially Lansing, Calumet City and Burnham. On the North Side, the last vestiges remained around Belmont and Clark and on Lincoln Avenue up to the 1970s.

Current migration patterns:

The number of Hungarian immigrants to Chicago, both legal and illegal, is not significant in the late 20th century. One of the main forms of immigration is through the visa "lottery." Some Hungarian scholars in Chicago, mainly those working in computer science, can get immigrant status because of their achievement as outstanding scholars. The amount of reverse migration is insignificant too. Most Hungarian Americans return just to visit, although after the collapse of the communist regime in Hungary more people, mainly elders, consider the possibility of return.

Language:

Hungarian.

Religion:

The immigrants, mirroring the population of the homeland, were about 60% Roman Catholic; 30% Protestant, either Calvinist or Lutheran; and 10% other affiliations, such as Jewish, Eastern Orthodox Catholic, Baptist and Adventist.

Important traditions:

Hungarian family traditions are no longer maintained to the extent they were before communism got a firm hold in Hungary. Most Hungarian Americans marry outside the Hungarian community. A major family tradition that prevails today is connected with funerals. Several funeral homes on the South and the North Sides are utilized by Hungarian families. Language is mainly perpetuated by the Hungarian churches, which also have Sunday schools. Hungarians may not live in closely settled ethnic communities anymore, but Hungarian-affiliated churches and several Hungarian organizations make a great effort to maintain the Hungarian community of Chicago, its language and cultural traditions. The Catholic Church of St. Stephen King of Hungary Church and the Protestant Church of Westside (Norridge United Church of Christ) offer Sunday services in both English and Hungarian. The Treasure Chest of Hungarian Culture is an organization for the support of Hungarian culture. The Hungarian Cultural and Education House publishes the literary periodical *Szivárvány*. Its Literary Circle meets regularly and sponsors literary and music events. The Hungarian Scout Association, founded in 1946 when scouting was banned in Hungary, offers Hungarian language courses in addition to scouting activities. The Chicago Pannonia Sportsclub organizes sports events and balls, at which the Hungarians of Chicago can come together as a cultural community.

Holidays and special events:

Besides the traditional holidays of **Christmas**, **New Year's Eve** and **Easter**, Hungarian Americans generally celebrate three major national holidays: the **Revolution of 1848** (March 15), **St. Stephen's Day** or **Constitution Day** (Aug. 20), and the **Revolution of 1956** (Oct. 23). In Hungary, St. Stephen's Day is celebrated with fireworks and flower carnivals. In Chicago it is celebrated with a community gathering and cultural events. Though Hungarians are no longer involved in wine-making, it is a strong tradition for Hungarians in Chicago to hold **harvest festivals** in late September or early October.

Foods for special occasions:

Foods for the special holidays are very traditional. On Christmas Eve both Catholic and Protestants abstain from meat and eat fish. On Christmas Day and Easter, Hungarian ham or American turkey is the main course. A pastry called *beigli* (poppy seed- or walnut-filled yeast dough) and *torta* (coffee cake) are eaten for dessert. Although not closely related with any special occasion, Hungarian *goulash* (a thin, spicy stew-like mixture of meats and vegetables eaten as a soup) is the most popular dish.

Names:

The common Hungarian names are slowly changing. Some Christian given names, such as Erzsébet, Margit and Magda for women, and István, László, József, Imre, Zoltán and Péter for men, are still very frequently given to Hungarian children. Surnames often represent jobs, as in Szabó (tailor), Kovács (smith) or Molnár (miller). Others are named for the region they came from, like Szathmáry.

Major issues for community:

The major current concern for American Hungarians is the relationship between the American and Hungarian governments, both politically and economically, especially because of the crisis in the Balkan peninsula. As a neighboring country, Hungary is eager to see the U.S. help bring about a peaceful solution in that region.

Political participation:

Hungarians who live in America traditionally have been members of one of the two main political parties. Some have had very strong Democratic ties. The Republican ties also have been strong since Lincoln, who had several Hungarian generals and high-ranking officials during his presidency. The Hungarian population of Chicago does not exercise any political clout. Most of the older generation are American citizens.

Links to homeland:

Hungarian Americans maintain an active interest the political life of Hungary. They often express their critical views in various periodicals including the Toronto-published weekly, *Amerikai Magyarsag*, whose editorial staff includes a representative in Chicago. In recent years, Hungarian American travel agencies, bookstores and charity organizations in Chicago have provided financial help to hospitals in Hungary, for the acquisition of modern medical equipment.

Myths & misconceptions:

Myth: Hungarians are gypsies and Hungarian music is gypsy music.

Fact: Hungary does have a gypsy population, as do several other countries in Europe, and many Hungarian gypsies are musicians. The historical country of origin and the cultural traditions of the two peoples are not identical, however.

Etc.:

The capital of Hungary is Budapest and not Bucharest (Romania). Hungarians are not historically related to the Slavs and the Hungarian language does not belong to the Slavic language group.

— By Dr. Eva Becsei, a candidate for a second doctoral degree, this one in history at the University of Illinois at Chicago

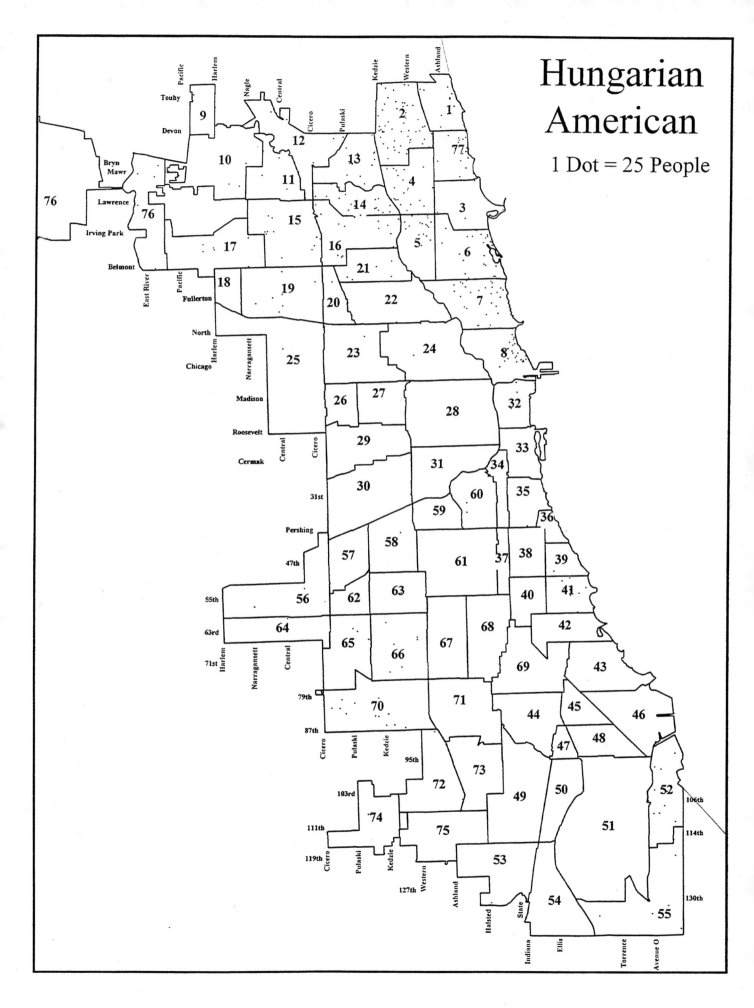

Hungarian American

1 Dot = 25 People

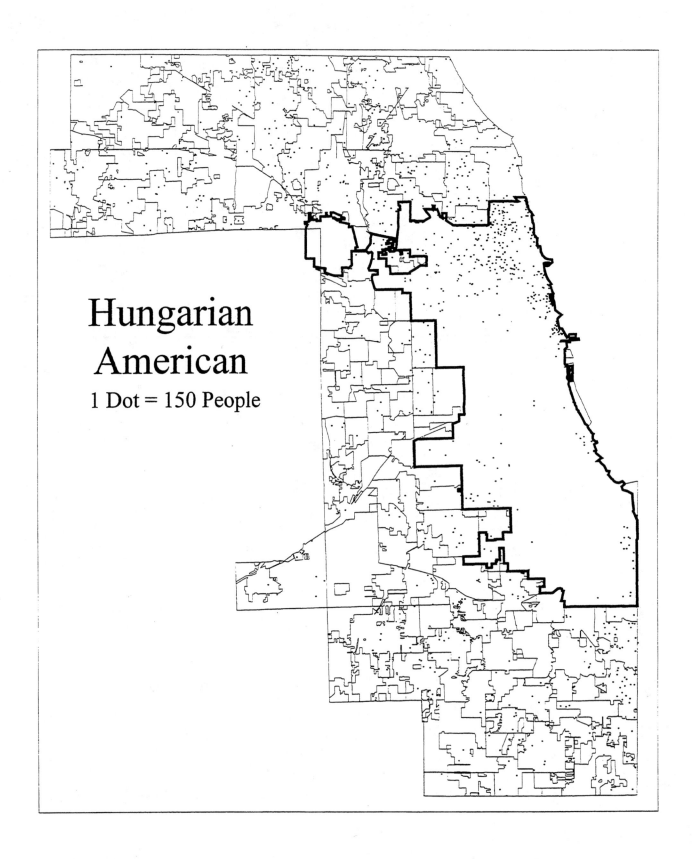

Hungarian
American

1 Dot = 150 People

Indian Americans (Asian)

Chicago population:
16,386 (1990 Census)
30,000 (1996 community estimate)

Metro area population:
57,992 (1990 Census)
100,000 (1996 community estimate)

Foreign-born:
More than 75%

Demographics:
According to the 1990 Census, most Indians (72%) live outside the city, with the suburban Indian population concentrated in Cook and DuPage counties. DuPage has 23% of the Indians in Illinois. In Chicago, Indians are concentrated on the North Side in West Ridge and Rogers Park, as well as other North and Northwest neighborhoods. In the suburbs, the Indian population doubled from 1980-90. Northwest and west suburbs such as Skokie, Schaumburg, Hoffman Estates, Mount Prospect, Naperville, Oak Brook and Downers Grove have seen the greatest increase. Indians in DuPage have a median household income of $55,366. The median for Chicago is $28,600, while that for the whole metro area is $44,000. Indians are very highly educated; 25% of those in Chicago and 33% in the suburbs have a bachelor's degree. Yet many live below poverty level, ranging from 7% in the metro area to 18% in the city. Over 36% of Indians in the metro area are in professional or managerial jobs, compared with 28% in the city; fewer than 10% of Indians are laborers. Most came from India as married couples; bachelors commonly go back to find marriage partners. Most Indians speak English very well, having learned it in school as the colonial legacy of British rule.

Historical background:
Indian immigration to Chicago began with the 1965 Immigration Reform Act, which paved the way for highly skilled professionals to enter the United States. The best and brightest urban middle-class Indians from every region came from elite medical colleges and engineering and scientific institutions. They also came from other countries of the global family of Indians, such as England, Canada, South Africa, Tanzania, Fiji, Guyana and Trinidad. They were well accepted because they quickly acquired prestigious, high-paying jobs and were seen to assimilate easily. At first, Indian immigrants settled on the Far North Side, along Broadway and Sheridan Road and west along Lawrence and Devon avenues, where they found a congenial atmosphere in the cosmopolitan mix of ethnic groups, plus convenient access to the central city. But like other immigrants before them, they moved on to the suburbs as soon as they could afford it, in search of better schools and a safer environment. Wide dispersal in the suburbs is one of the most striking characteristics of Indian settlement patterns in Chicago.

Like other immigrants before them, they moved on to the suburbs as soon as they could afford it, in search of better schools and a safer environment.

The growth of Devon Avenue as an Indian ethnic neighborhood is tied to the second wave of immigration in the 1980s.

From 1990-94, 15,943 Indian immigrants came to the Chicago area, making Indians the third largest group coming here now.

Indians arrange marriages among their own kind because they believe marriage needs family support to be successful.

• The growth of part of Devon Avenue as an Indian ethnic neighborhood is tied to the second wave of immigration in the 1980s, when families of the first immigrants came. Known as "Indiatown," Devon Avenue is a strong draw for the estimated 150,000 Indians in the Midwest, who go there to shop for Indian goods and eat Indian food. These relatives of the earlier immigrants were less skilled, faced an economy plagued by unemployment, and took up occupations in retail trade or other small-scale businesses that did not call for special skills. This led to greater economic stratification and a sharper divide between city and suburban Indians.

Current migration patterns:

The increasing shift to a service-oriented economy in Chicago is drawing more and more computer professionals from India. From 1990-94, 15,943 Indian immigrants came to the Chicago metro area, making Indians the third largest group coming here now, after Mexicans and Poles. Though small numbers of undocumented aliens are trapped in low-paying jobs, mostly in the food and retail industries, continued legal immigration has made Indians one of the fastest-growing and economically successful ethnic groups in Chicago. But India now has a vibrant, newly liberalized economy, which may slow future immigration to the U.S.

Language:

Most Indians speak English fluently, but they also speak their native language. India has 15 major languages and 844 different dialects and most of the major languages are represented in the Chicago area, namely Gujarati (spoken by about 50%), Hindi, Punjabi, Telugu, Malayalam, Tamil, Kannada, Sindhi, Urdu and Bengali. Each of these languages has a rich literature and ancient cultural heritage.

Religion:

An estimated 80% are Hindus (the same proportion as in India). Muslims are about 15% of the population and estimate their numbers for the metro area at 20,000. There also are Sikhs, Jains, Christians, Zoroastrians, Buddhists and Jews. Hindus, Sikhs and Jains have built houses of worship in the Chicago area, each with a distinctive architectural style.

Important traditions:

Indian Americans are afraid their traditions will be lost unless vigorous efforts are made to preserve them. At temples and mosques, Indian parents try to offer, through religious education and social and cultural activities, a viable alternative to excessive Westernization, which they equate with a permissive lifestyle. Dating is frowned upon. There is conflict in many Indian homes where teenage children, taught in school to think independently, clash with Indian parents who demand unquestioning obedience.

Caste considerations are usually ignored in social life here but become important when it comes to marriage. The four major groups in the Indian Hindu community are: Brahmins, who traditionally formed the priesthood; Kshatriyas, who were kings and warriors; Vaishyas, producers or merchants; and Sudras, who performed the most menial tasks. (The "Untouchables" are considered so low in the caste hierarchy that they are outside of it.) In the early days of immigration in the 1960s and '70s, when Indians were few in number, they were reconciled to assimilation and intermarriage, if not with other Americans, at least with other Indians regardless of caste or regional origin. With the increased immigration of the '80s and '90s, there is closer observance of caste rules. The Indian population here is dominated by Gujaratis, who are more prone than other Indians to observe caste rites and rituals, and to marry only within their own caste. (The Patels and Shahs who abound in Chicago are Gujaratis.)

Indians arrange marriages among their own kind because they believe marriage needs family support to be successful. Alarmed by early trends toward interracial and intercultural marriages, Indian immigrants have started organizing marriage fairs, where eligible second-generation men and women are brought together under the watchful eye of their parents. In a typical arranged marriage, parents "advertise" their eligible son or daughter's availability in ethnic newspapers in the U.S. and in India or subscribe to a matching service or computerized data bank. A suitable candidate is picked after the families correspond, and the boy and girl meet to socialize and make up their own minds. Most Indians brought up in the United States insist on the right to reject a prospective spouse. This dating period lasts only a few months, sometimes only days.

The second generation appears to be working toward a middle ground, anticipating they will probably marry another Indian, perhaps someone their parents might introduce them to, but definitely someone with whom they will be comfortable.

Unmarried and married women wear a *bindi,* or dot, on their forehead as a cosmetic adornment. (Hence the name "dotbusters" for the white racist groups that launched a series of attacks, some fatal, on Indians in New Jersey in 1994-95.) Widows aren't permitted to wear bindi because they are not supposed to do anything to look attractive. Because language is seen as vital to cultural preservation, classes are offered at temples, mosques and *gurdwaras* (Sikh houses of worship). The temple is also the venue for christenings, *upanayanam* (initiation ceremony for the young Brahmin male), and weddings, all performed in traditional style by Indian priests. Education is highly valued in the middle-class Indian community and children consistently excel at their studies. Sometimes they complain of the pressure by parents to achieve at school and choose prestigious careers in medicine, engineering and law.

Holidays and special events:

Independence Day commemorates Indian independence, Aug.15, 1947, and is celebrated with a parade of floats. Other holidays are religious and there are many. A few of the more prominent ones include: for Hindus, *Janmashtami*, the birthday of Lord Krishna, celebrated in August with night-long prayers, religious hymns, and a re-enactment of scenes from his early life; *Navratri*, *Dussehra*, and *Durga Puja*, a 10-day festival in October or November that celebrates the triumph of good over evil, with each regional association in Chicago arranging functions at Hindu temples and community centers; and *Divali* (October or November), the festival of lights observed by Hindus all over the world, which celebrates the return of Lord Rama from his 14-year exile in the forest. For Divali, oil lamps and lights are lit in homes and public buildings and fireworks and festivities mark the occasion, as people worship *Lakshmi*, the goddess of prosperity. Devon Avenue is gaily decorated and merchants set out special wares to attract customers. For Muslims, *Eid-ul-Fitr* (date varies, each year falling about 10 days earlier than the preceding year) is when a month of fasting (Ramadan) is brought to an end with much feasting and rejoicing. Muslims gather with Muslims of other nationalities in mosques to pray, and visit friends and relatives to exchange greetings. Another important Muslim festival is *Eid-ul-Adha*, which is celebrated 70 days after Eid-ul-Fitr in memory of the prophet Abraham and his sacrifice to God. The Jain community observes *Mahavir Jayanti* (March), the birthday of the founder of Jainism more than 2,500 years ago. *Baisaki*, (April) is of special significance to Sikhs, who celebrate it as a harvest feast and revere it as the day in 1699 when Guru Govind Singh organized them into the brotherhood of the *Khalsa*.

Foods for special occasions:

Indians celebrate practically every major festival and life-cycle ritual, such as birthdays and weddings, by preparing rich sweetmeats and offering them to friends and relatives. Foods prepared at religious functions are generally vegetarian and Divali is the most important festival for preparing special delicacies, such as *barfi* (a thick, dry milk cake) and *laddoo* (a sweet round ball of graham flour and sugar).

Dietary restrictions:

Meat and fish are widely eaten, but some communities are strictly vegetarian, especially Hindus and Jains. Most Hindus avoid beef because the cow is a sacred animal to them, and Muslims refrain from eating pork. Jains, who have very strict dietary laws, avoid eating even root vegetables because it violates their belief in non-violence against even the smallest creature on earth.

Names:

There is tremendous variety in Indian names, which usually refer to the natural environment or human sentiments, such as Usha (the dawn) or Priya (beloved). Other common names are the names of gods, such as Gopal (another name for Krishna) or Lakshmi (the goddess of prosperity), Zia (light), Shaan (glory) or Habib (friend). It also is common to name a child after an elderly grandparent. Surnames usually reveal a person's regional origins, caste or sub-caste. The naming of a child is generally a religious ceremony the 10th day after birth.

Major issues for community:

Racial discrimination, both at the social level and on the job, cuts across class, gender and ethnicity, hitting both highly paid executives in the form of the glass ceiling and unskilled factory workers facing unemployment. People also are concerned about proposed anti-immigration laws that threaten to cut off new immigration from India. Another issue is maintaining Indian traditions, deeply rooted in family ties, which are considered essential to social stability. The family reunification clause in the 1965 Immigration Law helped Indians build a stable immigrant society and they want it preserved. New immigrants with less education and fewer marketable skills are being helped by community activists through self-help social service programs. There also is the plight of elderly immigrant parents who have followed their children to America. In Indian culture, aged parents are the responsibility of their sons, but here many live isolated, lonely lives without the traditional support system. A final issue is the policies of the U.S. government seen as hostile to India, such as supplying arms to Pakistan.

Political participation:

Between 1984-93, 11,159 Indians were naturalized, the third highest number after Mexicans and Filipinos. But these numbers do not necessarily translate to high voter participation; they are more a reflection of immigrants' desire to sponsor family members for immigration. Well-established Indians contribute money to politicians in return for recognition and the coveted "photo-op." But Indians have not come together as a voting bloc, in part because they are scattered. Indians are only now gaining the numbers required to wield political power. City dwellers tend to vote Democratic, while the well-heeled suburbanites may favor Republicans. The Indo American Democratic Organization works with Latinos and African Americans to increase voter registration. Indians have tried repeatedly to get elected to office as city councilmen or village trustees but failed. The only Indian elected to office in the area is Raj Ambegaokar, an alderman in Darien.

Links to homeland:

Though most Indians accept America as their new home, they maintain strong ties with India because they are proud of their heritage. They travel frequently to India and are avidly courted by airline and telephone companies because they spend so much on international air travel and phone calls. Indians send money home regularly, not only to support family, but also to invest in India's economic development. They set up factories in India's underdeveloped areas and lend professional expertise in hospitals and laboratories. Indian Americans also contribute funds and expertise to village and urban projects in India. And when disaster such as an earthquake strikes India, people here are quick to respond with charitable contributions.

Myths & misconceptions:

Myth: Indians are monolithic people and speak "Indian."
Fact: There is no such thing as the "Indian" language. Indians are a diverse, multicultural people who speak different languages and belong to different religions.
Myth: Indian women are oppressed, treated as chattel and denied freedom to express themselves.
Fact: Indian women, many highly educated, manage to overcome barriers and achieve their goals, sometimes while conforming to their own culture, sometimes by breaking out of it. They share many of the same disadvantages as American women, but their homemaker role is more valued and honored than in Western society.

Etc.:

Because Indians did not come to the United States fleeing intolerable conditions in their homeland but rather to pursue economic and professional opportunities, they are not as eager to sever ties as other immigrant groups. This group is called Indians elsewhere in the world but call themselves Asian Indians here so as not to be confused with American Indians.

— By Dr. Padma Rangaswamy, a Postdoctoral Fellow at the University of Illinois at Chicago who authored the chapter on Asian Indians in Ethnic Chicago

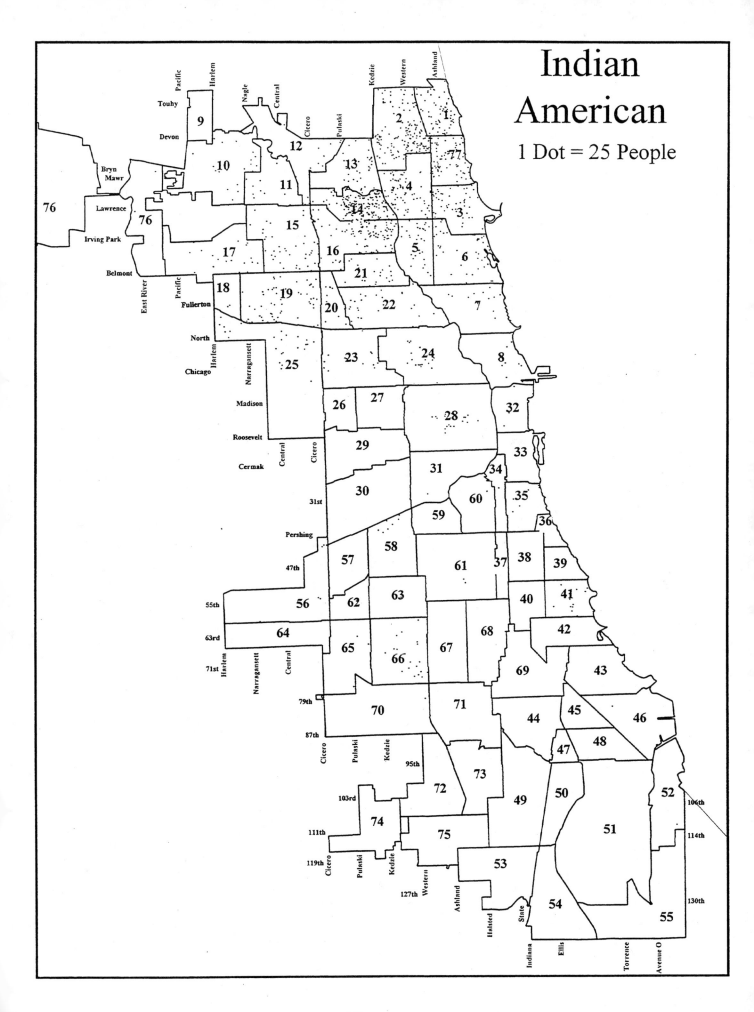

Indian American

1 Dot = 25 People

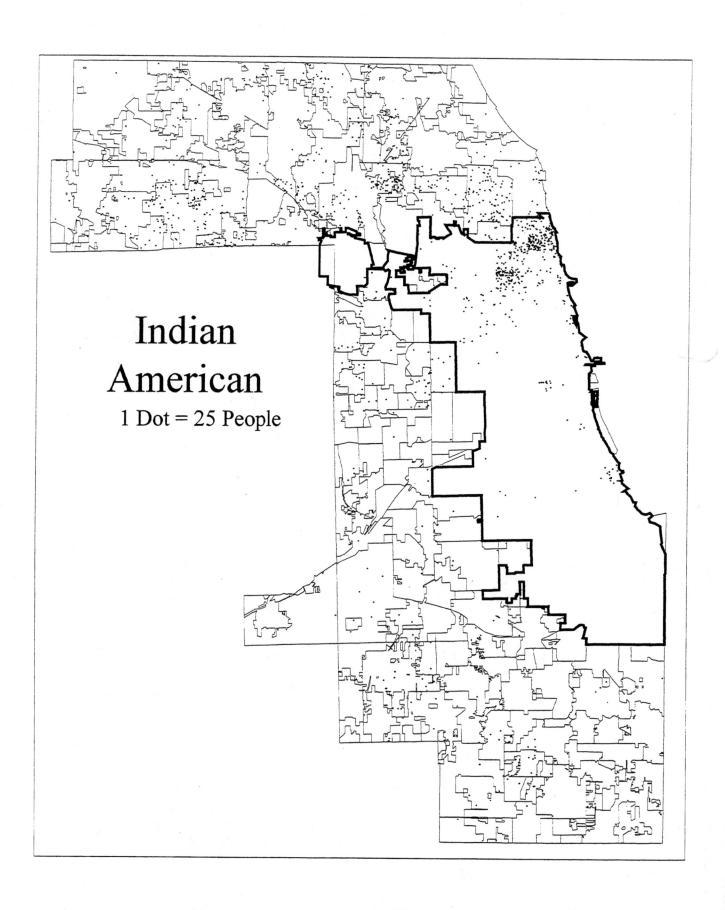

Indian
American

1 Dot = 25 People

I AM WHO I AM

By Moin "Moon" Khan

It was on a late September afternoon that I first encountered my identity crisis in the United States. Deplaning from a flight from New York, I was at the Atlanta airport where I asked a person how to get to the University of Georgia campus and how long it would take. A well-mannered and cooperative person, James Howard, gave me a detailed description of the university and its Bull Dogs football team. First of all, I got mixed up between football and soccer. After all, this was my first day in this country, and while preparing for GRE and TOEFL exams, I had learned many new American words, like "mall," "condominium," etc., but I never imagined Americans would be so innovative that they would change the name of the most famous world sport.

When Mr. Howard finished his orientation lecture, he gently asked me about my nationality. He said he could guess but he might be wrong, because Khan is such a universal title that a person with this surname could come from any continent in the world. I replied, "I'm an Indian." Mr. Howard could not control his laugh, and said, "You can't be an Indian; you're kidding." I felt very bad; I was shocked. It was not bad if I did not know the difference between football and soccer, because I was never a sports buff. But how could I not know who I was?

Mr. Howard advised me to call myself an "Asian Indian" or a "person from India." Traveling in a shuttle bus from Atlanta to Athens, Ga., I was dwelling on his advice while undergoing a private transformation in how I thought of myself. Until now, I had identified myself only as an Indian, and I was proud of it because I was a nationalist and a patriotic Indian. I took part in Indian politics as a student leader, and despite being a member of a minority linguistic and religious community of India, I always involved myself with the mainstream issues. I embraced issues pertaining to the minority community but without feeling limited by them. Thus, it was impossible for me to think I was not an Indian.

Next day, I was at the UGA admission office, filling out various forms. On one, I was asked for my ethnic identity. To my dismay, there was no category for "Indian" or "India." My friends suggested I write "Asian" in that box.

My friends also advised me to go to UGA's International Students Office. I started thinking about the words "international students" because I had an F-1 visa, known as a "foreign student visa." I could not comprehend how a foreign student became an international student overnight. Things were changing very fast.

At ISO, I was encouraged to get in touch with officials of the South Asian Students Association, which would help me find an ethnically suitable roommate. South Asia consists of India, Pakistan, Bangladesh and Sri Lanka. Governments and sometimes people of these countries don't get along very well. I started wondering how people of these countries lived together here.

To my surprise, I got accommodations in a building where students from more than two dozen countries were living together without any obvious signs of animosity. It was a place where you could find salsa, gyros, rye bread, humus, egg rolls, sausage, pizza, apple pie and chutney.

In a few days, I changed my identity several times. In other parts of the world, identity is not so fluid. You are born with it. But in the United States, I realized while filling out my admission forms, identity is constructed. Indeed, I was at a crossroads in my personal and academic journey.

A big debate started in myself. What was my identity or ethnicity? Was it limited to one of the five racial orders (Asian, black, white, Latino and Native American)? I started realizing that my multi-faceted identity was not mutually exclusive but mutually inclusive.

I began to reconstruct my identity, and in that process it occurred to me that I was not limited to just one identity: I was Indian by birth, American by choice, Asian by legal classification, and Muslim by faith. All these identities were part of my comprehensive ethnicity.

Now, I am trying to pass on this legacy of multi-dimensional ethnicity to my child. When God blessed my wife, Shanu, and me with a child in 1994, we gave him a universal name that reflected several ethnicities and identities. We named him Shaan. It sounds Irish, but also is popular among African Americans. It is easily understood by Asian Indians, my first ethnicity. My one Hindu friend has a child named Shaan. Also, in Islamic tradition, Shaan means "Glory of Almighty." In brief, we wanted to develop in him a stronger, more cosmopolitan, richer sense of self-worth than the restricted one in which I am confined.

The respect and acceptance of numerous ethnicities, or rather "ethnorities," in the United States has brought a global cultural bazaar to this country of experiments. About 70 million Americans make up minority groups with about $620 billion in purchasing power, according to *Progressive Grocer* magazine. Ethnic foods had a volume of more than $21 billion in 1994.

Although people may start with one race or a one-dimensional model for self-identification, due to legal pressures, they gradually acquire a meaning of self through actions with family, friends and others in the immediate community. In fact, self-identity is an ongoing process, particularly in the United States, which has lured people from almost all ethnic backgrounds.

I believe convergence of various ethnicities in the United States has enriched this country. In fact, ethnicity can bind people to several groups, as my multi-faceted image connects me to the 400,000 American Muslims, more than 300,000 Asian Americans, and tens of thousands of Asian Indians in Chicago. At the same time, it connects me to my native soil of India and my mother tongue, Urdu. It keeps my childhood alive in my subconscious while it connects me to the new Americana. With this multi-dimensional ethnic approach, I am related to everyone in the world, and everyone is in my family.

Moin "Moon" Khan is secretary of the Federation of Indian Associations.

Irish Americans

Chicago population:
161,180 (1990 Census, first ancestry),
75,953 (Census, second ancestry)
1996 community estimate: NA

Metro population:
645,491 (1990 Census, first ancestry),
424,195 (Census, second ancestry)
1996 community estimate: NA

Foreign-born:
Less than 4% in the city, less than 2%
in the metro area

Demographics:

People who claimed Irish ancestry on the 1990 Census are scattered throughout the city and suburbs, especially Cook and DuPage countries. Irish Americans are the second largest white ethnic group, after Germans, in the metro area. In Chicago, Irish are in virtually every neighborhood. The highest concentrations are in the Southwest Side neighborhoods of Beverly Hills, Mt. Greenwood and Ashburn. On the North Side significant numbers can be found in Lincoln Park, Lake View and the Near North. There also are fairly high concentrations in Edgewater, Norwood Park, Irving Park and Portage Park. Contrary to popular perceptions that Bridgeport is essentially Irish, large numbers of Italians, Poles, Latinos and others make up the majority of residents. In the Cook County suburbs, where 420,000 list Irish as first or second ancestry, the highest concentrations are in Arlington Heights, Evanston, Oak Lawn, Oak Park, Schaumburg and Tinley Park. Virtually every suburb has some Irish Americans. In DuPage County, with about 160,000 reporting Irish as first or second ancestry, the highest concentrations are in Downers Grove, Elmhurst, Naperville, Lombard and Wheaton.

Historical background:

Irish Catholic immigrants came here to escape hunger, poverty, and British religious, economic and political oppression.

• The first Irish community appeared in Chicago in 1837. Most were attracted by the work offered on the Illinois and Michigan Canal, which connected Lake Michigan with the Mississippi River valley system, and later by the railroads. By 1843 foreign-born Irish made up 10% of the 7,580 people in the city.

• In the late 1840s a potato blight destroyed the major staple of the Irish peasant diet. The resulting famine led to the death of up to 1.5 million Irish and the emigration from Ireland of as many more. The famine institutionalized emigration for Irish families, who would rather see their children leave to seek their fortunes elsewhere than remain in Ireland vulnerable to poverty and future catastrophes. In 1860, the Irish were approximately 18% of the city's population. By 1870, the influx of other immigrant groups diminished the Irish-born share to 13%, and by 1890 the Irish were only 7% of the city's one million inhabitants.

• Irish peasant immigrants started on the lowest rungs of the

The potato famine led to the death of 1.5 million Irish and the emigration of as many more.

The Irish responded to Anglo-Protestant hostility by building their own communities within the Catholic parish system, with schools, hospitals and orphanages.

A generation ago, it was customary for the Irish to give a girl a form of "Mary" in her name, after the Blessed Mother. Hence, there were many Mary Pats, Mary Janes, Mary Kays and Maries.

socio-economic ladder. Men worked at unskilled jobs on the docks, at construction sites, on rail-roads and in packing houses. Women were domestic servants. Poverty and the traumatic transition from rural Ireland to urban America created major social problems such as crime, alcohol abuse, dysfunctional families and juvenile delinquency. This, plus their Catholicism, provoked nativist hostility from Anglo-Protestants, who saw the Irish Catholics as a subversive force endangering American institutions and values. As a result, the Irish suffered discrimination in the workplace and at school. They responded by building their own communities within the Catholic parish system, with schools, hospitals and orphanages.

• The Irish played a major role in Chicago politics. Political skills had been honed in Ireland, in agitating for Catholic emancipation and repeal of the union with Britain; and the Irish spoke English, which gave them an advantage. By the end of the 19th century, Irish Catholic men were prominent in City Hall and were employed in positions of political influence in the police and fire departments and on construction projects with city contracts. They dominated the Chicago City Council and ward committeeman posts and contributed eight mayors to Chicago. While the Irish built their own Catholic subculture in the city to protect them from nativist hostility, their institutions also encouraged assimilation by equipping their children with an educational foundation to compete in American society. They advanced to the skilled labor ranks and, inspired by the nuns who taught them, Irish women became significant in nursing and teaching. Irish success was reflected in residential shifts from the center to the outskirts of the city and into neighboring suburbs. Starting in the 1940s, the GI Bill helped the Irish complete their journey into the middle class. When Chicago neighborhoods experienced racial change and white flight in the 1960s, many Irish joined the exodus to the suburbs.

Current migration patterns:

From 1992-94, about 2,400 Irish immigrated to the Chicago area, according to the INS. At the start of the '90s, Congress authorized a lottery of 40,000 extra visas per year for three years to people from countries whose citizens formerly came in large numbers but no longer could do so under current regulations. Some 40% of those visas went to the Irish. Many were already in this country with temporary or expired visas.

Language:

English

Religion:

Roman Catholic

Important traditions:

Much of native Irish culture was lost through centuries of British oppression, as well as American nativist hostility that pressured the Irish to become "respectable" and assimilate. Therefore, Catholicism became the primary source of tradition for the Irish. Christenings, communions, confirmations, weddings and funerals are important rites of passage in their lives. Since the 1960s, a search for ethnic roots has led to renewed interest in Irish history, literature, dance, music and theater. Many Irish fests have sprung up in the Chicago area and have been very popular.

Holidays and special events:

Religious holidays and observances associated with the Catholic faith are important in Irish culture. **St. Patrick's Day** (March 17) has been the most noted Irish holiday in Chicago. There are two major parades, the St. Patrick's Day Parade in downtown Chicago, and the Southside Irish Parade in Beverly Hills. Many restaurants and taverns cater to this celebration with traditional Irish folk music, various Irish brews, Irish stew, corned beef and cabbage, and soda bread. Gaelic Park in Tinley Park has an annual **Irish Fest** on Memorial Day weekend. St. Xavier University sponsors an Irish Fest Labor Day weekend. Besides folk music and various sorts of entertainment, these fests have lecture series on Irish topics, poetry readings, and a Gaelic Mass. Loyola University has had an Irish studies program that attracted national and international students and attention. Notre Dame's Fighting Irish football team has a strong following among Chicago Irish. The Chicago White Sox were found by Irish American Charles Comiskey.

Foods for special occasions:

Due in part to Ireland's impoverished condition, Irish cuisine is not noted for its diversity. The foods that Irish Americans think of as traditional "comfort" foods are Irish soda bread, Irish stew, corned beef and cabbage (which is more Irish American), fish and chips (British Isles), and, of course, various forms of potatoes.

Dietary restrictions:

The only restrictions are dictated by fast days of the Catholic Church, which are far less frequent than in the days before Vatican II.

Names:

A generation ago, it was customary for the Irish to give a girl a form of "Mary" in her name, after the Blessed Mother. Hence, there were many Mary Pats, Mary Janes, Mary Kays, Marions, Maras and Maries. Other popular names were Patricia or Patrick, Kevin, Joseph, Bridget, Kathleen, Colleen, Eileen, Noreen, Maureen, Michael and Daniel. More recently, names such as Sean, Brendan, Seamus, Colin and Shannon have become popular. Surnames beginning with "O" (O'Brien, O'Connor) mean "grandson of" and those starting with "Mc" or "Mac" (McGuire, McCarthy) mean "son of," in the old Celtic clan system.

Major issues for community:

Recent Irish immigrants, especially from Northern Ireland, are very concerned about the situation there. Many are interested in seeing immigration legislation that is favorable to the Irish. There also is strong support for the MacBride Principle, which Illinois and other states have passed, prohibiting American businesses in Northern Ireland from discriminating against Catholics.

Political participation:

The Irish have a long tradition in political and civic affairs, as explained above. Despite their small numbers in the city, Chicago has an Irish mayor, prominent aldermen such as Edward Burke, Tom Hynes as County Assessor, and many judges. The Irish still turn out in support of their candidates. Irish Americans have tended to be Democrats because Republicans at one time were anti-Catholic and are seen as anti-immigrant. Since the Reagan Administration, some have become Republican. Traditionally, Irish Americans are very active voters.

Links to homeland:

Because the Irish began immigration to the United States and Chicago so long ago, many of their personal ties to Ireland have been diminished. In the 19th century, Irish immigrants could not expect to "go home" but they sent a portion of their meager earnings to their families. Many of the more recent Irish immigrants, who came since WWII, maintain ties to family and return to visit because of accessibility of air travel. These ties sometimes diminish with the passing generations, however.

Myths & misconceptions:

Myth: The Irish are drunks.

Fact: Irish Americans have had drinking problems, but according to the National Opinion Research Center, Irish Americans have no higher an alcoholism rate than urban Anglo-Protestants. But, as the Rev. Andrew Greeley has asked, "Have you ever heard a joke about a drunken Englishman?"

Myth: The Irish are poorly educated and working-class.

Fact: Irish Catholics are notably above the national average for other whites in terms of education, occupation and income.

Myth: Irish men are male chauvinists.

Fact: The Irish are more likely than other Americans to approve of a women working outside the home, and they are more likely to vote for a woman for president, according to the National Opinion Research Center. Irish Americans are more supportive than other Catholics of the idea of ordaining women priests.

— By Dr. Eileen McMahon, an Irish and Irish-American Historian who teaches at Loyola and St. Xavier universities

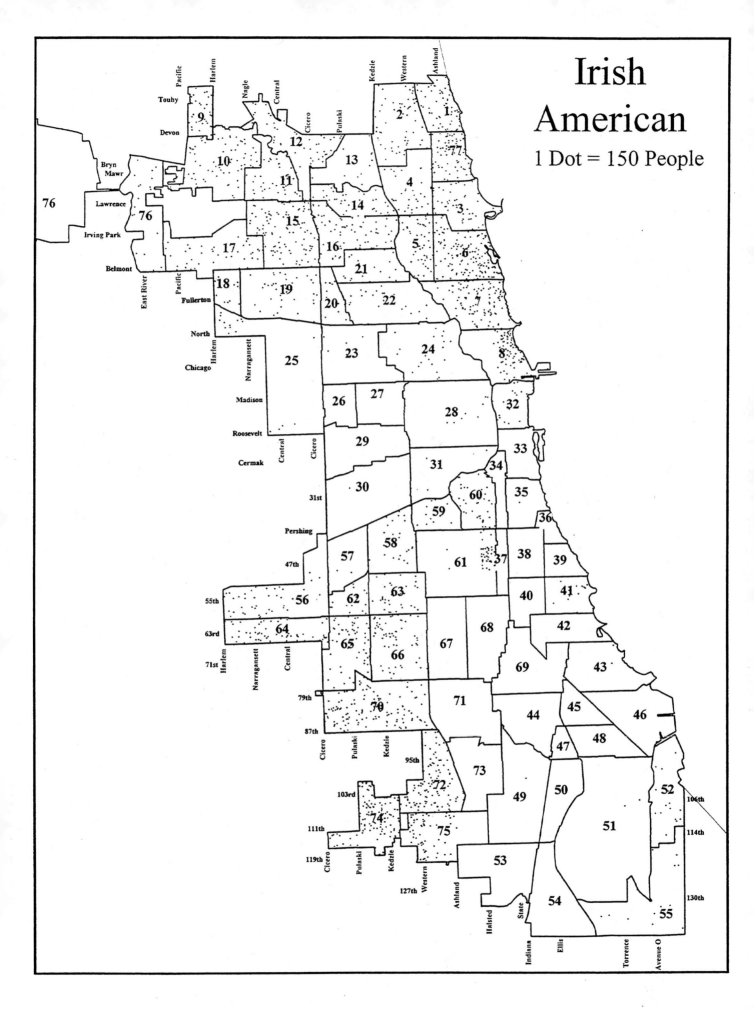

Irish
American

1 Dot = 150 People

Irish
American

1 Dot = 150 People

Italian Americans

Chicago population:
93,840 (1990 Census, first ancestry)
25,857 (Census, second ancestry)
250,000 (1996 community estimate)

Metro area population:
440,660 (1990 Census, first ancestry)
141,159 (Census, second ancestry)
600,000 (1996 community estimate)

Foreign-born:
NA, but believed to be small

Italians tended to live in enclaves with others from their village or region.

In the '40s, '50s and '60s, urban renewal encroached on Italian neighborhoods.

The negative stereotype and defamation of Italian Americans as involved in organized crime is the main issue that binds the community together.

There has been little migration during the past decade.

Demographics:
There are heavy concentrations of Italian Americans on the Northwest Side. Substantial numbers of Italian Americans live in Clearing, Dunning, Edison Park, Montclare, and the area around O'Hare, as well as in Armour Square, Bridgeport and areas to the southwest. In the suburbs, there are concentrations in Addison, Bloomingdale, Elmwood Park, Harwood Heights, Highwood, Hillside, Melrose Park, Rosemont and Chicago Heights. Little other Census data is available. It does show, however, that about 2,400 people of Italian heritage in the city don't speak English well or at all. The community estimates that income levels are above average and few are in poverty, which was virtually eliminated in two generations. Italian Americans are well-represented in small-business ownership, law and medicine. Outmarriage is estimated at 50%. Most Italians came here legally, with estimates of the undocumented at less than 1%.

Historical background:
A handful of Italians came to Chicago in 1850 from Northern Italy, but large numbers didn't arrive until years later.

• There was heavy migration from the 1890s to WWI (1914), under open immigration policy. They came for economic reasons, mainly from Southern Italy and Sicily, but several migration chains came from the Veneto and Tuscany regions of the north. Italians first settled on the near West Side (Taylor Street), and on the North and South Sides, including Bridgeport, 24th and Oakley, Grand Avenue and the Roseland/Pullman neighborhoods. The Italian neighborhood on the Near North Side was known as "Little Sicily." About 16,000 Italians lived in Chicago in 1900. They tended to live in enclaves with others from their village or region. The early immigrants were unskilled and often found jobs as railroad and construction laborers. Many were young men who planned to earn money and return home. Some did, but many stayed. The early immigrants had an ambivalent relationship with the Catholic Church, partly because in Italy it was identified with landowners, partly because in Chicago it was dominated by English-speaking Irish clergy. In 1903 the Scalabrini Fathers came to Chicago to minister to Italians here, eventually starting or taking over about a dozen churches. Italian immigrants in Chicago were subjected to prejudice and insult, often called dirty and lazy. Still, they were determined to assimilate into the life of the city.

• By 1920, Italians made up more than 7% of the population.

Some settled in the suburbs in the early decades of the century, especially Blue Island, Chicago Heights (which was half Italian in 1930), Highwood and Melrose Park. More came in the 1920s. While most were in unskilled jobs, others were small merchants, selling fruit and vegetables, shoes and clothing. There was always a significant group in small business, music and the arts.

• In the 1940s, Cabrini-Green housing project supplanted Little Sicily. In the late '50s and early '60s, urban renewal and industry began to encroach on other Italian neighborhoods. Taylor Street, which once held the most Italians, was carved up by the expressways and the University of Illinois. In the late '60s and early '70s, Roseland/Pullman residents were driven out by block busting.

• Until war broke out between the U.S. and Italy in 1941, support was strong for Benito Mussolini, dictator and founder of Italian fascism. Then second-generation Italian Americans went to war for America and that support diminished. During WWII, Italian Americans without U.S. citizenship were required to register as enemy aliens. After WWII, through the 1970s, Italians came to Chicago at a lively pace, with a mixture of economic migration and reuniting of families. In 1980, there were nearly 45,000 foreign-born Italians here.

Recent migration patterns:
There has been little migration during the past decade. In 1996 migration from Italy to anywhere is at a standstill.

Language:
Italian, with regional dialects. Fluency over the generations is weaker than many other Chicago ethnic groups, because of enemy alien status during WWII and U.S. Americanization policies. Most Italian Americans know a few words of Italian but 5% or fewer speak Italian only.

Religion:
Italian Americans are overwhelmingly Roman Catholic. There also is a small number of Protestants and Jews.

Important traditions:
Italian Americans have big christenings, weddings, wakes, funerals and birthdays, all rooted in the expectation of strong family ties. Dozens of feast days are celebrated, some with street fairs, others by individual churches or communities. Weddings are lavish and it is traditional to give money as gifts to help defray the cost of the event. The wedding day is considered the most important day in a woman's life, and it is the marriage of families as well as individuals.

Holidays and celebrations:
These include the basic Christian holidays, with a big emphasis on **Christmas Eve**, **Easter**, **St. Joseph's Day** (March 19) and feasts of village patron saints. **Festa Italiana** (summer), **Our Lady of Mount Carmel** (mid-July) in Melrose Park, **All Saints Day** (Nov. 1) and **Italy's National Day** (June 2) and other various street festivals are observed. **Columbus Day** (Oct. 12) is a major event for Chicago's Italian Americans and is celebrated with a big parade.

Foods for special occasions:
Italian Americans traditionally have a Mediterranean diet, high in olive oil, fruits and vegetables. They place a high value on food and consider cooking an art and eating a celebration. There is an elaborate seafood dinner for Christmas Eve. The exact content depends on the region in Italy from which the family comes, but a dinner might include eels, squid, octopus, cod, and smelt. On *Pasqua* (Easter), lamb and pasta dishes are served, along with special breads with whole eggs baked inside, and pies with ricotta cheese, eggs and sausage. On St. Joseph's Day, many Italians Americans create St. Joseph's Day tables, a Sicilian tradition in which the fortunate provide buffet tables of food outside their homes for the poor. On this day, a special pasta, replacing cheese with breadcrumbs and sugar, is served. Also, *zeppole* (pastries) are eaten. Very few holidays are celebrated without an appropriate pasta dish.

Specialty dishes, bread, pies and *dolci* (sweets) are produced for a variety of holidays. Italians often serve wine with their meals and some dilute their children's wine with lemon-lime soft drinks.

Major issues for community:

The negative stereotype and defamation of Italian Americans as involved in organized crime is the main issue that binds the community together. There also is concern about the negative stereotypes of the Italian government. Also, with more than 100 separate organizations, loosely united under the Joint Civic Committee of Italian Americans, the community has suffered from a lack of unity and a need to institutionalize its culture. Recent efforts to change this include: organizing parents to get Italian taught in schools; working closely with the Italian government to produce high-quality educational and cultural events here; gaining the resources to help establish programs and endow chairs at academic institutions; creating Italian and Italian American business expositions; and establishing a strong political presence. The Villa Scalabrini (Italian Home for the Aged) in Northlake and the Italian Cultural Center in Stone Park are the major institutions founded by the Italian American community.

Political participation:

Italian Americans are trying to gain a statewide political presence in Illinois. They vote in large numbers and are politically active. Most were Democrats up into the Kennedy era, but many have moved up socio-economically and may now be predominantly Republicans. Although no Italian has run for mayor of Chicago, there have been several aldermen (not so many now as a decade ago), county officials, a state treasurer, judges, and mayors of suburban towns. Italian Americans have begun to organize voter education, registration, informational forums and candidate support through the Italian American Political Coalition.

Links to homeland:

Italian Americans are linked to Italy by the Italian Consul General, Italian Cultural Institute, regional clubs, and lively commercial interaction via the Italian Trade Commission. At the end of WWII there was a big effort to get relatives in Italy not to vote Communist. Whenever there is an earthquake the community lobbies for more U.S. aid. About 70% of those over the age of 50 have visited and look after relatives in Italy.

Names:

Early generations named children for grandparents, using saints' names such as Anthony, Joseph, Dominic, Marco, Bruno, Primo and the feminine equivalents, like Maria. Most surnames end in vowels. Emphasis is usually on the next to last syllable.

Myths & misconceptions:

Myth: Italian Americans are over-represented in organized crime.
Fact: The crime rate among Italian Americans is extremely low. Even the highest estimates of the number of Italians in organized crime here amount to much less than 1% of the Italian American population.
Myth: All Italian Americans are like those in movies and on TV — blue-collar, low-educated, street toughs and gangsters.
Fact: As with most ethnic groups, few mass media productions or best-selling novels depict Italian Americans in non-stereotypical terms. Italian Americans are above average in income and education.
Myth: Italian American society is male-dominated.
Fact: Women have played a strong role in family affairs and the number of Italian American young women in college is at or above the national average.

Etc.:

Italians here have continued to identify with people from their own region, as well as with Italians in general. While differences between the North and South are exaggerated, historically those from the North have paid more attention to language retention in the U.S. and were more familiar with industrial and urban settings, while the South produced more small-business people who come from rural towns in Italy.

— By Dr. Dominic Candeloro, Adjunct Professor at Governors State University and former President of the American Italian Historical Assn.; and Dr. Fred Gardaphe, English Professor at Columbia College and author of two books on Italian Americans

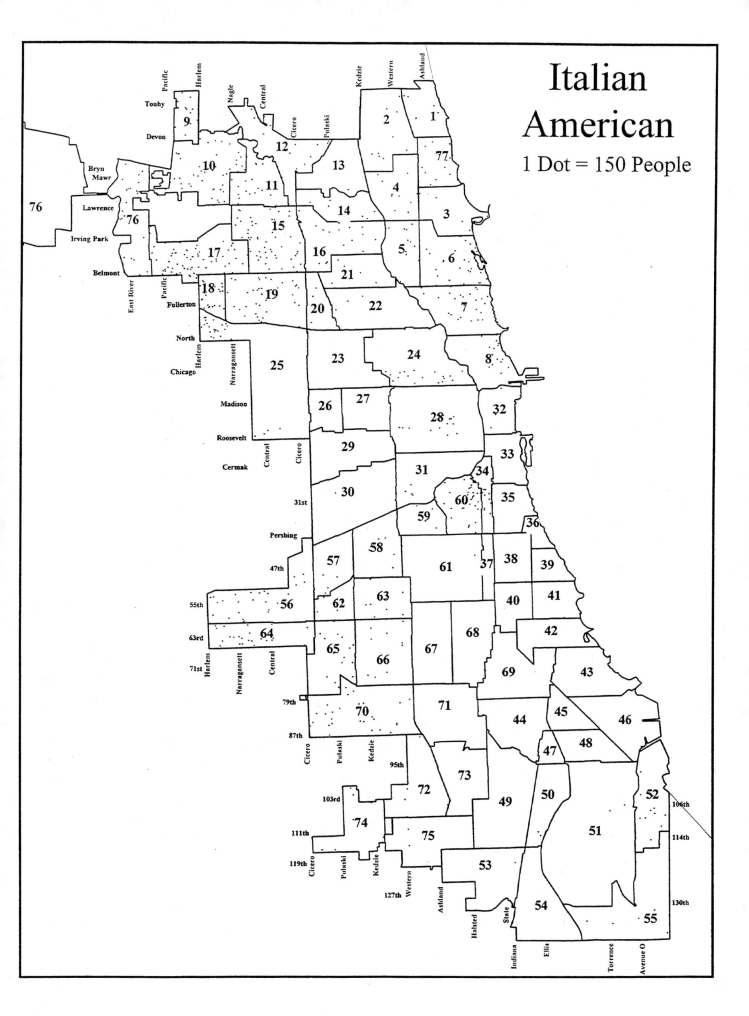

Italian
American

1 Dot = 150 People

Italian
American

1 Dot = 150 People

THE PEOPLE NEXT DOOR

By Fred L. Gardaphe

Between 1920 and 1950, the number of Italians immigrating to the United States diminished each year. No longer were Italians leaving their homeland by the thousands. Living conditions in Italy had greatly improved since the late 19th century; the U.S. government was limiting the number of people who could immigrate to America from any one country; and Mussolini prohibited it. However, the end of World War II brought a new wave of Italian immigration, and these immigrants would change the definition of Italian America.

For us, the children and grandchildren of the first major wave of Italian immigration, these new arrivals came as the enemy we had defeated, the people we had liberated. They came as our people, and most of us wanted nothing to do with them. But no matter what we wanted, their arrival would change our attitudes toward our own immigrant grandparents.

My grandparents never did fit into what I believed was American. I was often embarrassed by their mixture of Italian and English, especially when they would "speaka likea thisa" to me while I was with my non-Italian American friends. And whenever we would do something wrong, they would yell to us, "Look at that American!" as though being an American was something that shamed our family.

We finally became Americans when the Fazzolo family moved in next door. They were the new Italians, and even though our lives were separated only by a picket fence and a small garden the previous owners had neglected for years, we were worlds apart.

Until they moved in, whether or not we wanted it to be, we were America's Italians. In spite of the fact that our speech was only seasoned with the Italian that was our grandparents' primary language, and that hamburgers and hot dogs had begun replacing lunches of *"pasta e fagioli"* or escarole and beans — we were still the Italians, if only because others saw us as having different names, noses, or skin color. But this all changed the day the Fazzolo family moved in next door.

It was early spring when their moving van pulled up outside our home. I was playing outside, pretending not to notice them as they carried boxes and furniture from the street onto their front porch. My mother yelled for me to lend them a hand, and I pretended not to hear her. She came out of our house, grabbed me by the arm, and dragged me over to where they had gathered to take a break. When my mother tried to speak to them in English, they could barely respond, and so Mr. Fazzolo asked if she spoke Italian. She tried, but she spoke a dialect that hadn't changed in over 30 years, which made them snicker and scratch their heads. As though in some form of retaliation, I decided it was OK to laugh and mock their broken English. I helped them only because my mother had forced me, and throughout the whole ordeal not a word passed between us.

These were the Italians who immigrated to America during the 1950s. We called them immigrants with wings, for they came to America in airplanes, unlike my grandparents, who had crossed the Atlantic in an overcrowded boat. These people came with a truck load of possessions, not like my grandparents who were lucky if they could carry along a cardboard suitcase or a sack stuffed with what they had to bring to America.

You'd have thought there would have been a natural affinity between the two groups of immigrants, but nothing could have been further from the truth. They came better-educated and with a greater knowledge of America than their turn-of-the-century predecessors. They had been prepared by years of association with American soldiers, and the subsequent media invasion of their culture. They arrived more like Americans, yet they remained quite different. To us they were the new greaseballs, and we wouldn't let them forget it.

It took a few years for the Fazzolos to become more like us, but in the process we were becoming more like them. Mrs. Fazzolo would send over samples of her homemade cooking. My grandfather worked with Mr. Fazzolo to triple his yearly production of wine. My grandmother joined Mrs. Fazzolo in their back yard to dry tomatoes into paste. Our neighbors rejuvenated my grandparents' Italian and kept the sound alive so that later, when I finally decided to study my ancestral language, my pronunciation would be near perfect.

Years later, after I had learned Italian, I went back to my old neighborhood and spoke, for the first time, at length with the people next door in what I came to call "our language." I learned that Mr. Fazzolo had been a *"partigiano"* during the war and had spent three years in a fascist prison until he was freed by Allied soldier. He told me of having witnessed the machine-gunning of innocent people by the Nazis; he told me of how his father had been shot by a firing squad; he told me of how his whole family had been driven out of their village for fear of their lives. And all that he told me made me ashamed of how we had treated them when they first moved into the house next door.

Essentially their immigration had created two types of Italian Americans. They maintained contact with Italy, and every few years took trips back. But as the years passed, and the trips grew fewer and farther between, the people next door eventually grew to be different from contemporary Italians so that if for some reason a new emigration had begun, our next-door neighbors would be viewed by the new immigrants as American.

This forced me to question just what it was that the whole experience of immigration to America could do to a human being. In our efforts to preserve an Italian-American culture, are we just preserving a memory that is frozen in time? For the people next door had a different memory of Italy than my grandparents, and than I have since I've traveled back. It made me realize that with each wave of immigration the image of Italy changes, just as the experience of being American changes. In their own peculiar way, the people next door brought me closer to my Italian heritage, but only after I realized that my idea of being American was falsely rooted in trying to distance myself from them. For I thought, and wrongly so, that the only way for me to be American was to alienate the people next door.

Fred L. Gardaphe is a professor of English at Columbia College, and author of two books on Italian Americans.

Japanese Americans

Chicago population:
6,696 (1990 Census)
1996 community estimate: NA

Metro area population:
18,820 (1990 Census)
1996 community estimate: NA

Foreign-born:
28% in city, 4% in metro area

Demographics:

Japanese Americans are dispersed into many Chicago neighborhoods, with concentrations living in Uptown, Edgewater, Lake View and West Ridge. In the metropolitan area, Japanese Americans also tend to be dispersed, although larger concentrations live in the north and northwest suburbs such as Evanston, Morton Grove, Skokie, Lincolnwood and Arlington Heights. There are 15,725 Japanese in Cook County, 1,473 in DuPage and 1,108 in Lake. The numbers in other collar counties are very small. Further local Census breakdowns were not available, but nationally Japanese Americans have a high school graduation rate (for males 25-64) of nearly 98%, with 37% employed as managers or professionals, a per-capita income of $19,373, and only 7% in poverty. In Illinois, the likelihood of intermarriage for a U.S.-born Japanese American male is 38%, and for a U.S.-born Japanese American female, it is 43%. The rate of outmarriage seems to increase with each new generation.

Historical background:

• The internment of the 120,000 West Coast Japanese Americans during WWII, as a result of Executive Order 9066, became a stimulus for migration to areas like Chicago. Many were given permission to leave the detention camps to find jobs away from West Coast security zones. In the early 1940s just several hundred Japanese families lived in Chicago, but during the migration from the camps, Chicago became the leading destination for those resettling to inland areas. Over 30,000 internees and West Coast evacuees settled here during the '40s and many found work in the manufacturing-based companies of that era. Some also worked in hotels and restaurants. The original areas of resettlement here were on the South Side in Kenwood, Hyde Park and Woodlawn, and on the North Side in Uptown. A major problem faced by Japanese Americans in Chicago was the refusal of cemeteries to sell them burial plots. The Japanese Mutual Aid Society bought a small communal plot at Montrose Cemetery and, amid considerable publicity, negotiated with other cemeteries for additional sites.

• By 1950 most who had resettled to Chicago returned to the West Coast, leaving a population of about 11,000. Eventually, the majority of the Japanese American population would settle in Uptown and Edgewater on the North Side of the city and, during the 1950s, in the suburbs of Lincolnwood, Morton Grove and Skokie.

Many were given permission to leave detention camps to find jobs away from the West Coast. Chicago was the leading destination for those resettling inland.

A major problem faced by Japanese Americans in Chicago was the refusal of cemeteries to sell them burial plots.

Most Japanese Americans are several generations removed from their ancestral homeland.

Current migration patterns:

Today, most Japanese Americans are descendants of the immigrants who came to America during the period 1900-24, before the Asian Exclusion Act blocked immigration. Current immigration from Japan is negligible, consisting of temporary students and businessmen with their families.

Religion:

Although there are no precise figures, it is thought that a majority (50-60%) of Japanese Americans identify with Buddhism, the dominant religion of Japan. Most of the remainder belong to various Christian denominations.

Language:

Japanese, though most of the population is second-, third- or fourth-generation and therefore speaks English.

Important traditions:

Many of the traditions practiced by first-generation immigrants who came to America at the turn of the century have been altered or lost with the passage of time. Among those still maintained are Buddhist funerals where priests recite *sutras* to the accompaniment of bells and gongs, and the New Year's Day celebration. Third- *(Sansei)* and fourth- *(Yonsei)* generation Japanese Americans have displayed a curiosity about the culture and traditions of their ancestral homeland. This is demonstrated by their participation in ethnic festivals and pursuit of classes in Japanese language, *ikebana* (flower arranging), *judo*, *kendo* and musical instruments such as *taiko* drums.

Holidays and special events:

New Year's Day (Jan. 1) is celebrated with a preparation of traditional Japanese foods. Often, family and friends are invited to celebrate the New Year to offer good will. In addition, New Year's celebrations are held by prefecture associations (groups that originate from specific locales in Japan) and business organizations. **The 60th birthday** is celebrated as a milestone signifying that certain of life's responsibilities have been fulfilled and it is time to undertake new directions.

Food for special occasions:

The New Year's Day celebration features traditional Japanese food, including some that carry meaning, such as *kuromame* (black beans) signifying good health, and *tai* (whole fish) used to celebrate happy occasions. A popular New Year's item is *mochi*, a glutinous rice cake used as an ingredient in a traditional soup or toasted and eaten by hand with soy sauce. Until recent years the production of mochi was a community endeavor and the men, using wooden mallets, would pound the rice to the proper consistency while the women would shape or cut it. Mochi is considered a good-luck omen.

Names:

Before 1868 Japanese commoners were known by their first name and where they worked or lived (e.g. Jiro from Kobe). After the abolition of the feudal system, people chose family names that related to their environment or to sentiments that appealed to them, such as Yamamoto (foot of the mountain), Yoshino (good field), or Ogawa (large river). In Japan, women's names are generally those of flowers, seasons and sentiments, such as Haruko (spring child). Men's names often refer to their numerical position in the family, like Goro (fifth son). Japanese Americans rarely choose Japanese first names for their children, but Japanese middle names frequently are used.

Major issues for community:

In recent years, the Chicago Japanese American community has been concerned about the welfare of its aging and elderly population. This resulted in construction of Heiwa Terrace, a retirement residence, and Keiro, a long-term care facility. At a different level, Japanese Americans remain concerned about issues of defamation and discrimination. Stemming from their historical experience in America, Japanese Americans are very conscious about the emotional backlash from economic criticism that is directed toward Japan, because such criticism often leads to acts of defamation and incidents of anti-Asian sentiment and violence inflicted on Asian Americans.

Political participation:

Japanese Americans were among the first of the Asian American groups to become politically active in Chicago. Following their resettlement here during and around WWII, the Japanese American community actively sought passage of federal legislation to allow naturalization of the immigrant generation who were prevented by law from becoming citizens. Their efforts finally resulted in passage of the McCarran-Walter Act in 1952. This successful legislative effort necessitated communication with their members of Congress as well as with other public officials — a practice that has been maintained to the present time. A Japanese American has not been elected to public office at the state or local level in Illinois, although they have been involved actively in party politics. In states with sizable Japanese American populations such as Hawaii and California there is considerable involvement in the political process. At one time during the 1980s, five Japanese Americans served in Congress, a large number relative to their ethnic population. Among the various Asian American ethnic groups, Japanese Americans have one of the highest rates of voter registration.

Links to homeland:

Most Japanese Americans are several generations removed from their ancestral homeland, thus their linkage is not as strong as for more newly arrived ethnic groups. During and immediately following WWII, Japanese Americans distanced themselves from Japan as a means of protecting themselves from the perception of having any association with an "enemy" nation. Today there is much less tendency by Japanese Americans to distance themselves from their ancestral homeland. They often travel to Japan for various reasons including business, tourism, and to visit relatives. As a community, however, Japanese Americans do not try to influence foreign policy issues involving Japan, except to encourage that any debate surrounding issues such as trade relations with the United States be devoid of emotional messages that may lead to acts of defamation directed at Japanese Americans. They remain sensitive to tragedies that occur in Japan. Following the Kobe earthquake in 1995, they contributed to relief organizations.

Myths & misconceptions:

Myth: All Asian Americans are the same.

Fact: Asian Americans are not a monolithic group. Each Asian ethnic group is separated by language, religion, history and culture. In addition, in the United States, the groups often are separated by economic class. Some are American-born, tracing their history to the mid-1800s, while others have immigrated since 1965, when a change in law allowed Asians to come here in substantial numbers. Their issues differ greatly, ranging from the concerns of a fourth-generation Japanese American executive trying to scale the corporate ladder to those of an unemployed Hmong unprepared for survival in an urban environment.

Myth: Discrimination does not affect Japanese Americans or other Asian Americans.

Fact: Many Asian Americans believe discrimination is still pervasive, accounting for their underrepresentation in managerial positions in the workplace. This may be due to stereotyped notions that Asian Americans lack aggressiveness, possess poor communication skills, or that they can't advance beyond their technical skills. A 1992 report by the U.S. Commission on Civil Rights indicated that U.S.-born Asian American men were 7-11% less likely to be in managerial positions than white (non-Hispanic) men with the same measured characteristics.

Etc.:

The terms "Jap," "slant-eyed" and "nip" are racial slurs. These terms are offensive to Japanese Americans because historically they have been used to demean and dehumanize. Japanese Americans paid a price for the emotional message of these terms, as during WWII, when virtually all Japanese Americans were forced from their West Coast homes and incarcerated because of racism, and the use of slurs to reinforce this hatred was allowed to persist unabated.

— By William Yoshino, Midwest Director of the Japanese American Citizens League

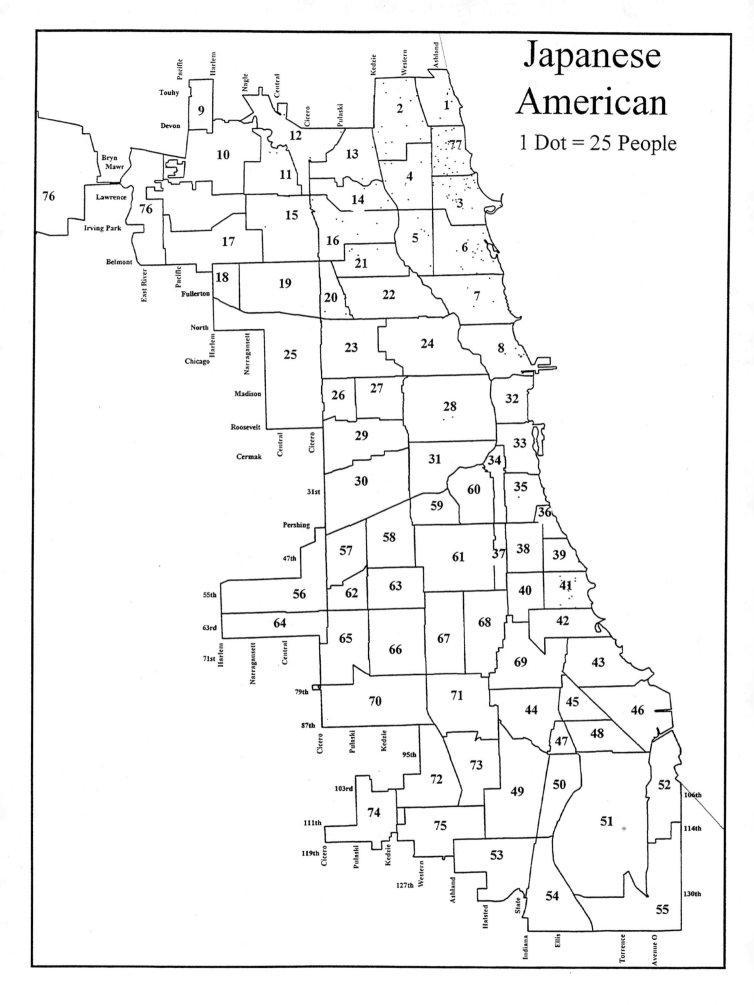

Japanese
American

1 Dot = 25 People

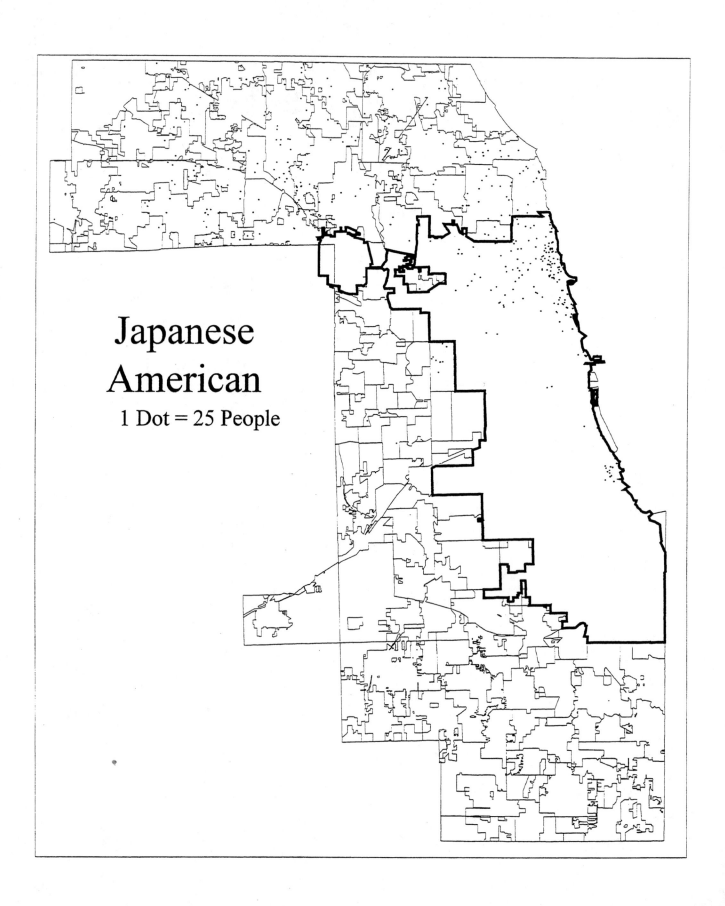

Japanese
American

1 Dot = 25 People

Jewish Americans

Chicago population:

1990 Census not available
87,600 (1990 community estimate)

Metro area population:

1990 Census not available
261,000 (1990 community estimate)

Foreign-born:

NA but relatively small

(Note: The Census Bureau does not collect information on religion or give people the opportunity to check off Jewish ancestry. The data here are from the *1990 Chicago Jewish Population Study* of the Jewish Federation of Metropolitan Chicago.)

Demographics:

Chicago's Jewish population ranks fourth in the United States after New York, Los Angeles and Philadelphia. It is about two-thirds suburban, reflecting a heavy out-migration from the city beginning in the late 1940s and early '50s. The population is overwhelmingly native-born. Most are second-, third-, or even fourth-generation Americans. The notable exception to this pattern is the 23,000 Jewish immigrants who have come in the past 15-20 years from the countries of the former Soviet Union. As products of Soviet culture, this group can be differentiated from the rest of the community. Also a very small number of Israelis have settled here permanently. In Chicago, Jews traditionally have been concentrated in West Rogers Park, with lesser numbers in Albany Park, Hollywood Park, Peterson Park, the North Side lakefront, the Gold Coast, the Near North area in general, and Hyde Park-Kenwood on the South Side. The largest concentrations outside the city are in the North Shore suburbs of Skokie, Evanston, Wilmette, Winnetka, Glencoe, Highland Park, Northbrook and Deerfield. There also are significant communities in Oak Park and River Forest west of the city and in Homewood, Flossmoor and Olympia Fields to the south. In recent years, the northwest suburbs of Buffalo Grove, Schaumburg and Vernon Hills have seen a significant influx of Jews, and there has been growth in DuPage County, particularly in Naperville and surrounding communities. National data suggest the Jewish community is relatively affluent and well-educated compared with other ethnic and religious groups. Occupationally, they are concentrated in business and the professions, and to a lesser extent in education and social services.

Historical background:

• Jews have lived in Chicago since the 1830s. For the next 50 years they came primarily from Central Europe, especially from Germany. The early Jewish citizens lived in the central area of Chicago, but after the 1871 fire most moved to the South Side. They were mostly in business and, to a lesser extent, the professions. The community's growth was steady but slow, probably totaling less than 6,000 after 50 years.

Chicago's Jewish population ranks fourth in the U.S., after New York, Los Angeles and Philadelphia.

Jews have lived in Chicago since the 1830s. For the first 50 years, they came primarily from Central Europe, especially Germany.

The 1880s saw the start of a dramatic increase, as tens of thousands came, mainly from Eastern Europe and Russia.

Jews have been very active politically, perhaps more so than any other ethnic community.

• The 1880s saw the start of a dramatic increase in the Jewish population, as tens of thousands of immigrants came, mainly from Eastern Europe and Russia. They concentrated in the Maxwell Street area. This period was a difficult one. As the community struggled to absorb increasing numbers of immigrants, tensions arose between the older, better-educated and assimilated Reform Jews of German origin and newcomers who were poor, often uneducated, and mostly Orthodox. Moreover, the new immigrants were more likely to be shopkeepers or laborers whereas the earlier settlers were already several steps higher on the socio-economic ladder.

• The next several decades saw the Jewish population balloon to an estimated 300,000 by 1930. This number may have increased slightly after WWII, but the population began to decline in the 1950s, as war refugees stopped coming, the birthrate declined, and migration to other parts of the country, particularly California, increased. The population had spread west to Lawndale after WWI. Almost half the Jewish population of Chicago lived in this area well into the 1940s, then people began to move to neighborhoods elsewhere in the city. From the beginning, the community developed institutions to take care of its own. Synagogues and temples multiplied with the population increase, as did community centers, Yiddish theaters, religious schools, health-care facilities, and other communal organizations. Today an extraordinary network of services is provided by and for the community.

Current migration patterns:
The community is now relatively stable There is some immigration of Jews from the former Soviet Union and Jews in their 20s who are attracted to Chicago after college. But a low birthrate and considerable intermarriage keep the Jewish population from increasing significantly. Movement to the suburbs continues, especially among those whose children are reaching school age. Increasing numbers are moving to south and northwest suburbs. There seems to be some reverse migration from suburbs to city, particularly among empty-nesters.

Language:
Chicago-area Jews, by and large, are not bilingual, though significant numbers, particularly the Orthodox, know Hebrew. Yiddish, the lingua franca of the immigrant generation a century ago, has all but died out. In the 1990 Census, 341 in Chicago who spoke Yiddish did not speak English well. Russian is spoken by immigrants from the former Soviet Union.

Religion:
An estimated 60% of the population is formally affiliated with Orthodox, Conservative, Reform and Reconstructionist congregations. The remainder are unaffiliated, with the majority probably considering themselves Reform, Conservative or "just Jewish." Of the affiliated Jews, about 15% are Orthodox; 40% Reform; 40% Conservative; and the remainder are Reconstructionist or "other."

Important traditions:
Rites of passage include the *Brit Millah* (ritual circumcision), commonly called *bris,* for a boy; naming for a girl; *bar-* or *bat-mitzvah,* at which the young person demonstrates knowledge of Judaism and ability to read the Torah and thus is welcomed into the adult community (Orthodox Jews don't have bat-mitzvahs); and confirmation (usually for 16-year-olds) for Reform and, to a lesser extent, Conservative Jews. A Jewish wedding ceremony is peformed under a *chupah,* or wedding canopy, symbolizing the new home the couple will build together. The ceremony includes the breaking of a glass, symbolizing the destruction of the Temple in Jerusalem. When a person dies, Jews do not tamper with the body. Under normal circumstances, there is no autopsy, no cremation and no embalming — and because of the latter there is speedy burial, usually within 24 hours. Mourning, or "sitting *shiva,*" for a family member who has died also is important Instead of flowers, donations are given to life-affirming causes. These traditions are observed even by those unaffiliated with a congregation.

Holidays and special events:
The Jewish year is based on lunar calculations and Jewish holidays do not fall on the same day each year. **Shabbat,** the Jewish Sabbath (from sundown Friday to sundown Saturday), is observed to varying degrees by a signicant percentage of the community. The High Holy days,

from **Rosh Hashanah** (the Jewish New Year) to and including **Yom Kippur** (the Day of Atonement) are the most important. This period, in September or October, is known as the Ten Days of Penitence and is devoted to praying for forgiveness of sins and for a good year. Yom Kippur is the holiest day of the year, marked by 24 hours of fasting from sundown to sundown. The Pilgrimage festivals are second in importance. These include **Passover** (March or April), **Sukkoth**, the Feast of Booths or Harvest Festival (September or October), and **Shavout,** the giving of the Torah on Mt. Sinai (May or June). Each of these days has agricultural, historical and spiritual significance. Passover marks the exodus of the Jews from Egypt and is celebrated with a *seder* meal. Sukkoth commemorates the 40 years of Jewish wandering in the desert on the way to the Promised Land. Many celebrate by building a *Sukkah* (booth) to symbolize the first stopping place of the Israelites on their flight. The Sukkah is decorated with fruits of the harvest and is often covered with tree branches. The lesser or minor festivals include **Chanukah,** the festival of Lights (November or December) and **Purim,** the Feast of Lots (February or March). Chanukah (often spelled Hannukah) marks the heroic battle of the Maccabees in 165 B.C.E. Jews light candles (one the first night, two the second, and so on). On these nights, children play the *dreidel* game, and it is traditional to give them small coins, or *gelt,* although many Jews also give toys, perhaps because of the competition with Christmas. (The dreidel game dates back to early times when it was forbidden to study Torah. Young boys snuck out to the woods to study. When the Roman soldiers came, they hid the Torah and pretended to play the dreidel game.) Purim commemorates the downfall of the wicked Haman, the confidante of King Ahaseuras of Persia. Adults and children dress up as one of the characters from the Purim story. **Yom HaShoah,** commemorating those killed in the Holocaust, and **Yom Ha'atzmaut,** celebrating the birth of modern Israel, also have become important in recent years. (Both are in April or May.)

Foods for special occasions:

Jewish food reflects history and celebration and, as in other cultures, explains traditions and preferences that define Jews. Virtually every holiday has a special dish associated with it, reflecting Eastern European (Ashkenazic) or Mediterranean (Sephardic) roots. In Jewish homes where Shabbat is observed, families make or buy *challahs,* (special braided egg breads). At Rosh Hashanah these breads may be round and filled with raisins. Challahs have religious significance and no meal is complete without some. On Rosh Hashanah, honey cake or sweetened apple slices signify a sweet year. After the fast associated with Yom Kippur, many Jews enjoy a breakfast of bagels, lox and cream cheese. During Sukkot, they eat fruits and vegetables. Chanukah is often celebrated with foods made in oil to commemorate the miracle of a small amount of oil lasting eight days while the Jews fought a battle for freedom, like *latkes* (fried potato pancakes) and *soufganiot* (doughnuts). For Purim, *hamantash* (a three-cornered pastry filled with poppy seeds, honey or preserves) symbolizes the festivities.

Dietary restrictions:

Jewish law regarding food *(Kashrut)* is complex. Among other things, it requires separating meat and dairy products (and the utensils and dishes used for them), forbids eating shellfish and meat from animals without cloven hoofs. It also requires that animals used for meat be slaughtered according to specific rules. A significant minority of Jews observe Kashrut completely; others maintain a strictly kosher home but will eat out in non-kosher restaurants or homes; still others merely avoid eating proscribed foods or do not observe any form of Kashrut at all.

Names:

In the minds of many, there are clearly identifiable surnames that have for hundreds of years been identified as Jewish, mostly coming from Europe. Many such names have occupational origins. Some, like Cohen (the priestly class) or Levy (guardians of the temple) have religious roots. Others, particularly first names, have clear biblical origins, like Sarah, David, Jonathan and Rachel). It is becoming harder to identify "Jewish names." Many American Jews, like other Americans, have adopted ethnically neutral names, perhaps reflecting the level of assimilation of Jews in American life.

Major issues for community:

The critical issues are Jewish continuity and the maintenance of Jewish identity in a secular society; Israel's safety and security; anti-Semitism in the United States and abroad, and the security of Jewish communities in other parts of the world, particularly the former Soviet Union. The community also is concerned about such domestic issues as the separation of church and state, immigration policy, the future of quality public education in America, and prejudice and discrimination in American life generally.

Political participation:

Jews historically have been very active politically, perhaps more so than any other ethnic community. The percentage of Jews who vote regularly is twice that for the general population. They have been very active as volunteers and financial supporters for candidates at the local, state and national levels. Jews have traditionally voted for Democrats though they have tended to be more independent in recent years, especially at the state and local level.

Links to homeland:

The religious, communal, social, political and psychological links to Israel are central to the community's definition of itself. Many Chicago Jews have family in Israel and a significant minority have visited there, some many times. A number of Jewish organizations focus primarily on ties with Israel. While Israel is not literally the homeland for America's Jews, it is the historic homeland of the Jewish people and occupies a far more central role in the life of the community than homelands do for some other ethnic groups.

Myths & misconceptions:

Myth: Jews are all rich.
Fact: Jews occupy all rungs of the economic ladder, including the lowest ones. It is estimated that close to 20 percent of the Jewish community in Chicago is near or at the poverty level.
Myth: Jews care more about Israel than they do about the United States.
Fact: Jews do care a great deal about Israel; but they have been, are, and will remain first and foremost Americans. There is a deep love and appreciation on the part of Jews for America and all it means.

Etc.:

Clothing and comportment distinguish Orthodox Jews from Conservative, Reform and Reconstructionist Jews. The most observant Orthodox Jews dress in a manner designed to separate them from secular society. Men wear black hats and suits. They do not cut their sideburns or shave. Women cover their legs, arms and hair and never wear pants. More modern Orthodox Jews, however, look and dress like secular society except that men (and sometimes women) cover their heads. Men may wear hats or *kippot* (small skullcaps, sometimes called *yarmulkes*). Modern Orthodox women may only cover their heads at religious services, or may wear a hat or *shetl* (wig) at all times. Some wear skirts that cover the knee and blouses that cover the elbow, but others wear pants. Orthodox men and women maintain separation. Typically, they do not shake hands. Physical contact is reserved for husbands and wives or, in some cases, family members. Orthodox Jews tend to be more formal in speech and physical comportment. In religious settings, Orthodox Jews are gender-separate. Conservative Jewish men sometimes cover their heads with kippot outside of worship and women usually wear skirts or dresses for worship. Women usually do not cover their heads, though they may wear a *kovah* (small lacy hair covering) during prayer. Reform and Reconstructionist Jews dress similarly to secular society.

— By Jonathan Levine, Executive Director of the American Jewish Committee

Korean Americans

Chicago population:
13,863 (1990 Census)
40,000(1996 community estimate)

Metro area population:
36,189 (1990 Census)
100,000 (1996 community estimate)

Foreign-born:
About 80% in the city, 75% in metro area

Demographics:

Koreans are concentrated on the North Side of Chicago and in the northern suburbs. In Chicago, according to the 1990 Census, more than 8,000 live in the four communities of Albany Park, West Ridge, Lincoln Square and North Park. It is estimated that about half of Korean American families here are in small businesses, about one-quarter of them dry-cleaning businesses. The Korean American Dry Cleaners Assn. boasts a membership of more than 1,200 businesses, while the Korean American Merchants Assn. has 800 members. Aside from dry-cleaning, popular businesses are general merchandise, beauty supply, clothing, snack shops and import/export. The Korean business community is evident in Albany Park, along Lawrence Avenue. There also are Korean businesses along Bryn Mawr, Lincoln, Foster, Clark, Peterson and Devon. About one-quarter of Korean Americans in the city are below poverty level. Nearly 5,000 Koreans in Chicago do not speak English well or at all. In the metro area, nearly 10,000 do not speak English well. With 15,824 recorded in the Cook County suburbs in 1990, Korean Americans have heavy representation in Skokie, Lincolnwood, Glenview, Park Ridge, Morton Grove, Northbrook and Schaumburg. They also are scattered through DuPage (3,587) and Lake (1,923) counties. More than 60% of the population now lives in the suburbs and Korean businesses are opening in Glenview, Northbrook, Morton Grove and Schaumburg, following the residential migration. The Chicago metropolitan area is home to about 5% of the Korean American population in the U.S.

Historical background:

• The massive influx of Korean immigration (all from South Korea) began in the late 1960s as the U.S. immigration law was amended to accommodate people from the Eastern Hemisphere. In the late 1960s, many who came first were students, children of the wealthy Korean elite who could afford to send them abroad for better educational and economic opportunity. Other early Korean immigrants came for educational and economic opportunities for their children. This is the generation that grew up under Japanese occupation and then lived through the Korean War. The early Koreans settled in Wrigleyville and Uptown. Some qualified for subsidized housing but most lived in cheaper rental apartments until they saved enough money to buy a modest home, usually within 5-10 years of arrival. Many worked in nursing, unskilled labor, janitorial services and

Many who came first were students, children of the wealthy elite who could afford to send them abroad for better educational and economic opportunity.

Immigration has slowed since the late 1980s because South Korea is experiencing economic prosperity and political stability under democracy.

One-fourth of the people in Korea are Protestants. Here, the number is much higher.

Because the community is relatively new, Korean Americans are not active in grassroots politics.

driving buses.

• From the early 1970s on, the Koreans who immigrated were college-educated and tended to be in their 30s, including many nurses and engineers. Later they brought their parents here. In the 1970s, South Korea was economically and politically unstable. The economic boom was not felt until the 1980s, with the 1988 Seoul Olympics a turning point.

Current migration patterns:

Immigration has slowed since the late 1980s because South Korea is experiencing prosperity and has regained political stability by restoring democracy. About 4,200 arrived in Chicago from 1990-94. Word has traveled back home that the American Dream is very hard to achieve. The Los Angeles riots in the aftermath of the Rodney King verdict in 1992 put some real pictures to the rumors that life was hard in the States. In the 1990s, there is some reverse migration back to Korea, with an estimated 5,000 a year returning from the U.S. as a whole.

Language:

Korean. The spoken language is monolithic, with no regional variations. It is written in unique Korean characters, though some Korean words originated from Chinese and can be written in Chinese characters. Most second-generation children attend Saturday Korean schools. They can understand Korean but most cannot speak it fluently.

Religion:

One-fourth of the people in Korea are Protestants. Here the number is much higher, perhaps because the church functions as a networking organization and settlement house, so virtually every Korean in the U.S. is a church-goer. Some are Catholics and some Buddhists. Confucian values are important to all, regardless of religion. Confucian fundamentals include respect for elders, especially in the family unit; introversion and patience; and allegiance to family, church and — lastly — nation.

Important traditions:

Korean culture is hierarchical. Therefore, respect for elders is essential. When a person greets someone who is older, he or she bows and greets in a language befitting the elder. "Hi. How are you?" in the American casual way would not be acceptable. On New Year's Day, it is traditional to wear Korean dress and visit parents and grandparents and bow on one's knees *(jul)* to elders. In turn, the elders wish younger people good fortune, health and prosperity, and give them money. In the Korean American community, the "1.5 generation," those born in Korea but raised here, have a special responsibility to be the bridge between Korean Americans and the mainstream. Thus, they must learn the best of both cultures.

Holidays and special events:

The *Lunar New Year* (Jan. 1), and *Chusuk* (Aug. 15), the Harvest Day when the moon is brightest, are major holidays. Although the Lunar New Year is based on the lunar calendar, Korean Americans in Chicago have adopted Jan. 1 as the day to celebrate the New Year. Likewise, they've adopted the solar calendar for Chusuk (in Korea late September), when Korean Americans celebrate with traditional games and special events, including a parade around "Koreatown," along Lawrence Avenue in Albany Park.

Foods for special occasions:

Korean food is very seasonal. For example, during the hot summer, Koreans enjoy eating *naeng myun* (a cold buckwheat noodle soup). In the winter, there are hot (both spicy and steaming) soups to go with the cold season. One very traditional and special food is eaten on New Year's Day. No matter whose house one may go to, *duk mandoo guk* is served. This is a steamy beef broth-based soup with dumplings and rice cakes in it. *Kimchee* (fermented salad made from Chinese cabbage, hot peppers and garlic) is a side dish at almost every meal. Korean Americans also eat a lot of hot broth, like egg drop soup.

Names:

Most first-generation Korean Americans transliterated their names, putting the surname last instead of first as in Korea. Many are naming second-generation children with English first names and Korean middle names. Most Korean first names are two syllables, one shared by all siblings and the other unique. Each syllable has a distinctive meaning. The surname Kim is held by more than 20% of all Koreans. Other last names include Lee, Park, Choi and Chung.

Major issues for community:

One is socio-economic mainstreaming. Korean Americans tend to be relegated to labor-intensive trade in "high risk" neighborhoods. The second is political participation (see below). The third is an effort to enhance harmony between Korean American merchants and African American consumers.

Political participation:

Because the community is relatively new, Korean Americans are not active in grassroots politics. Yet political empowerment is one of the issues that most concerns the community. Such empowerment is difficult for newcomers, including Korean Americans. Although some individuals have access to government officials because of financial contributions, the community as a whole is not active in politics. The current anti-immigrant climate in the Congress is spurring citizenship and voter-registration activity, however. In the 20- to 30-year history of Korean Americans, the community has concentrated on bread-and-butter issues. As the community matures and understands the system, it will be better equipped compared with other recent arrivals because of the financial security achieved through entrepreneurship. Koreans do not gravitate specifically to either political party.

Links to homeland:

There are eight major Korean news media in Chicago, including three daily papers and one TV station. News from Korea is transmitted every day to Chicago via satellite. Also there are Korean bookstores and video rental stores featuring Korean drama and entertainment. Trade and visits back and forth increase the ties.

Myths & misconceptions:

Myth: Koreans are entrepreneurial and many of them are inner-city merchants.
Fact: Some Koreans (25% in Chicago) live below the poverty line and less than 10% of Korean American stores are in the inner city.
Myth: Korean American merchants in the inner city do not hire local people.
Fact: Three-fourths of their employees are neighborhood people, according to a study by Korean American Community Services.

Etc.:

The Los Angeles riots and boycotts of Korean American stores by some African America groups have left an image of Korean Americans that is hard to erase. The sensational coverage of both events left impressions that "all" Korean Americans have problems with African American customers; that "all" Koreans Americans are involved in inner cities. Korean American businesses exist elsewhere in the city and in the suburbs as well. Korean Americans are busy trying to achieve the American Dream that was so deftly marketed to them. It is important to remember, also, that for every family involved in business, there is one that is not. Korean Americans may look different from most other Americans, but they are Americans with Korean ancestry and are here to stay. They name their children Eric, Benjamin, Victoria and Thomas and want for them what all Americans want for their children: a better life than the one they have known.

—By InChul Choi, Executive Director of Korean American Community Services; and
Jae Choi, Founder and Past President of the Korean American Citizens Coalition

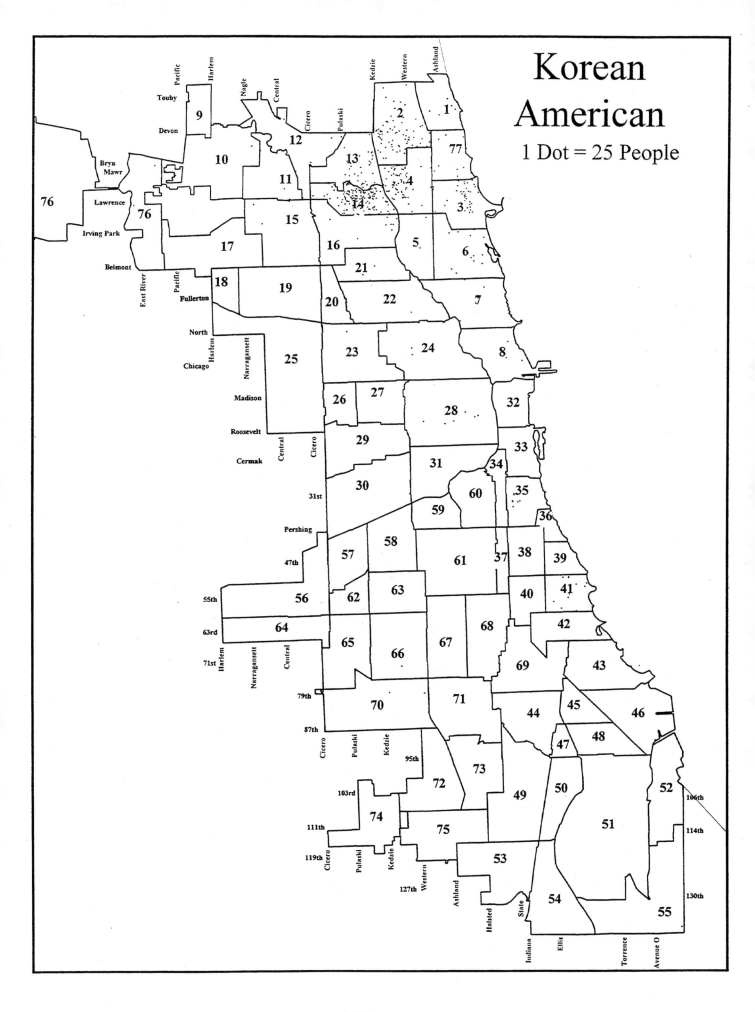

Korean
American

1 Dot = 25 People

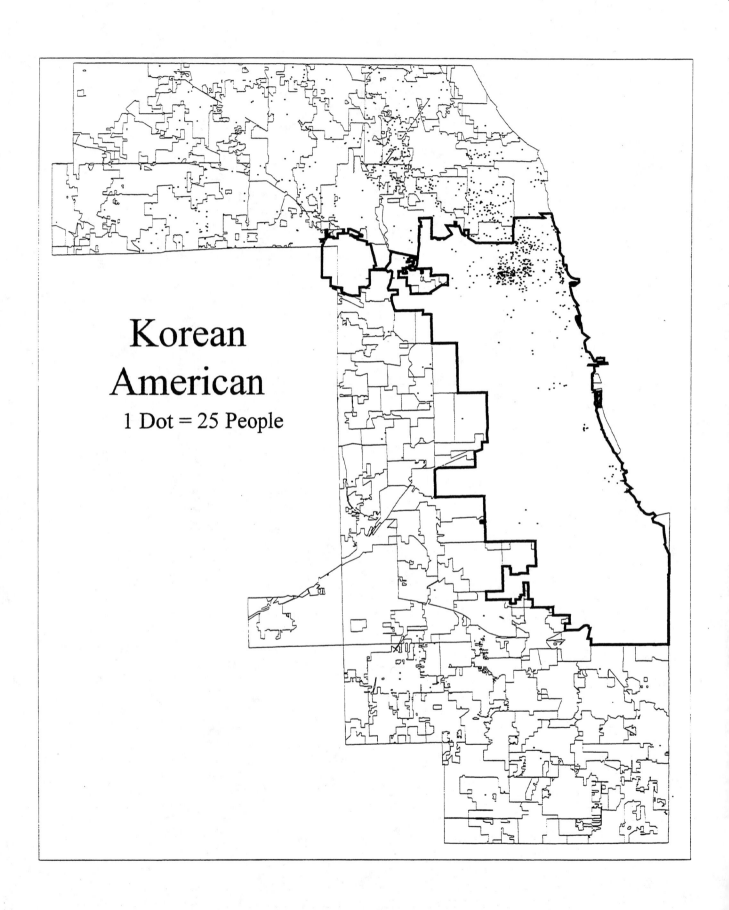

Korean
American

1 Dot = 25 People

THE 1.5 GENERATION

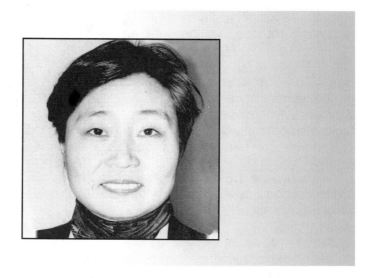

By Jae Choi

I am a 1.5 generation Korean American. No one knows quite where or when that terminology was coined, but we use it as if the whole world knows what it means. The 1.5 generation refers to Korean Americans who were born in Korea but educated mostly in the United States. We came as little children to this country, holding our parents' hands, and adopted America as our own.

I came to this country at the age of 9 and have lived here 25 years. This is my *"gohyang"* (my home, my place of growth). My culture is Korean; I was reared by Korean parents. But my consciousness, values and thoughts were formulated here. My country is America.

Being a 1.5 Korean American carries a lot of responsibility. As the term suggests, I'm someone in between Korean and American. When I'm among people who consider themselves to be Korean, I'm not quite one of them. My thinking and values are different from those of traditional Koreans. And yet, when I'm with "Americans," I am not quite one of them either. I may think and act "American," but others do not view me as American. To them I am Korean no matter how many times I say that I'm not just a Korean, I am a Korean American. Sadly, Asian Americans live with this stereotype. In the mind of America, Asian Americans are forever foreigners.

The 1.5's are expected to be a bridge between the mainstream and the marginalized Korean community. As newcomers in this country, the first-generation, immigrant Korean Americans have put their energy into providing food and shelter for their family. Their reason for being is to work, save, and buy a house in a good neighborhood so that their children can get a good education. That is the American dream. They work and sacrifice so their children can achieve and become a "somebody" in this country. And the 1.5 generation must then work incredibly hard, to vindicate their parents' hard work and sacrifice by being successful.

I did not always have a Korean American identity. When I first immigrated as a child to Chicago, I attended a racially mixed grammar school. I identified myself as a Korean because the first question people asked of me was, "Where did you come from?" Throughout high school I identified as a Korean. I participated in cultural days, proudly presenting my food, song and dance. It was not until I went to college that I developed a new identity.

In college, at the University of Chicago, I met foreign students from Korea. Interacting with them, I realized I was different. By that time, I had forgotten my Korean. When they ridiculed me and said I was not a Korean because I could not speak the language, I learned to speak it out of anger. I wanted to prove I was Korean. Although I eventually spoke the language fluently, I still knew I was different from them. My thought processes, my values and my mannerisms were different from theirs.

It wasn't until I graduated in 1983 that I called myself a Korean American. Rather than going off to graduate school or getting a job in the mainstream market, I decided to join my parents in their small garment business because they were having difficulties. Working with my first-generation parents allowed me to experience first-hand just how hard it was to be an immigrant pursuing the American Dream. They sacrificed so we could be financially secure and become fully American.

But neither financial security nor education can make us American, because by today's standards Americans are either white or black.

Today I feel confident calling myself a Korean American, because of my community service and advocacy work over the past decade. The Korean American community wants so much to build relationships with other communities and groups. We want to be a part of America. We simply don't know how to yet. As newcomers, we lack the savvy, the social and communication skills to share our dreams and sentiments. Within the community, hopes are high that the 1.5 generation can do that in the future. Unfortunately, most of us are going to college and then moving on to mainstream America without a relationship with the Korean American community. Too few are returning to the community with mainstream skills to be that bridge.

The Rodney King verdict in 1992 was a rude awakening for my community. The Los Angeles riots threw Korean Americans onto the center stage of America for a brief moment. Images of Korean American shopowners in conflict with their neighbors were beamed across the country, out of nowhere and without context.

Korean Americans have been scapegoated for an unjust social system and institutional neglect of poverty that we neither created nor had any control over. Half the loss during the riots was sustained by Korean American businesses, and we suffered irreparable damage to our image as people. Only disembodied images of us were presented to America. Korean Americans felt betrayed and bitter that the police did not protect our civil rights and property. Government failed to respond to our needs. We now know the price of being economically strong but socially and politically invisible.

To explain to the rest of America what it means and how it feels to be a Korean American is the responsibility of the 1.5 generation. To become a bridge between the immigrant families and the rest of society at large; to become educators, not only teaching the Korean American community about other groups and cultures, but educating America about us.

That is my role as a member of the 1.5 generation: to help Korean Americans become part of the American discourse, so that we can be part of the American fabric.

Jae Choi is founder and past president of the Korean American Citizens Coalition.

Lithuanian Americans

Chicago population:

18,592 (1990 Census, first ancestry)
6,955 (Census, second ancestry)
50,000-70,000 (1996 community estimate)

Metro population:

60,627 (1990 Census, first ancestry)
30,218 (Census, second ancestry)
180,000-250,000 (1996 community estimate)

Foreign-born:

17% in Chicago, 11% in metro area

Demographics:

In the early 1900s most Lithuanians were concentrated on the near South Side in Bridgeport and Town of Lake (Stockyards). They spread to adjoining neighborhoods — Brighton Park, Gage Park and Marquette Park — and to Roseland in the far South Side. Today the heaviest concentrations are in the Chicago Lawn and Brighton Park neighborhoods. Over the past 25 years, significant numbers of Lithuanians have moved throughout the metropolitan Chicago area, to places like Palos Hills, Oak Lawn, Downers Grove, Waukegan and Chicago Heights. The establishment of the Lithuanian World Center, a 130,000-square-foot cultural, educational and religious center in suburban Lemont, was a magnet for Lithuanian Americans to move to that area. Today the number in the suburbs outnumbers those in the city by better than 3:1. The estimate for the metro area varies depending on how second, third, and fourth generations are classified, especially if they married non-Lithuanians and have children with multi-ethnic backgrounds. The Chicago area has the largest concentration of Lithuanians outside of Lithuania.

Historical background:

Chicago's Lithuanians came from two Lithuanias — Lithuania Major (Republic of Lithuania) and Lithuania Minor (East Prussia). The first Lithuanian to make a significant contribution to this land was Alexandras Carolus, a native of the Kursas region, the first schoolteacher in New Amsterdam (New York), 1659-1661. Today his proud descendant, Guenter Korallus, owns the largest Volvo automobile dealership in the Midwest, located in Lisle, while other descendants of Lithuanians from the Kursas region maintain three Lithuanian Protestant churches here: Lithuanian Evangelical Home Church and Lithuanian Evangelical Reform Church in Marquette Park, and Zion Evangelical Lithuanian Church in Oak Lawn.

    • Large-scale economic migration from predominantly Roman Catholic Lithuania Major occurred when incessant rains, followed by drought, caused more than 20 percent of the population to emigrate, between 1868 and 1914. The majority came to the United States where, after 1903, they formed their largest community in Chicago. Once here, Lithuanians were often classified as Russians because they had lived under Russian rule. Further confusion resulted when Lithuanians were classified as Poles, because both were Roman Catholic, whereas

The Chicago area has the largest concentration of Lithuanians outside Lithuania.

Lithuanians were often classified as Russians because they lived under Russian rule, or as Poles because both were Roman Catholic; Protestant Lithuanians were confused with Germans.

Lithuanians organized 20 banks in Illinois between 1897 and 1926.

Protestant Lithuanians were confused with Germans. University of Chicago researcher Carl D. Buck tried to count the number of Lithuanians in 1903 and calculated between 10,000-15,000. Arriving without any education or occupational training, they entered the lowest level of the work force. Many worked in factories. But once they learned English, sizable numbers ventured into entrepreneurial enterprises. Guided by the peasant custom of mutual assistance between neighbors, they formed self-help associations that helped them create savings and loan associations, banks and automobile dealerships. These in turn generated capital for investment in other businesses, as well as enabling the majority of Lithuanians to become homeowners. Lithuanians organized 20 banks in Illinois between 1897-1926. In 1919, the founder of the Lithuanian Chamber of Commerce, Stanley Balzekas, Sr., opened his automobile dealership which, to this day, is carried on by his son, Stanley Balzekas, Jr., founder of the Balzekas Museum of Lithuanian Culture.

• When the USSR invaded and occupied Lithuania in 1940, the Chicago Lithuanian community helped form the Lithuanian American Council, which lobbied President Franklin Roosevelt, who assured a delegation that Lithuania would one day be free again. LAC sponsored and resettled 10,000 Lithuanian refugees arriving in Chicago between 1948-52. These second-wave emigres in the post-WWII era found the first wave well-established in social, political, economic and educational spheres of urban Chicago — especially in the neighborhoods of Bridgeport, Brighton Park, Town of Lake and Marquette Park. There were 16 Roman Catholic parishes and schools, two hospitals, a Lithuanian press and two cemeteries (Lithuanian National Cemetery and St. Casimir's Lithuanian Cemetery). Using the established communal base, the second wave went on to create a bevy of new organizations and institutions clustered around the Lithuanian World Community, the Ateitis Federation, the multimillion-dollar philanthropic Lithuanian Foundation, and the Lithuanian Scouts Association, as well as other political, professional, cultural and academic organizations for all age groups and interests.

Current migration patterns:
The March 11, 1990, independence of Lithuania from the Soviet Union has initiated a new cycle of economic immigrants. An estimated 5,000 -10,000 have arrived in the Chicago area since 1990. Of these, several thousand are probably undocumented. This "third wave" is beginning its own structural assimilation into multi-ethnic Chicago. Whereas the immigrants from 1948-52 were political refugees, the most recent ones are here primarily for a better economic life. Some have gone back to help in Lithuania.

Language:
Lithuanian, with its archaic tense structure, is the oldest living Indo-European language. It derives from Sanskrit and is akin to Latvian.

Religion:
Predominantly Roman Catholic, with some Lutherans and Jews.

Important traditions:
These are primarily tied to Roman Catholic sacraments such as baptism, holy communion and marriage. Wakes and funerals are traditional Roman Catholic. Lithuania has a strong folk craft tradition, so that most Lithuanians have at least some amber, wood carvings, woven linen, and art and straw Christmas ornaments.

Holidays and special events:
The major holidays are religious: **Christmas Eve** and **Easter**. The community commemorates **Independence Feb. 16, 1918,** after 130 years of Russian occupation; and the more recent **Independence March 11, 1990**, after 50 years of Soviet occupation. **St. Casimir's Day** (March 4), for the Patron Saint of Lithuania, is celebrated with St. Casimir's Fair, which takes place locally at the Lithuanian Youth Center, 5620 S. Claremont, on the closest Sunday. **Day of Sorrow** (June 15), recalls the June 15, 1940, occupation of Lithuania by the Soviet Union, and the start of killings and deportations, as well as the June 1941 massive deportations to Siberia. Other special

local events include **dance festivals** and **annual operas** in the spring. On political holidays some participants wear folk costumes.

Foods for special occasions:

Easter eggs are decorated, with some used for games such as egg rolling and going around the traditional Easter table to exchange greetings and see whose egg will survive tapping from the others. Christmas Eve has a tradition of 12 meatless dishes. Christmas wafers are shared with others at the Christmas Eve table. Each person takes the other's wafer and kisses or shows some other sign of affection. Pancakes are the specialty on Shrove Tuesday. Other special dishes include *kugelis* (grated potatoes baked with bacon, onions and eggs), *cepelinai* (potato dumplings filled with ground beef), *virtiniai* (meat, cheese or mushroom dumplings), Napoleon torts (about 20 thin layers of baked dough with butter cream and layers of fruit in between), *baravykai* (a mushroom that is a delicacy) and *saltibarsciai* (cold beet soup).

Dietary restrictions:

None, except for meatless Fridays during Lent for Roman Catholics.

Names:

Names often end in "is," "as," and "ys." The tradition is to give a child a saint's name and a traditional Lithuanian name. For example, the co-author's first name is Alexander (a saint's name) and second name is Rimas (a traditional Lithuanian name).

Major issues for community:

Main concerns are preservation of the Lithuanian language and culture in face of assimilation into the broader American society; relations between Lithuanian Americans and Lithuanians in Lithuania and worldwide; and preservation of Lithuania's freedom, which remains threatened by Russian words and actions.

Political participation:

Lithuanian Americans actively vote and participate in their communities. Few run for elective office, though Congressman Richard Durbin, a Lithuanian American, was elected to the U.S. Senate in 1996. Participation was at its maximum during Lithuania's recent struggle to regain its independence after Soviet occupation, in terms of both voting and lobbying. Lithuanian Americans are a mix of Republicans, Democrats and Independents.

Links to homeland:

Citizenship in Lithuania was not available during the Soviet occupation. Since Lithuania regained its independence, a number who were born in Lithuania have maintained dual citizenship to the extent allowed by United States law. There are strong ties among Lithuanians worldwide, with most families having relatives in Lithuania as well as in other parts of the United States, Canada and Australia. Relatives visit back and forth, with food, clothing and money deliveries by Lithuanian Americans to relatives in Lithuania. They also give generously to people in need in Lithuania, through Lithuanian Mercy Lift (over a hundred 40,000-pound containers of medical and pharmaceutical equipment sent in the past five years), Lithuanian Children's Aid, Dental Assistance to Lithuania and other charitable assistance. The Leonas Kriauceliunas Family Foundation of Lemont recently built and equipped the small animal clinic of the Lithuanian Veterinary Academy with a $1 million donation.

— By Dr. Antanas J. Van Reenan, Professor of History at Columbia College and author of <u>Lithuanian Diaspora: Königsberg to Chicago</u>; and Alexander Rimas Domanskis, Past President and Board Chairman of the Lithuanian World Center

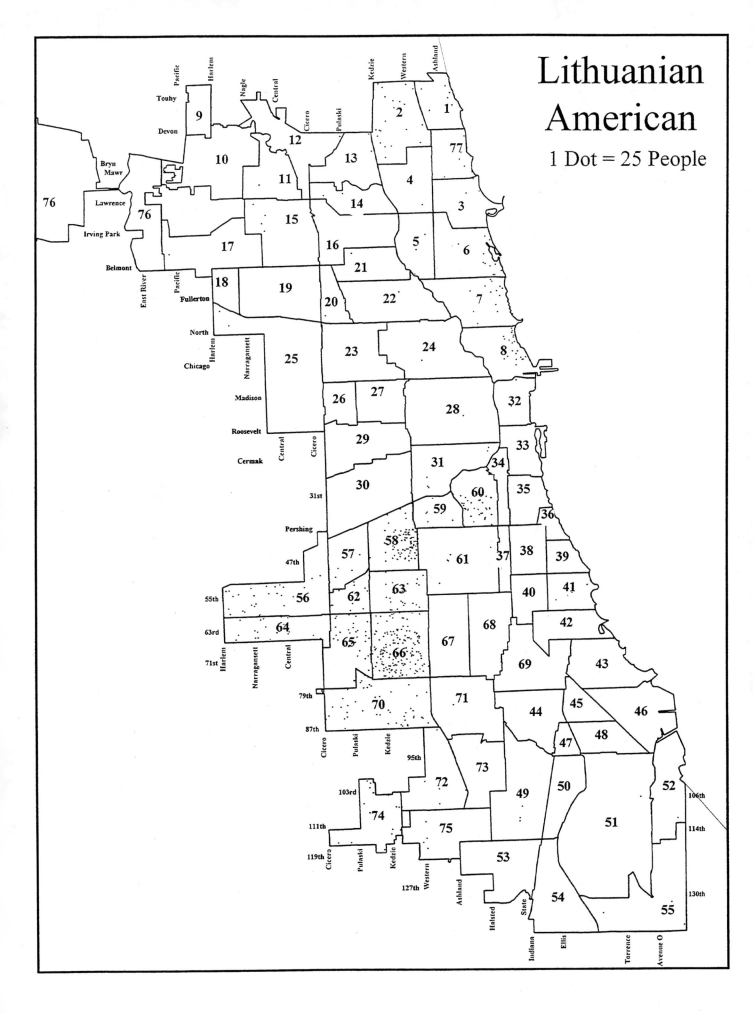

Lithuanian American

1 Dot = 25 People

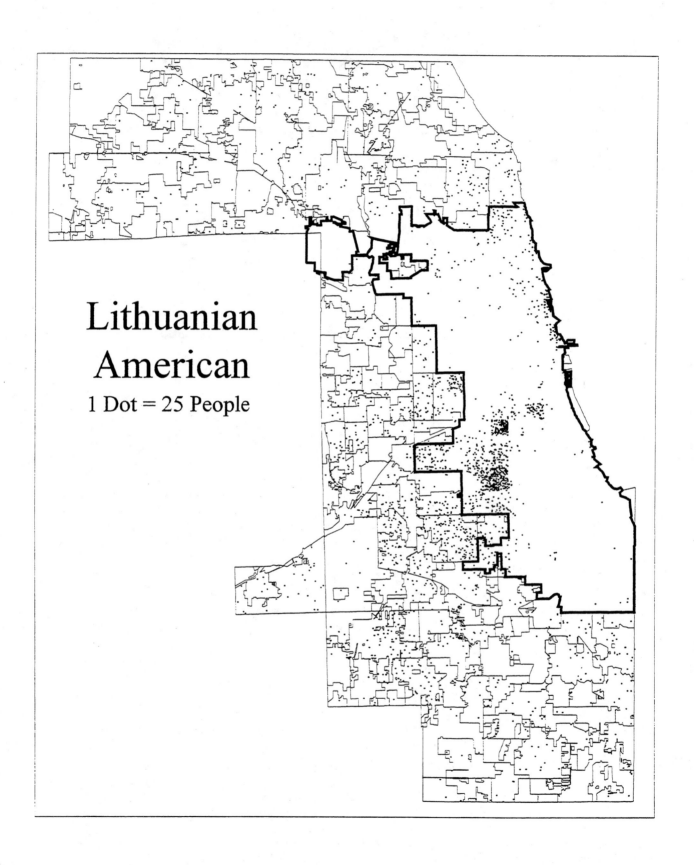

Lithuanian
American
1 Dot = 25 People

BETWEEN TWO WORLDS

By Alexander Rimas Domanskis

Throughout life we choose what we do as individuals and as members of a community. In Chicago, I live in the broader metropolitan community and in the vibrant Lithuanian American community as well. Raised by parents who immigrated to the United States several years before I was born, I was faced with the questions many others face — what is my place in America and do I accept or reject my ethnic roots? I have embraced both, but find myself not fully part of either. I am between two worlds.

Today I live in Western Springs with my Lithuanian American wife (whom I met at a Lithuanian Club meeting at the University of Michigan) and two children. We belong to two Catholic communities, one at the Lithuanian World Center in Lemont, where our children attend Lithuanian Saturday School, and one in Western Springs, where they are in elementary school.

We speak Lithuanian and English at home. My wife, as a psychologist, and I, as an attorney, use our Lithuanian language skills in our practices, though our clients cover a wide spectrum of American society.

I was born in 1952 on the West Side into a world of post-World War II Lithuanian refugees. Then as today, metropolitan Chicago had the most residents of Lithuanian descent of any place outside Lithuania. Since the first Lithuanians arrived in Chicago in the 1800s, many have assimilated, intermarried and could be called part of the "melting pot." Those who are most active today in the Lithuanian community tend to be from families who came after WWII.

My parents and older brother arrived in 1948 from post-war Germany where they were displaced persons, having fled the occupation of Lithuania by Stalin's Soviet Union. Similar to Hitler's deportation to prison camps and killing of many Jews and other East Europeans, Stalin's reign of terror resulted in deportations to Siberia and deaths even exceeding those caused by Hitler. Over 30 percent of Lithuania's population was deported, fled or was killed during WWII. I doubt any Lithuanian American family was spared. My father and his family were on deportation lists for Siberia. Other family members were deported, and my great grandmother is buried somewhere in Siberia.

Like most other immigrants, my parents came to this country with nothing but their hopes, fears and willingness to do anything to improve their lives. My father, a mechanical engineer, worked with heavy metals and machinery at the Sunbeam factory. My mother, a physician, moved from late-night short-order cook and waitress at White Castle at Division and Western to laboratory jobs. Weeks after I was born, she took and passed the foreign medical licensing exam and became the first woman and first foreign medical graduate to complete an internship at Presbyterian (now St. Luke's) Hospital. She later developed a practice in ophthalmology. Several years after I was born, my father secured a mechanical engineering position. Thus I experienced little of the difficult immigrant experience or economic struggles my parents and brother had.

I have always been proud I am American-born. As a child I would dream of being either president or pope; but only Italians were popes then, so I had a better chance of being president.

And because a fervent hope for an independent Lithuania permeated the Lithuanian American community, I daydreamed about leading the liberation of Lithuania, after reading about American revolutionary guerrilla war leaders. I pulled out maps and plotted how to infiltrate behind Soviet lines.

Growing up in a predominantly Irish Catholic parish, I was the only child who spoke Lithuanian — and one of only a few who spoke any foreign language. I was proud, independent and sometimes lonely. When the Irish in my school were allowed to go out of uniform and wear green on St. Patrick's Day, I took the liberty of wearing Lithuanian colors on St. Casimir's Day. My teacher told me to remove the colors, but I convinced her I was entitled to wear them. I bonded with the rare foreign child who came through our school — the Mexican American blind boy and the Yugoslavian immigrant, who were my best friends in third and fifth grades, respectively.

The Lithuanian American community today maintains the parallel societal structures I grew up with. I attended Lithuanian Saturday School and Lithuanian scout and religious camps. We spent many a summer day at Lithuanian resorts along Lake Michigan. We attended Lithuanian opera, folk dance and folk song festivals. Many of my generation grew up so immersed in Lithuanian American society that they chose either to remain totally immersed or to minimize their ethnic heritage. I have chosen to be part of both American and Lithuanian American society.

During the 1950s and '60s, contact with my father's brother and parents in Lithuania was nonexistent. In those Cold War years and continuing in the 1970s, any contact was spied upon. After my visits with relatives in Poland in 1966 and Lithuania in 1971 and '74, I felt a stronger personal bond with my Lithuanian heritage.

In 1988 I joined with others to purchase the former DeAndreis Seminary in Lemont to establish the Lithuanian World Center, for which I became the first president. At the same time, Lithuania was experiencing breakthroughs in its struggle for independence.

The near-impossible dream of restored freedom began to take shape, with the Lithuanian World Center becoming a meeting ground and support center. In the autumn of 1988 we hosted the International Lithuanian Symposium of Arts and Sciences, which for the first time included a sizable contingent from Lithuania, including Vytautas Landsbergis, soon to become the first president of the restored nation. In 1989 during the Soviet Union's economic blockade, we organized to coordinate political action. Our children started political protesting early.

In 1989, I began taking yearly trips to Lithuania. They were exhilarating and cathartic because I felt I was part of the rare moment in history when a nation regains its freedom. Many Lithuanian Americans shared this exhilaration, which gave meaning to all we had done to keep our heritage alive. When Lithuania's independence was fully restored in 1990, we were overwhelmed that little Lithuania had stood up to the Soviet Union and regained its independence. And we felt part of that struggle.

Alexander Domanskis is an attorney in Chicago.

Mexican Americans

Chicago population:
352,560 (1990 Census)
456,600 (1996 community estimate)

Metro area population:
570,257 (1990 Census)
702,560 (1996 community estimate)

Foreign-born:
51% for city, 49% metro

Demographics:

The vast majority live in Chicago and Cook County. They live throughout the city but are most heavily represented on the Lower West Side, in Pilsen (40,227), South Lawndale (69,131), New City, West Town, Brighton Park, South Chicago, South Deering, and the far Northeast Side. They also have lived in many Cook County suburbs for several decades. The largest Mexican populations in suburban Cook County are in Berwyn, Cicero, Palatine, Stone Park, and Hanover, Wheeling and Thornton townships. In recent years Mexicans have immigrated directly to various places in the six-county metropolitan region or moved to these areas from Chicago. Aurora (Kane County) has one of the largest Mexican populations outside of Chicago (24,494). So does Elgin. The Mexican population of Lake County numbers about 27,000; DuPage, led by Addison Township and Winfield Township, counted almost 24,000 Mexicans in 1990. Almost 20,000 Mexicans live in Will County, most of them in Joliet (11,000). Among Mexicans 25 and older, mostly immigrants, approximately 17% in Illinois have less than a fifth-grade education. Of those between 18 and 24 years of age, more are U.S.-born or arrived at an early age, so over 48% are high school graduates; 22% have at least some college. Approximately 27% of Mexicans in Chicago do not speak English well, if at all, according to the Census. Only 7% of employed Mexicans in Chicago are managers or professionals, while almost 73% are in service, unskilled and skilled occupations. As a result, median family income for Mexicans in Chicago is $25,994. U.S.-born Mexican Americans and non-citizens who arrived before 1979 fare considerably better than those who came after 1980, earning $30,232, as a statewide median. The Latino Institute's estimate of undocumented Mexicans is 120,200 in Chicago and 138,800 in the metro area as a whole.

Historical background:

Large-scale Mexican immigration to Chicago has come in several distinct waves.

• After the 1910 Mexican Revolution began, Mexicans first found their way to Illinois in large numbers, mainly as factory replacement workers for European immigrants during WWI and after. They were recruited to the meat-packing, steel and railroad industries and settled on the near West Side, in Back of the Yards, in South Chicago, and around Hull House, near already established Polish, Italian, Irish, and Slavic commu-

Many whites fled to the suburbs, so Mexicans' neighbors are now usually other Hispanics.

Trends are changing, with almost 100,000 Mexicans expected to take advantage of amnesty and become U.S. citizens in the next few years.

Interest in local civic participation among Mexicans was sparked by school council elections, which do not require citizenship.

About 80% of Mexicans are practicing Roman Catholics, but a growing number have converted to Protestantism, particularly evangelical Protestantism.

nities. This first generation of immigrants consisted mostly of single young men who came as contract workers for specified terms in the *bracero* program. By the end of the 1920s, however, Chicago was the fourth most popular destination of Mexican immigrants crossing the border, and the city was home to almost 20,000. During the Great Depression, unskilled Mexican laborers were more vulnerable than other immigrants, and many were voluntarily and sometimes forcibly repatriated to Mexico. In 1940 the number of Mexicans had dropped to about 16,000.

• With WWII came the second big immigration. Americanization programs, settlement houses and the economic rigors of the Depression had erased some of the ethnic tensions of the early years. New immigrants joined the Mexican Americans who had remained during the Depression. Many were *braceros* — contracted laborers who came to work in the defense industries — and they usually settled in the already established neighborhoods.

• During the 1950s and early 1960s braceros continued to come to the Midwest, as farmworkers who later found their way to the city. Some overstayed their contracts; others went home to seek legal visas to return to Chicago. By the early 1960s, despite the huge impact of Operation Wetback — a concerted national effort to return undocumented workers to Mexico during the 1950s — the number of Mexicans in Chicago had reached over 60,000. Most settled in the original *colonias*.

• The later '60s and 1970s saw many changes in immigration patterns and urban landscape that directly affected Mexicans and Mexican Americans in Chicago. In 1965, changes in the U.S. immigration laws increased the proportion of migrants coming from Central and South America and dramatically multiplied the number of legal and undocumented Mexicans coming to the city. The building of the University of Illinois campus on the near West Side dispersed Mexican settlers to the Pilsen neighborhood a few blocks south and to various western and southern suburbs. Since 1970 Pilsen and Little Village have been the primary recipients of new Mexican immigration. With the decline of the meat-packing and steel industries, these newest immigrants have more often worked in restaurants, hotels and landscaping. Some have moved directly to suburbs like Aurora for manufacturing jobs. After the flight of many whites to the suburbs, Mexicans' neighbors are now usually other Hispanics: Puerto Ricans and Central and South Americans who also have come in ever-larger numbers since the 1965 immigration law changes.

Current migration patterns:

More than 70% of foreign-born Mexicans have, until recently, remained non-citizens, thinking one day they would return to their homeland. Since the amnesty laws were passed in the late 1980s, many Mexicans have regularized their status and thousands have been naturalized in the past five years. With the recent decline in Mexico's economy, many more Mexicans will opt to stay in Chicago. Legal immigration to the metro area from 1990-94 was 96,843, according to the INS.

Language:

Spanish. Of the 404,918 Mexicans over the age of 5 in Cook County, 348,566 speak Spanish; 203,922 do not speak English "very well;" and 32,169 live in "linguistically isolated" homes, primarily in Pilsen (almost 90% Spanish-speaking) and Little Village (about 85% Spanish-speaking).

Religion:

About 80% of Mexicans are practicing Roman Catholics, but a growing number have converted to Protestantism, particularly evangelical Protestantism.

Important traditions:

Many of the rites of passage are associated with the practice of Roman Catholicism. At birth, children are baptized with the aid of *Madrinas* (Godmothers) and *Padrinos* (Godfathers). Most children receive communion at the age of 7 or so, and confirmation in the Roman Catholic religion at the age of 12 or 13. At age 15 many girls are feted individually at a *quinceañera*, which marks their entry into society as young women. Some young women have opted to join together in celebrating this event in a cotillion, where they receive the blessings of the community and of the Church. Marriage and family are central values to Mexican people. Immigrant families are primarily patriarchal. U.S.-born children and long-time residents have adapted more readily to the egalitarian American model of family relationships.

Holiday and special events:

Important customs include serenading at **birthday celebrations** (*mañanitas*); the *posada* at **Christmas**, which represents Joseph and Mary's search for shelter; **Day of the Dead** (Nov. 2), a day of remembrance that represents a melding of ancient Aztec ritual with Christian sentiment; The **Day of the Kings** (12th day of Christmas); and **Good Friday** (re-enactment of Jesus carrying the cross). Two of the most important days of celebration are **Cinco de Mayo** (May 5), which marks the expulsion of the French from Mexico in 1867, and **El Grito** (Sept. 16), when the first cry of revolution against Spain was sounded in 1810.

Foods for special occasions:

Tacos and *enchiladas* in various configurations represent regional variations and tastes and are common national foods, along with *huevos rancheros* (a spicy egg dish), and various spice combinations that make up regional *mole* sauces. *Salsas* — green and red—are relishes that use the native chiles of Mexico in combination with onions and tomatoes. They have become so popular in the United States that they have replaced catsup as the most frequently requested condiment. Along with chile, native maize (corn) is a staple in almost all Mexican cooking and can be used in soups as well as tacos and *tortillas* (unleavened flat bread). The food most often thought of as festive, because it usually is prepared communally for Christmas and other holidays, is *tamales*, a fritter-like concoction made of corn-meal mash stuffed with any combination of sweet, savory or meat fillings, wrapped in corn husks or banana leaves and steamed. The food itself is part of a holiday celebration; and making it fulfills the value of family and community that is so much a part of Mexican life.

Names:

The most often-used given names are Spanish variations of those also common in other Christian countries: Jesus, Juan (John), Jose (Joseph), Miguel (Michael), Samuel, Guillermo, Maria, Josefina, Cristina, Carmen and Guadalupe.

Major issues for community:

One major issue is immigration restriction, which in the past has led to undifferentiated harassment of Mexicans and other Latinos. Another is the need to improve education, with a special concern for transitional bilingual education, which would enable young people to prosper in school without losing the ability to communicate with their parents and grandparents. Economic and housing development also are urgent needs in the community, to help alleviate overcrowding and lift many newer immigrants from poverty status.

Political participation:

Traditionally, Mexican immigrants have maintained the citizenship of their homeland, where political participation is relatively low because of skepticism about the 60-year reign of the PRI (Institutional Revolutionary Party). In 1990, of the 232,044 foreign-born Mexicans living in Cook County, only 56,000 were naturalized and eligible to vote. Of 227,956 native-born Mexican Americans, over 50,000 were under the age of 17. Recently trends are changing, with almost 100,000 Mexicans expected to take advantage of amnesty and become U.S. citizens in the next few years. Interest in local civic participation among Mexicans was sparked by school council elections, which do not require citizenship. Recent redistricting, which increased the number of slots available to Mexican candidates for Chicago City Council and Illinois State Legislature, also have spurred interest among immigrants. Mexican Americans in Chicago tend to be predominantly Democrat. As they move to the suburbs they become more Republican.

Links to homeland:

From the first, Mexican immigrants have sent much money back to relatives. Postal money orders were important to the Mexican economy in the 1920s. Even today money orders make up an important part of the gross national product of Mexico. That is why immigration policy is among the issues of great importance to Mexicans in Chicago and the Midwest. Only slightly less important is trade policy, like that represented by NAFTA. On neither of these issues, however, is the community totally united. Many Mexicans and Mexican Americans support an open immigration policy, particularly as it pertains to the reuniting of families. Others, particularly those who have lived in the United States for a long time, feel their own jobs might be vulnerable to continued immigration or to the export of local industries to the Mexican border. Most Mexicans are kept informed by the international Spanish-language television networks — Telemundo and Univision — which instantly link them with news and cultural developments in the homeland.

Myths & misconceptions:

Myth: Mexicans are lazy.

Fact: Recent studies have shown that Mexicans work extremely hard for minimum wages. They have a lower unemployment rate than almost any other ethnic group.

Myth: Mexicans, especially undocumented immigrants, are a drain on social services and cost the taxpayers money.

Fact: Mexicans contribute to Social Security and income taxes through wage deductions and use social services in much lower proportion than their tax contributions.

Myth: Mexicans too often are public charges and do not pay their own way.

Fact: The 26th Street retail corridor generates the second largest sales tax receipts in the city, making that neighborhood one of the most viable and its residents very much a part of the larger community's lifeblood.

Myth: Most Mexicans do not become a part of the American mainstream.

Fact: While it is true that recent immigrants have not always immediately moved to the suburbs, and they do still predominantly use Spanish, the evidence shows that U.S.-born Mexican Americans and earlier immigrants have adapted to American social and cultural life. Their children follow the second-generation pattern of many other immigrant groups, including intermarriage. However, Mexican neighborhoods continue to be replenished with new immigrants from Mexico. So those who remain maintain a bilingual and bicultural way of life.

Etc.:

With so many other nationalities from Latin America coming to Chicago, the general label "Latino" is often applied, making it difficult to distinguish Mexicans from other groups. Mexicans prefer to be identified as such, rather than as Latinos or Hispanics.

—By Dr. Louise Año Nuevo Kerr, Associate Professor of History at the University of Illinois at Chicago and author of a book, Mexican Americans, due out in 1997

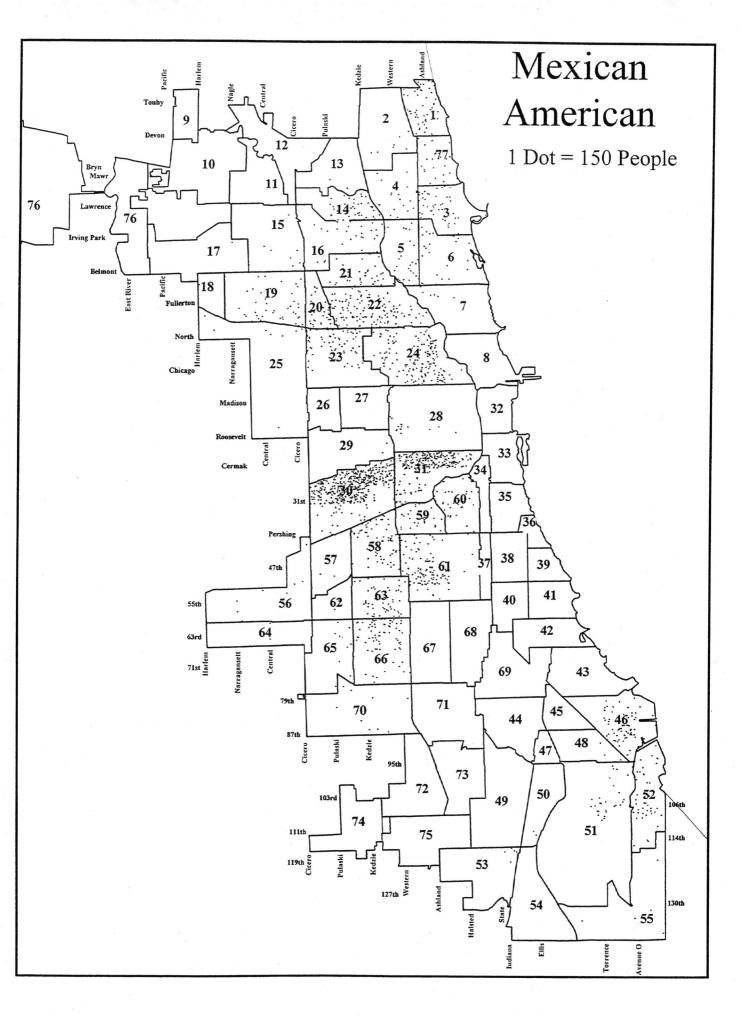

Mexican
American

1 Dot = 150 People

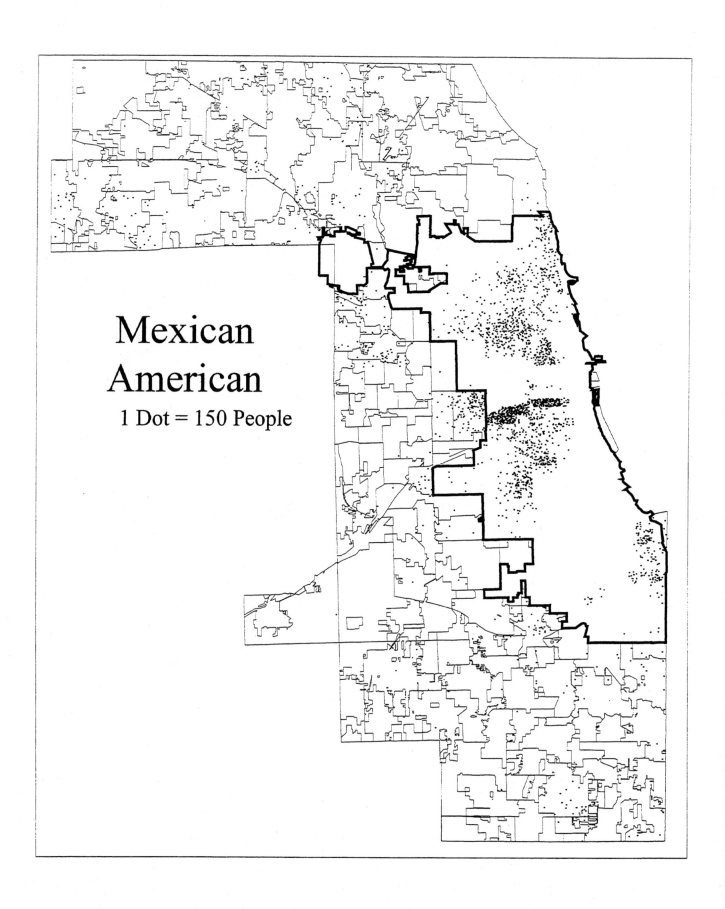

Mexican
American

1 Dot = 150 People

WHERE ARE ALL THE PEOPLE?

By Cecilia Rubalcava

I began my life in America when I was but three months old. My parents, Jesus and Teresa, decided to move our family (which included my brother Jesse, 3, and my sister Claudia, 1) from Mexico to America. They had hoped to work in the United States and save up enough money to start a small business in their hometown of Aguascalientes. Their stay was to be temporary. But two years into it, my brother Omar was born and my father found a good job as a machine operator, which postponed our plans to return to Mexico.

It was April and snow was still covering the ground when we arrived in East Moline. My mother had never seen snow and thought it was beautiful; but the novelty soon wore off. The desolation of the small town was foreign to her. She still laughs when she recounts the times Jesse, as a child, would sit in front of the window, longingly looking out, and would ask, *"Momi, donde estan toda la gente?"* ("Mommy, where are all the people?")

My mother explained to me that she was used to such a different lifestyle. In Aguascalientes you are constantly among people. She missed the sounds of her town: the din of the morning's activities, the shouting of newspaper vendors, the clanging of church bells. She was used to walking to the markets to purchase food for the meals of the day and running into people she knew along the way. I sensed my parents' longing for the life they left behind and the cultural dislocation they felt, when they recounted their memories of Mexico.

What strikes me most about being a "Mexican American" is that I have grown up with two different cultures. I have the opportunity to learn from both and the freedom to choose what I accept or deny of each. But as the term applies to me, it suggests I am neither wholly Mexican nor American; this leaves me with a sense I can claim neither identity. This feeling of displacement renders me voiceless at times, unable to have a strong grasp of my own identity.

Having grown up in East Moline, a small Midwestern town with a very small Latino community to identify with, I did not notice the duality of our world. It was just so automatic to live in Spanish in our home and in English outside our door. They both spilled over enough into each other that it all melted together somehow. Although the rule of the house was to speak in Spanish, our television and radio would be speaking or singing to us in English. While outside of the home, everywhere we went we would carry our Spanish culture with us.

I began to take more notice when my siblings and I reached the ages when we would become interpreters for our parents. I grew to dread this task at times, for there were situations in which I did not fully understand what it was my parents wanted, so I would have a difficult time communicating it to the third party. It was such a feeling of entrapment, because I certainly did not want to humiliate myself in front of a complete stranger, nor did I want to deal with my parents' disappointment because I did not carry through for them. But as I grew up, I appreciated my bilingualness more and more.

It was not until my summer trips to Mexico that I was fully able to come to terms with my Mexican identity. During my first trip there, at the age of 8, I was enraptured by the vibrancy of the colors I saw — from the brilliant hues of fruit in the marketplace to the deep, rich colors of the traditional dress of Mexico's indigenous cultures. I had never come across these colors in the United States and the experience piqued my curiosity about cultures all over the world.

I began a hunt for my own history. I found a source for building my own identity by reading about Mexico's rich but bloody history; I was fascinated by the Indian culture, yet repulsed by its brutal conquest by the Spanish and the ensuing repression of Mexico's indigenous peoples that continues to this day.

I pursued these studies in college. I took courses in Mexican history and culture. And in my costume design course, I focused on the clothing of native cultures. This education has enabled me to feel like an ethnic person with an American lifestyle. Because most of our family still lives in Mexico, we visit often; these visits keep us aware of Mexican culture and its constant changes.

I still am uncertain which side is dominant in me, but I have come to understand that my passions are definitely an outgrowth of my Mexican heritage and its rich cultural diversity.

Cecilia Rubalcava is a 1996 Columbia College graduate who works in costume design.

Native Americans

Chicago population:

6,761 (1990 Census)
8,000-12,000 (1996 community estimate)

Metro area population:

14,666 (1990 Census)
16,000-20,000 (1996 community estimate)

Demographics:

The Native American population is about evenly divided between city and suburbs. The largest concentration is in Uptown, but that is less than 10% of the city's American Indian population. The population has flowed north and west of Uptown as well as jumping to suburbs and other areas of the city. Median household income is $20,899 for the city and $29,143 for the six-county metropolitan area, according to the 1990 Census. In Chicago 36% are not high school graduates, 16% are college graduates or higher. In the metro area those figures are 27% and 16%. In Chicago, 22% of American Indians in Chicago are below the poverty level. The problem is compounded by family structure: 66% of American Indian households have children, over 40% of those households are female-headed and 50% of female-headed households with children are at or below poverty level. And 19% of married couples with children, generally the most economically stable group in American society, are in poverty. About 7% of workers are in managerial positions and 31% in service occupations. There is extensive outmarriage. A recent national poll showed 60% of Native Americans have married non-Indians. There are significant numbers of African Americans with American Indian heritage, and many Hispanics, especially from Central America and Mexico, are indigenous people as well.

Historical background:

Native Americans have lived in and passed through the Chicago area for hundreds, even thousands, of years. Even after the treaties that culminated in 1833 forced American Indian nations to leave Illinois, individuals remained behind, and members of area tribes continued to travel through Chicago as in the past.

• In the 19th and early 20th centuries, Native Americans came to Chicago to sell fish, berries and other foods, and handicrafts; they came as entertainers, sometimes as part of Wild West shows, other times to establish encampments at major events (such as the 1893 and 1933-34 World's Fairs and the annual celebrations of American Indian Day in the 1920s); and they came as parts of delegations traveling from western reservations to meet with federal officials in Washington, D.C. A small population, numbering in the hundreds, included Dr. Carlos Montezuma, the renowned Yavapai stomach surgeon who made Chicago his home for a quarter of a century until just before his death in 1923. Indian people

In the 1950s the federal government established a relocation policy, in which it recruited Indians to move from reservations to six major cities, including Chicago, and paid partial expenses.

Chicago's American Indian community is still considered fluid, with many families traveling back and forth between Chicago and home reservations.

Feasts are an important cultural base for many American Indians, and most get-togethers for any occasion include a feed-out.

149

living in the city included professionals as well as entertainers and laborers. Women often worked as maids. Many of Chicago's early American Indian residents had been forced to attend federal boarding schools, where they were taught manual-labor skills, but got little intellectual training. In the early and middle 20th century, the city's Indian population was concentrated in two neighborhoods, on the South Side near Hyde Park and on the Near North Side, especially along Clark Street.

• Beginning around WWII, the Native American population in Chicago boomed. Because of depressed reservation economies, as well as experience serving in the armed forces, many American Indians came to the city to find work in factories. Then, in the 1950s the federal government established a policy of relocation in which the Bureau of Indian Affairs (BIA) recruited Indian people to move from reservations to cities, and paid partial expenses. Chicago was one of six major cities involved in this program, which sent Indian people from all over the United States to these designated urban centers. For this reason, members of over 100 tribal backgrounds make up the Chicago Indian community. The BIA housed many of the new arrivals in Uptown, and others who came on their own moved to this area as well. Many of these new arrivals viewed the city as a temporary home and returned to their home reservation; others stayed. Jobs often were outside of Uptown, and as families became financially stable they moved to other parts of the city or the suburbs to be nearer to work. Until the early 1980s, Uptown remained the heart of the American Indian community. In 1953 the community had formed the All-Tribes American Indian Center, the first such urban center in the United States; today it is located on Wilson Avenue in Uptown. Many of the community's organizations, including health, social service, economic development and educational institutions, are still located in Uptown; others have followed patterns of population dispersal to the north and west.

Current migration patterns:
Chicago's American Indian community is still considered a "fluid" community in which many families travel back and forth between Chicago and home reservations in the United States or Canada. The Chicago region's Native American population seems to have stabilized in the past 20 years, but there is a constant influx and outflow of individuals and families.

Language:
Each of the more than 100 tribal groups has its own language. The most commonly used languages in Chicago are Choctaw, Ho-Chunk, Lakota, Ojibwe, Menominee, Navajo and Potawatomi.

Religion:
This is an individual choice. Some American Indian people are Christian; others practice their tribe's traditional religion. There is an active Native American Church, a religion with both Christian and Native American roots that was founded at the turn of the century. A few individuals belong to other religions as well.

Important traditions:
Many Native American languages are being lost and there is a strong attempt to maintain them. This is a difficult problem in a city with a diverse native population and relatively small numbers of people from any one tribe. Generosity has been a part of most Indian cultures, and is maintained in Chicago. Leaders are expected to help community members who are unable to manage successfully. The extended family is important.

Holidays and special events:
The fourth Friday in September is **American Indian Day**, as designated by Illinois State Legislature in 1919. Throughout the year, the most prominent community-wide special events are pow-wows, which occur several times a month and are sponsored by community organizations. Pow-wows are social events in which people get together to dance and renew acquaintance; their meaning varies from community to community. Two major contest pow-wows, in which dancers compete for prizes, are held in Chicago: **The American Indian Center Pow-wow**, held indoors in the fall since 1954, and the **NAES College Pow-wow**, held the second weekend in June at Mather Park since 1993.

Foods for special occasions:

These vary depending on the tribal background and affiliation. For woodland tribes, wild rice, fish or venison may be eaten on special occasions; for coastal tribes, it may be seafood or fish; for historically agricultural tribes, corn is among the foods cooked for feasting. Feasts are an important cultural base for many American Indians, and most get-togethers for any occasion include a feed-out.

Dietary restrictions:

No dietary restrictions exist community-wide; but some individuals do have restricted diets based on religion or clan affiliation. For example, in many tribes, members of clans are restricted from eating animals of that clan, bear for example. Also, American Indians are still dealing with the dietary changes wrought by colonialism, and are a high-risk diabetic population, so many individuals have dietary restrictions based on that.

Names:

Most American Indian people have common English names, but many also have tribal names. Customs for giving names vary widely based on tribal differences.

Major issues for community:

A primary issue is maintenance of culture. Many other issues overlap with concerns of other groups in Chicago's inner city: failure of the local schools to educate youth, gangs, drugs, poverty, unemployment and underemployment. The low educational levels of many adults means education at all levels is an important issue. Another problem is lack of recognition by the larger population that there are American Indians in Chicago. A Supreme Court case (Richmond v. Croson, 1989) requires cities to give minority contracts only to minorities the city can define as disadvantaged, but because Chicago's American Indian community is so small, the city did not think to include it in the guidelines. There is now an organized effort to change that.

Political participation:

The Native American population is too small and dispersed to create a strong voting base; however, individuals and organizations have worked on issues with the Mayor's Office for over 100 years. The first Chicago mayor to work with the American Indians was Carter Harrison, in the 1890s. Chicago's mayors have created various relationships with Chicago's American Indian community throughout the 20th century, but Mayor Harold Washington's administration was the most helpful and cooperative in its outreach. A relationship has continued with the Daley Administration. American Indians have worked on community issues with Illinois governors since the 1970s.

Links to homelands:

For many Potawatomi and Ho-Chunk people, the Chicago area is their homeland. For most Native Americans in Chicago, the connections to homeland are strong, as family members still live at home reservations; many retirees move back home to their own or their spouse's reservation; and many visit back and forth throughout the year.

Myths & misconceptions:

Myth: All Indians are experts on Indian culture and history. (This myth was identified by a group of American Indian youth in a Chicago summer enrichment program as being most destructive.)

Fact: With over 550 tribes in the United States, there are literally hundreds of cultural backgrounds and histories, which no one person can keep separate. There is not a universal "American Indian culture," although some commonalities do distinguish Indian cultures from Western culture. For example, one national Indian organization has identified generosity, importance of kinship, and responsibility to the community as "core cultural values" that define ways Indian individuals and communities act throughout the United States. When non-Indians demand information on "Indian Culture" it is demeaning and, when a person is unable to respond adequately, embarrassing. A myth related to this one in its destructive effect on youth is that American Indians are part of America's "frontier" western past and not part of current society.

Myth: Treaty rights are special racially based rights that the United States gave to tribes.

Fact: Indian tribes are sovereign nations within the United States. When 19th century treaties were negotiated, tribes not only sold land, but retained certain rights that they had always had, such as hunting and fishing. These rights are protected by the United States Constitution, as a large body of case law has established since the 1830s.

Myth: Because of gambling casinos, American Indians are now wealthy.

Fact: While about 100 of the 550 federally recognized tribes have gaming facilities, only a small handful of these casinos are successful enough to turn around economies that are among the poorest in the United States. The poorest U.S. county is Shannon County, S.D., home of the Pine Ridge Reservation. American Indian households, including those in Chicago, are far more likely to have children, to be female-headed, and to be poverty stricken than those of the general population. Most tribes, even with casinos, remain the poorest populations in their regions.

Myth: American Indians are subsidized by the government.

Fact: The United States has a trust responsibility to Indian tribes that dates to the 19th century, when tribes sold the valuable lands that make up the vast majority of this nation and kept for themselves small portions that were unfit to support their own populations. This is a legal responsibility recognized by the the legislative, executive and judicial braches of the U.S. government. While tribal governments, like state, county and municipal governments in the United States receive federal services and money, individual Indian people do not.

Etc.:

The strong American value based on property is not a primary value within the Indian community, where family and culture are much more the basis of decision-making (where to live, what to do for a living, etc.) In many American Indian cultures, it is the responsibility of aunts and uncles as much as of parents to discipline children. Extended families sometimes live all together in the same home rather than move away from one another, a condition that had caused social workers to break up Indian families to provide children with more space. The Indian Child Welfare Act (1978) is supposed to prevent such forced break-up from occurring, though this act is currently threatened in Congress.

— Compiled by David R. M. Beck, Director of the Center for Advanced Study and Research at Native American Educational Services (NAES) College

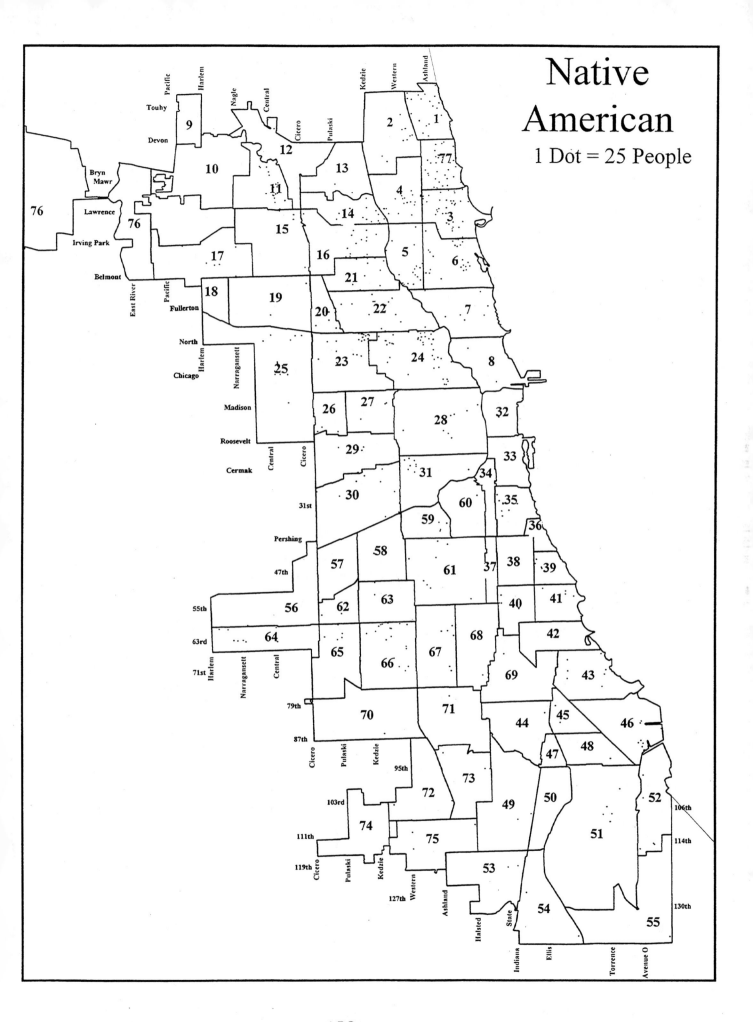

Native American

1 Dot = 25 People

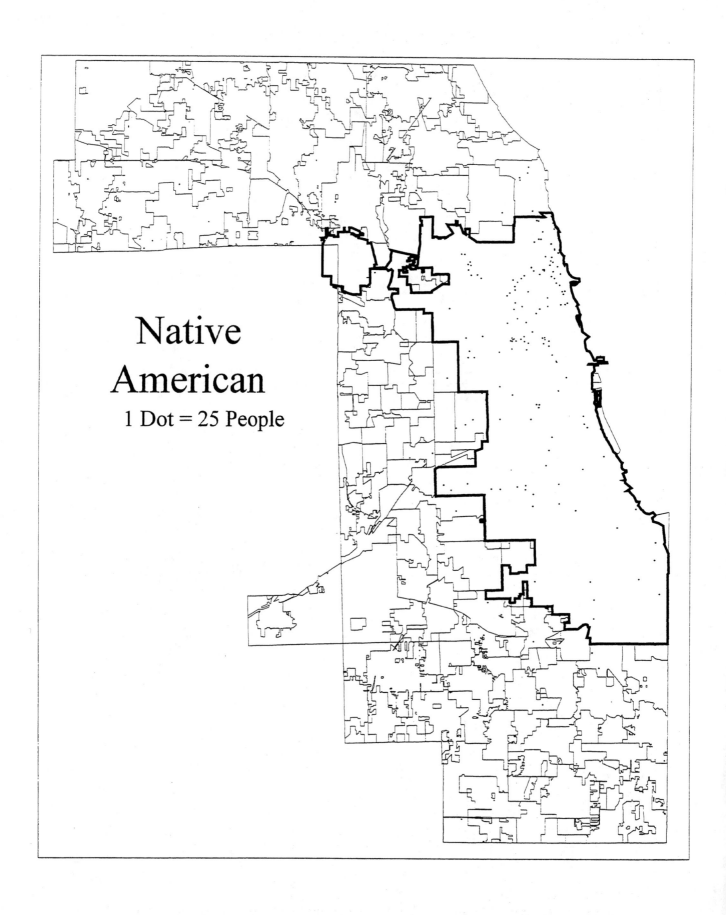

Native
American

1 Dot = 25 People

MY GRANDMOTHER'S GRANDMOTHER

By Rosalyn LaPier

My Blackfeet name is K-tia-i-tse-kus, or Not Real Beaver Women. It is the name of my grandmother's grandmother. I come from two very large families. My mother is Blackfeet, from Montana and Alberta, Canada. My father is Chippewa, from North Dakota/Manitoba. His family moved to Montana 150 years ago. On both sides, I have relatives in both Canada and the U.S.

The homelands of many tribes were unalterably changed with the creation of the Canadian/U.S. border we call the "49th parallel." At first, many tribes refused to admit its existence and continued with life as normal, which they were able to do because there were few white settlements and little enforcement at the border. But with the increased use of police against Native peoples, we eventually stayed on our respective sides. The process was heartwrenching.

At one point in the history of my father's family, the U.S. government declared them all Canadian citizens, rounded them up and under Army guard walked them to the Canadian border. But Canada refused them entrance, so they were forced to walk the hundreds of miles back to their homes.

As the years passed other ethnic groups have married into my family, including Irish, Spanish and French. All these people quickly integrated themselves into the family, and we have remained fundamentally Native. Both my Native families joke that any nefarious activity was brought on by their "white" blood.

Native Americans are unique in that America came to us — we did not come to America. Native Americans experienced reverse immigration. A new country surrounded and consumed our homelands. The borders of the present-day Blackfeet reservation in Montana were created only 100 years ago.

My grandmother's grandmother, for whom I am named, was a mother raising children at that time. She was trying to survive in a world she could hardly recognize. The old people around her remembered times of rapid change and deprivation. They told about those times to their grandchildren, who in turn are telling it to their grandchildren.

My grandmother's grandmother lived through the "Starvation Winter," when the Blackfeet were not allowed to leave the reservation to look for food and one-third of all tribal members starved to death, while many more suffered from disease.

All the while, new immigrants from far-away lands, moved to Montana and got

155

homesteads on land that once belonged to my grandmother's grandmother and her fellow Blackfeet. This disastrous time, as much as anything, shapes the present-day fabric of our home community. With the loss of land, a dramatic change in societal structure and the death of many family members, the Blackfeet were forced to reconstruct themselves within reservation boundaries. This reconstruction is at the root of present-day problems.

Many of the changes in the life of my families were brought by outside forces. The Blackfeet, who always had held land in common, were forced to take individual lots of land in 1907. We did not want to become Americans, but all Native Americans were made citizens by an Act of Congress in 1924.

The U.S. government has done everything in its power to force Native Americans to assimilate into American society. They outlawed our religions (until 1978). They forced previous generations to stop speaking Native languages in school and to wear "civilized clothes." They tried to change the societal and family structure and the gender roles of most tribes, making men take on women's work, such as raising crops, and forcing women out of their traditional role as spiritual and ritual intermediaries.

Fortunately, Native Americans have successfully fought every attempt at assimilation the government has tried and have maintained a heritage firmly based in our own values, which say the community and family come before the individual, and that there should be generosity and sharing of wealth. With this history of resistance, it is ludicrous for some to suggest Native Americans ever wanted integration. Most people assume we want what other minority groups in the U.S. want, but we want to maintain our separate societies.

I often am asked, "What do you people want from us?" There is a simple answer. We want the U.S. government to uphold the treaties they signed with us. Americans believe they have inalienable rights, as expressed in the Constitution. Native American rights stem from tribal systems that have existed for centuries, and also from their treaty rights, guaranteed by the Constitution.

This fundamental difference in how Native Americans view their legal rights in this country is something most people miss. We do not view ourselves as a minority group, but rather as distinct political entities within the United States.

Many of us have moved to cities like Chicago for a variety of reasons, some short-term others permanently. I came for educational and economic opportunity. Many Native people like myself view their residence outside their homeland as temporary, although it may last decades. Even fourth-generation residents here have a strong sense of their tribe's history.

Others may think Native Americans live in "two worlds" but I have never felt this dichotomy. I feel rooted in the Native community wherever I am. It is my husband, more than myself, who must live in two worlds. He was raised in the North Shore suburbs of Wilmette and Evanston and comes from a middle-class family of German and Swedish heritage. He has had to re-think his American-defined values and concepts to integrate himself into Native society, which he has done successfully.

Though I live in Chicago, Montana is still my home. I probably will retire there. When I see the mountains, prairies and river valleys, I am reminded of the long history of my people and can feel the spirit of my ancestors around me. Most of my family still lives there and will for generations to come. I may spend only one or two months a year there, but I think of my home and family every day.

My children need to know their grandmothers, aunts, uncles and cousins, so that they too can know what it is to be Native American. They also need to have that special relationship with the landscape that has shaped the values, language, religion, arts and culture of their ancestors. My children need to remember the things their grandmother tells them, and pass them on to their own grandchildren.

Rosalyn LaPier is an independent researcher for Native American organizations, an instructor at NAES College and a full-time mother of two.

Nigerian Americans

Chicago population:

3,136 (1990 Census, first ancestry)
105 (Census, second ancestry)
10,000 (1996 community estimate)

Metro area population:

3,763 (1990 Census, first ancestry)
169 (Census, second ancestry)
15,000 (1996 community estimate)

Foreign-born:

Virtually all adults

Demographics:

Nigeria, on the west coast of Africa, has 30 states with more than 250 distinct ethnic groups, each with its own customs, culture, traditions, values, and language or dialect. Nigerians in Chicago come from all those states. Each ethnic group here maintains its own customs and traditions. The dominant ethnic groups in Chicago are the Yorubas from the Western region and Igbos from the East. They account for an estimated 80% of Chicago's Nigerian population, with Yorubas the more prevalent. The rest include the Hausa/Fulani, Ijaw, Benin and TIV. The U.S. Census doesn't have a breakdown for Nigerians, but the community estimates about 20% of the population have become naturalized American citizens. In Chicago, an estimated 80% live on the far North Side in Rogers Park, Edgewater and Uptown, with others scattered about the city, including Hyde Park, Calumet Park and the West Side. The overwhelming majority marry other Nigerians, with about 2% marrying outside the nationality, according to community estimates. Because education is the main reason Nigerians came here, many have college degrees.

Historical background:

Before 1965 there were fewer than 100 Nigerians in Illinois. From 1965-79, the number in Chicago rose to several thousand, according to estimates, and by 1990 to more than 10,000, with an additional 5,000 in the suburbs. About 99% of the Nigerians who entered the United States after 1960 came as students, part of a "brain drain" that has brought many of Africa's best and brightest to the United States. After graduating they found a variety of jobs, from professions such as law and medicine to small businesses, accounting and, in some cases, driving taxi cabs. A few came here for reasons other than education, such as visiting relatives or for medical care.

Recent migration patterns:

Before 1980, the overwhelming majority of Nigerians returned home after graduation from college. But since 1981, only a tiny percent have returned to Nigeria because of unstable and deteriorating economic and political conditions there. Immigration slowed when it became more difficult to leave Nigeria and when students had to meet requirements to pay a full year's tuition upfront.

Nigeria has 30 states with over 250 distinct ethnic groups, each with its own customs, culture and language. Nigerians in Chicago come from all those states.

About 99% of Nigerians who came after 1960 came as students, part of a "brain drain" that has brought many of Africa's best and brightest to the U.S.

An estimated 80% in Chicago live on the North Side in Rogers Park, Edgewater and Uptown.

Language:

Virtually all Nigerians in Chicago speak English, because it was the official business language when Nigeria was under British rule. In addition, each ethnic group speaks its own dialect or language.

Religion:

The two dominant religions are Christianity and Islam, with roughly equal numbers in each. The Christians include Catholics and various Protestant denominations. Religion varies with ethnic group and region, with most Yorubas being Protestant and most Igbos Catholic. Those from the North are mostly Muslims. There are several Nigerian Christian churches and Nigerian Islamic Association places of worship, mostly on the North Side.

Important traditions:

Each ethnic group endeavors to transmit its customs, culture, values, traditions and language to the growing population of first-generation U.S.-born children in Chicago. Customs vary a great deal from one group to another, for example the dances and dress. Big events like weddings and graduations tend to be ethnic celebrations with guests coming from the same ethnic group. Respect for elders in the hierarchy of authority is important across the Nigerian community.

Holidays and special events:

The public holidays observed by Nigerians in Chicago are **New Years Day; Nigerian Independence Day** (Oct. 1), commemorating independence from the British in 1960; Christian holidays **Christmas Day** (Dec. 25), and **Easter Day;** and Muslim holidays **Maulid Eid al-Fitr** (end of Ramadan) and **Eid al-Adha** (feast of sacrifice, end of annual pilgrimage to Mecca). Nigerians also observe the American-declared public holidays such as July 4th, Labor Day and Memorial Day. Also, for the past two years there has been a **Nigerian Festival** in July at DuSable Museum, likely to become an annual event.

Foods for special occasions:

Nigerian foods are made up of rice, beans, yams, cassava, assorted vegetables, fruits, meat (cow, goat, fish, chicken, etc.), prepared into delicious dishes. These foods are almost always served at special occasions, such as weddings, naming ceremonies, festive graduations, anniversaries, picnics, ethnic parties and other social and cultural events.

Dietary restrictions:

None except religion-based restrictions for Muslims.

Names:

Some are given family names, others are named according to events in the life of the family, and some names are religious. A difficult pregnancy may result in a name for the baby that shows that difficulty. Religious people may use the name for God, such as Chuku (for the Igbos), Oluwa (Yorubas) or Allah (Muslims).

Major issues for community:

Despite the fact that Nigerians are tax-paying residents who make a significant contributions to the city with their education, skills and expertise, the economic interests of Nigerians have not been addressed adequately. They still have not built an economic infrastructure, in part because of difficulty getting loans for businesses.

Political participation:

Nigerians in Chicago are making a definite effort toward integrating into Chicago's political system. Although their participation is fragmented, the 20% who are naturalized U.S. citizens tend to vote in city, state and national elections.

Links to homeland:

Most Nigerian Americans who have become U.S. citizens maintain dual citizenship. All Nigerians here maintain very strong ties with their families in Nigeria. Many make at least one trip to Nigeria a year, visiting family and friends. Others may travel for business reasons. Nigeria has been ruled by military governments for 26 of its 36 years of independence from the British. Because the military leaders have mismanaged the Nigerian economy, the nation has suffered tremendous economic decline despite its massive natural oil resources. Furthermore, the current military government has implemented policies that have denied Nigerians their rights to enjoy the benefits of a democratic society. Human rights violations are persistently perpetrated against citizens. Because of these violations, Nigerians in Chicago have been actively involved in lobbying the U.S. government to support their efforts in calling for an end to military dictatorship in Nigeria.

Myths & misconceptions:

Myths: Nigerians tend to be involved in criminal activity, such as selling drugs. (This myth was promulgated by media coverage that generalized about all Nigerians from isolated incidents).

Fact: Most Nigerians, who are law-abiding well-educated people, many of them professionals, have nothing to do with drugs. Following one article that made it sound as if Nigerian organizations here were involved in a drug ring, the 20 organizations making up the Nigerian National Alliance came out strongly against drug dealing and urged people to report any incidents they learned about to officials.

— By Dr. Sam Enyia, Professor of Communications and Director of the Broadcast Program at Lewis University, and President of the Nigerian National Alliance

Palestinian Americans

Chicago population:

U.S. Census is not available
25,000-35,000 (estimate based on national statistics)
80,000-90,000 (1996 community estimate)

Metro area population:

U.S. Census is not available
50,000-70,000 (estimate based on national statistics)
150,000 (1996 community estimate)

Foreign-born:

NA for Chicago; 57% nationally

Note: Palestinians are not broken out locally by the Census. Community leaders say about 65% of the Arabs in the Chicago area are Palestinians.

Demographics:

The Palestinian community lives largely in the Chicago Lawn and Marquette Park neighborhoods on Chicago's Southwest Side. Palestinians also are found in Gage Park, West Elsdon and West Lawn. The intersection of Kedzie and 63rd Street is a hub for new arrivals from the Middle East. They also can be found in the southwest suburbs of Oak Lawn, Hickory Hills, Bridgeview, Burbank, Palos Heights, Palos Hills, Palos Park and Orland Park. Some Palestinians reside on the city's North Side, particularly in Albany Park around Kedzie and Lawrence, and are scattered throughout the Northwest Side, in a broad area west of Kimball and north of Diversey. The national Census figures for Palestinians show that half came after 1975 and 45% from 1980-90. Only 13% migrated before 1965, the year a new law lifted restrictions on the number of people from the Middle East, which resulted in more Arabs immigrating here. Nationally, 15% of Palestinian Americans live below the poverty line (that number is believed to be higher in Chicago) and one-fourth don't speak English well or at all. Most Palestinians are here legally. Scholars estimate a small percentage — less than 10% — enter the U.S. legally but overstay their visas.

Historical background:

Immigration from Palestine began in the late 1800s. Palestinians engaged in peddling and shopkeeping in cities and towns across the United States.

• The majority of Palestinians came here following the creation of the State of Israel in 1948, which resulted in nearly 1 million Palestinian refugees.

• Immigration from Palestine continued after the 1967 war, when Israel occupied the rest of Palestine, now called the West Bank and Gaza Strip. The policies of Israeli occupation, to rid the land of Palestinians to make way for Jewish immigrants, kept Palestinians coming into Chicago during the 1970s, '80s and '90s. The West Bank town of Beitunia now has more of its residents in Chicago than in the village itself. Those who came to the United States are from a variety of income levels.

The intersection of Kedzie and 63rd Street is a hub for new arrivals from the Middle East.

The majority of Palestinians came here following the creation of Israel in 1948, which resulted in nearly 1 million Palestinian refugees.

The Muslim tradition of writing a marriage contract and adhering to a formal engagement process is still alive in Chicago.

Elders are cared for by family members. Nursing homes are unheard of for Palestinians.

Like other immigrant groups, they maintained their tradition as small business owners, primarily of grocery stores.

Current migration patterns:

The Palestinians who came to Chicago in the 1990s did so as a result of continued hardship in their home country. In addition, the Gulf War resulted in 400,000 Palestinians being expelled from Kuwait, making some of them refugees for a second or third time. Many of these refugees came to the U.S. and to Chicago. Generally, Palestinians who settle on the Southwest Side move to the southwest suburbs as soon as they have the money to do so.

Language:

Arabic

Religion:

Muslim and Christian. Before WWII, Christian Arabs migrated to the West in larger numbers because of a perceived affinity with the West, and they tended to bring their entire families. But since 1965, Muslims have come in larger numbers, because of worsening economic and political conditions. Some Palestinian Christians are members of churches that follow Eastern (e.g. Melkite or Greek Orthodox) rites and others observe Western (e.g. Roman Catholic or Anglican) rites.

Important traditions:

The Muslim tradition of writing a marriage contract and adhering to a formal engagement process is still alive in Chicago. Some marriages are arranged, some are not; but either way, the family plays a big role in a young person's marriage. When Muslims die, they are not buried in coffins. Their bodies are washed, wrapped in a shroud and buried immediately. A person's death is followed by 40 days of mourning. On the 40th day, there is a remembrance ceremony. Palestinians encourage preservation of their language, folklore and social etiquette (hospitality, generosity and helping neighbors). There is a strong obligation to maintain close extended-family ties to cousins, aunts, uncles and grandparents. Elders are respected and cared for by family members. Nursing homes are unheard of for Palestinians. Social visits are frequent on all occasions, not just holidays. Storytelling and the oral tradition are very important.

Holidays and special events:

Muslims observe the **Eid al-Adha**, or feast of the sacrifice (when Abraham sacrificed a lamb in place of Ishmael). This feast is celebrated with prayers and an exchange of gifts. It marks the end of the *Hajj*, or pilgrimage to Mecca, Saudi Arabia, which all Muslims are encourage to make at least once in their lives. The **Eid al-Fitr** is a feast commemorating the end of Ramadan, 30 days of fasting between sunrise and sunset to renew piety as well as family ties. Ramadan and the Hajj are governed by the lunar calendar, so they do not occur at the same time each year. Christian Palestinians observe **Christmas** and **Easter**, although depending on the Christian denominations, these holidays fall on different days.

Foods for special occasions:

During Ramadan, Palestinian Muslims frequently prepare and eat special dishes like *katiyev* (a walnut-filled pancake). Special occasions often are celebrated by eating *mansaf* (goat or lamb served over rice with a yogurt sauce). Stuffed squash and rice with almonds also are popular. Spices like allspice, cumin and cardamon are commonly used.

Dietary restrictions:

The *Qu'ran* requires that Muslims refrain from eating pork and drinking alcohol. Christians do not have these restrictions.

Names:

All Arabic names have meanings. Common women's names include Sharifa (honest), Nawal (reward), Jameela (beautiful), Amal (hope) and Kareema (generous). In the Palestinian community, after the oldest child is born, the parents are referred to in terms of their relationship to that child. Thus, a father whose oldest son is named Jamal is known as Abu Jamal (father of Jamal) and the mother is called Um Jamal (mother of Jamal).

Major issues for community:

All Palestinians rally around the issue of their homeland. For decades they have been calling for an independent Palestinian state. They also have a genuine concern for the plight of all Arab peoples in the Middle East. Locally, they must combat anti-Arab stereotypes and slurs in the media, as well as a general misunderstanding of who they are as a people and the story of their dispossession.

Political participation:

Because of a strong feeling of marginalization from the American mainstream, Palestinians are not big in civic participation. Voter registration and participation are low. They have little clout and tend not to report crimes for fear of backlash. This is changing as the community builds from the grassroots and becomes more empowered. Third- and fourth-generation Arab Americans tend to meld into the mainstream and have been upwardly mobile and successful; sometimes they do not identify with the newer immigrants and their troubles.

Links to homeland:

Most Palestinians maintain a strong bond with their homeland, but because they are a stateless people, they have no citizenship and no passport. Those living in the West Bank and Gaza carry temporary residency cards. Most Arab countries won't give citizenship to Palestinians, partly because they are concentrating on looking out for their own citizens, partly to make a point that Israel has taken over the land that should be Palestine. Jordan, where many fled after the 1948 and 1967 wars, did give many citizenship and Jordanian passports, but that is the exception. Many Palestinians would like to return home, but because of ongoing Israeli control of the region, this is made difficult, if not impossible. The economic situation there has worsened in the past three years, as Israel has put more and more restrictions on the Palestinian movement into Jerusalem, where most of the jobs are. The border closures on the Gaza strip — 80% of whose population worked as low-paid day laborers in Israel — have created an unemployment rate estimated at more than 60%. Many Palestinians came to the U.S. to make money and send it home to family members and charitable organizations that build schools and provide needed social services. Palestinians lobby the U.S. government over its unconditional support for Israeli policies, which they say violates the human and civil rights of the Palestinian population.

Myths and misconceptions:

Myth: All Palestinians are "terrorists."
Fact: The vast majority of the Palestinian population has resisted nearly 50 years of Israeli occupation through nonviolent forms of resistance — educating the youth, building a civil society and maintaining their cultural heritage. The terrorist acts of fringe groups have been distorted to characterize the entire population.
Myth: Islam is divorced from the Judeo-Christian tradition. All Palestinians are Muslim.
Fact: Islam, Christianity and Judaism are all Abrahamic faiths. The Qu'ran accepts the revelations of Judaism and Christianity, which are seen as cousin religions. About 15% of Palestinians are Christians.

— Compiled by Mary Abowd, a Chicago journalist and board member of the Arab-American Action Network, who lived and wrote on the West Bank in 1992; also contributing: Dr. Louise Cainkar, Visiting Professor at UIC and author of a forthcoming book, Gender, Culture and Politics Among Palestinian Immigrants in the United States

Polish Americans

Chicago population:

218,559 (1990 Census, first ancestry)
43,340 (Census, second ancestry)
1996 community estimate: NA

Metro population:

647,047 (1990 Census, first ancestry)
206,695 (Census, second ancestry)
1996 community estimate: NA

Foreign-born:

24% in Chicago, 12% in metro area

Demographics:

Poles are the largest ethnic group in the following Chicago neighborhoods: Archer Heights, Avondale, Belmont-Cragin, Clearing, Dunning, Hegewisch, Jefferson Park, Montclare, North Park, Norwood Park, Portage Park, West Elsdon and West Lawn. Most Polish Americans now live in the suburbs, however. Although widely scattered, they make up over 20% of the population in each of the following suburbs, where they rank either first or second: Bridgeview, Burbank, Calumet, Forest View, Harwood Heights, Hickory Hills, Lemont, McCook, Niles, Norridge and Posen. A disproportionately high percentage of English-speaking Polish Americans own their own homes, 57% in Chicago, 80% in suburban Cook and 88% in the collar counties, and they have lived in their neighborhoods longer than most other ethnic groups. Median household income, education and jobs are slightly above average. The 1990 Census tells us that about 6% of Poles in Chicago speak English poorly or not at all.

Historical background:

Immigration statistics over the years have been somewhat inaccurate because Poland was occupied for 125 years, until the end of WWI, by Russia, Prussia and Austria, then by Germany during WWII, followed by a Stalinist communist government until 1989. Three main cohorts have immigrated here.

• The largest cohort of Poles entered Chicago from 1880-1932. It consisted mainly of peasants and village workers who came for economic reasons. They faced discrimination because they were peasants and many were illiterate. The 1911 *Dillingham Report* declared they would never be assimilated. These former agricultural workers found work in factories, mills and slaughterhouses. The peasants were accompanied by some bourgeoisie and members of the intelligentsia, who contributed to the building of a community, churches, schools and organizations.

• The second cohort, refugees and displaced persons, came during and after WWII. They had been citizens of a restored, independent Poland, were more educated and had experienced the war, often in the armed forces or labor camps.

• The third cohort left communist Poland in the 1970s, when that government variously expelled or loosened its hold on people, and it continues to come. This latest cohort tends to be younger, more urban, and

Although Poles had planned not to stay, most did because of political complications back home and increasing satisfaction with life in this country.

The low status, exemplified by the Polish jokes of the 1970s, really hurt individuals and the community.

More than 45,000 legal immigrants arrived in Chicago from Poland from 1990-94.

This cohort, brought up in communist Poland, is extremely suspicious of anyone who could possibly be associated with any government.

with a higher level of education, obtained under the communist system. While many came as formal immigrants, an even larger number entered on a temporary basis and remained illegally.

• Although most Poles of all three cohorts had not planned to stay, most did because of political complications back home and increasing satisfaction with life in this country. Chicago has long been one of the main centers of the national Polish American community, known as "Polonia." The main Polish settlement in the city has been on the Northwest Side, along Milwaukee Avenue. That community later extended into the Northwest suburbs. Poles also settled in Bridgeport, Pilsen, Back of the Yards and near the steel mills to the south. Many of the major fraternal, civic and religious organizations, some national and international in scope, were founded in the 19th century and continue to exist. Several of the long-lasting ones have an insurance base. The two largest fraternals are the Polish Roman Catholic Union, founded in 1883 with a religious focus, and the Polish National Alliance, founded in 1880 with a nationalist focus. Also important is the Polish Women's Alliance, founded in 1898.

Current migration patterns:

Poles continue to come to the Chicago area in large numbers; 45,192 legal immigrants arrived from 1990-94, according to the INS. Poles are coming through family reunification provisions, and the visa lottery. Some come because they have special employment skills. The lottery has resulted in an overwhelming outpouring of applications from Poles, especially because it is possible for people already in the U.S. to change their status if chosen in the lottery. Polish application for citizenship is high. It appears that few are returning to Poland.

Language:

Polish, though newer generations of the first cohorts may only speak English. Many recent immigrants speak Russian and the older ones who are Jewish often understand Yiddish. Poles ages 60 and over formed the largest subgroup (nearly 50,000) of Cook County residents who used English as a second language in 1994, though 67% of these people were U.S. citizens by birth and 22% were naturalized citizens. Language schools are very important here, to maintain the language among the young.

Religion:

Most Poles are Roman Catholics. An interesting development in Polonia has been the creation of a Polish National Catholic Church, founded in 1873 as a revolt against Irish influence and over papal control. The PNCC has local lay leaders and elected clergy who can marry. Only about 5% of Polish Americans joined the PNCC, but the religion has spread to the mother country, an unusual phenomenon. The election of Pope John Paul II and his several visits to the United States, including Chicago, has been a source of great pride for Polonia.

Important traditions:

Polonia marks events like weddings, baptisms, first communions and funerals with Catholic ritual enhanced by Polish touches. Because generous hospitality is part of the Polish self-image, such festivities always include much food and drink and an expansive guest list. Bride and groom depart for the church together after receiving the blessing of the bride's parents. Three-day wedding receptions were not uncommon as recently as a generation ago. The bride wears a sprig of myrtle in her hair for fertility. After her attendants remove her veil, they dress her in an apron decorated with toy dolls, and she dances with the groom. Similarly, at the end of life, after the burial service, everyone at the grave site is invited to dine with the family.

Holidays and special events:

Three main events in the Polish calendar have been carried over into Polonia. **Christmas** involves a highly decorated evergreen tree, once traditionally lit with candles, and a 13-course Christmas Eve dinner with a place set for the "hungry stranger" and hay laid under the tablecloth. Wafers, like communion wafers, are shared along with forgiveness for past offenses against one another and best wishes for the future. Gifts are opened after dinner. Even those who are not active Catholics attend Christmas Midnight Mass. Christmas day is spent visiting relatives. **Easter** is the second most important religious holiday and follows 40 days of self-denial during

Lent. The pious visit the decorated "graves" of Jesus at Polish churches on Good Friday. The third big holiday, **Polish Constitution Day** (May 3), celebrates Poland's Constitution of 1791, which was never put into practice because of the 1793 partition of Poland by Prussia, Russia and Austria. The holiday is observed with a parade. **Casimir Pulaski Day** (first Monday in March) is an official Illinois holiday that commemorates the Polish count who fought and died in the American Revolution. It is celebrated with a weekend parade, downtown lunch and event at the Polish Museum.

Foods for special occasions:

While Roman Catholics are no longer forbidden meat on Friday by their Church, the Christmas Eve dinner remains meatless by tradition. Easter breakfast foods, including butter molded in a the shape of a lamb, are taken to Polish parishes to be blessed on Holy Saturday. Easter dinner the next day includes beautifully colored eggs, sausage, ham, roast pork, lamb, and pig's feet in jelly. *Pierogis* (boiled and fried pockets of dough filled with fast-day foods such as sauerkraut, mushrooms, cheese or potatoes) are also favorites.

Names:

Polish is a gender-specific language. The surnames of women in a family end with "a" while those of men end in "i" unless the name itself ends in "a." There is differentiation between a woman who is a professional and a woman who is married to a professional. For example, *Pani* doctor is a woman doctor, while *pani doctorowa* is the wife of a doctor. *Pan* (sir) and *pani* (lady or madam) are used as titles in normal conversation and correspondence. Children are named for the saint on whose feast day they are born and celebrate a nameday rather than a birthday. Examples of girls' names are Elzbieta, Wanda and Zdzislawa; boys' names include Ryszard (Richard) and Krzystof (Christopher).

Major issues for community:

Of major concern to all Polish Americans, whether active in Polonia or not, is the social status of their group vis-à-vis other groups in America. The low status, exemplified by the Polish jokes of the 1970s, really hurt individuals and the community. Polonia also continues to be concerned over current events in Poland, especially the economic situation after the breakdown of communism. It also worries about the security of Poland from possible disorder emanating from neighboring countries of the former Soviet Union. Many are investing in joint ventures in Poland, assisted by the Polish American Enterprise Fund and various business organizations. Throughout Polonia's history, its members have contributed enormous sums of money and even a brigade of men to the Polish armed forces, to help win independence, rebuild the nation and, later, fight communism.

Political participation:

The organizational complexity of Polonia, concern about Poland, and an internal status competition have kept community members oriented inwardly, to the exclusion of concern with mainstream political life in the United States. The status competition makes for an unwillingness to support Polish American candidates, in part because of the common feeling that no one ought to claim higher status than any other, and in part because of the residual suspicion of one another bred into Poles by the long periods of occupation the nation suffered over most of the past 200 years. The newest cohort, brought up in communist Poland, is extremely suspicious of anyone who could possibly be associated with any government. This cohort also is antagonistic to established Polonia, feeling it has not sufficiently shared leadership. The main political association is the Polish American Congress, headquartered in Chicago.

Links to homeland:

Links to the home country have probably been stronger in Polonia than in most other ethnic communities in America, because of the history of the home country and efforts of its leaders to nationalize emigrants living abroad. The identification of the "fourth province of Poland" waned when both Polonia and Poland turned their attention to their own problems. The newest cohort and traditional Polonia have been very active in trying to influence the American government, first to help overthrow communism, later to provide economic and security assistance. Individuals are often moved by a characteristic nostalgia for the imagined homeland and its tragic past.

Myths & misconceptions:

Myth: Polish Americans are uneducated peasants. (This myth led to the very hurtful "Polish" jokes.)

Fact: American-born Polish Americans and newer immigrants tend to be very well educated. There is social class complexity in all cohorts and generations of the Polish American community.

Etc.:

Americans fail to acknowledge that during WWII the Nazis killed 22% of the inhabitants of Poland, 2.6 million of its 3 million Jewish citizens, 3 million other civilians and 320,000 in the military. (These losses compare with just over 2% of those in the Netherlands and 1.3% in France.) Most Polish Americans lost members of their families, sometimes whole branches, to the Nazi policy of extermination, but this tragic fact is not recognized by American society.

— By Dr. Helena Znaniecka Lopata, Professor of Sociology at Loyola University and author of nine books, including <u>Polish Americans</u>

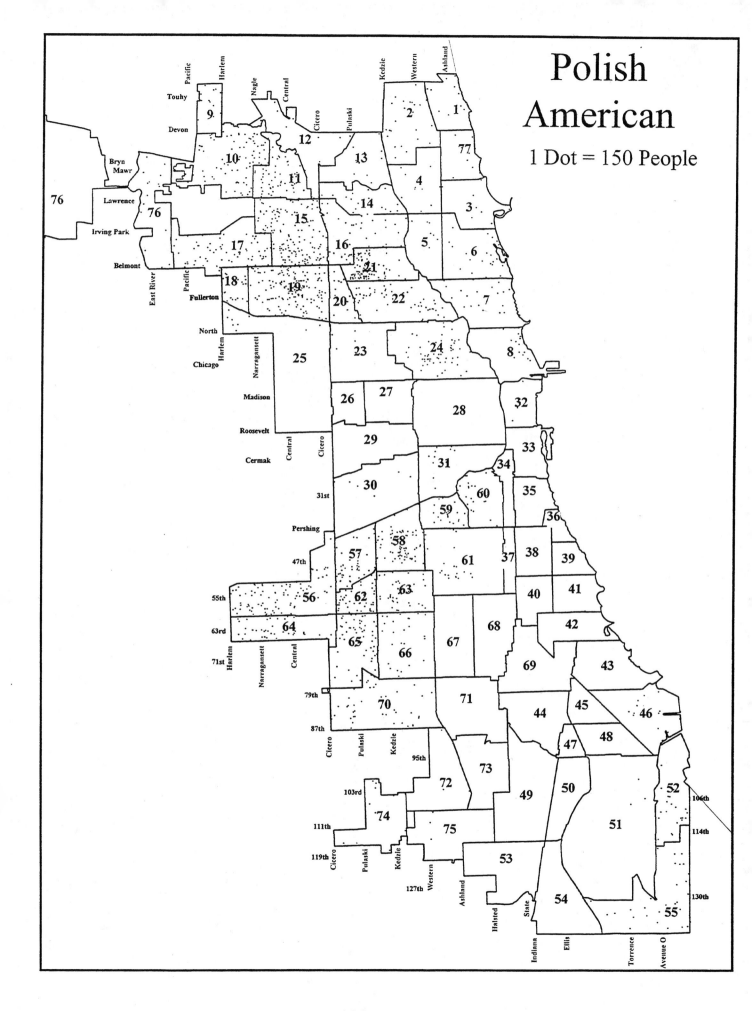

Polish
American

1 Dot = 150 People

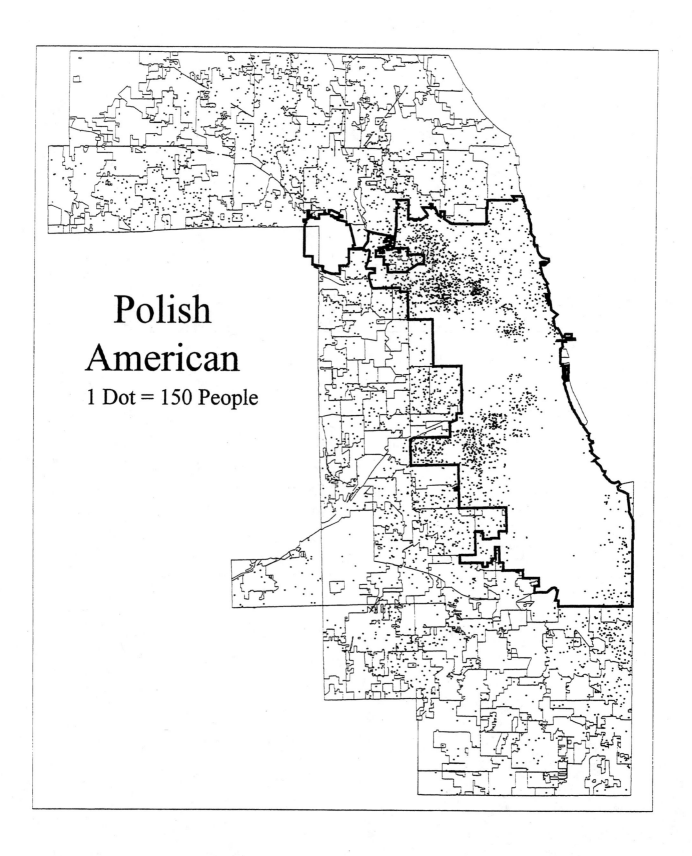

Polish
American

1 Dot = 150 People

Puerto Ricans

Chicago population:
121,209 (1990 Census)
1996 community estimate: NA

Metro area population:
142,745 (1990 Census)
1996 community estimate: NA

Born in Puerto Rico:
43%

Demographics:

Puerto Ricans live primarily in the city, around West Town and Humboldt Park. In fact, in 1992 a formal "entryway" for the neighborhood was erected on Division Street. Less than half (43%) were born on the Island, the lowest percentage of any Latino group to be born outside the continental United States. Puerto Ricans for the most part speak English; only 17% in the city reported they "do not speak English well," again the lowest percentage among Latino groups. Less than half (45%) have been awarded a high school diploma, and 6% possess a bachelor's degree. Their economic status is low: 34% report income below the poverty level, the highest of any Latino group. The median household income in 1990 was $20,698, below that of the total Latino population, which was $25,219. A very high percentage of Puerto Rican families (59%) live in female-headed households. Puerto Ricans are employed primarily in manufacturing (32%) and in service occupations (28%); only 14% report occupations as managerial or professional; 31% work in technical, sales and administrative support, and 30% are manufacturers or laborers. In the six-county metro area the median income rises to $22,022, still very low compared to other groups.

Historical background:

Puerto Ricans are relatively recent arrivals in Chicago. The 1950 Census grouped them together with Cubans, Central and South Americans, so the numbers were obscured. But we know that by 1970 about 78,000 Puerto Ricans lived in Chicago, a 125% increase from 1960. The 1980 Census reported a population of 129,000, an increase of 65% in 10 years. Now, it seems this population growth has ceased, perhaps because of the decline in manufacturing in the city. There are Puerto Ricans elsewhere in the Chicago metropolitan area (Waukegan, Aurora, Joliet), but their numbers are not very large.

• Puerto Rican migration into the continental U.S. has been dubbed the "airborne migration." Its most important characteristic is that this is not an immigration at all, because Puerto Rico is a territory of the United States, and Puerto Ricans have been U.S. citizens since 1917 (although ineligible to vote for President or Congress while on the Island). The population shifts are therefore just internal migrations. This characteristic precludes access to statistics on arrivals or departures.

The initial recorded arrivals were around 1953, when a few families were brought to Chicago through an organized program, males as factory workers and wives for domestic service.

This is not an immigration because Puerto Rico is a territory of the United States and Puerto Ricans have been U.S. citizens since 1917.

The arrival of Puerto Ricans has slowed in the '80s and '90s.

They tend to register and vote more than the average, and significantly more than other Latinos, who came as immigrants.

• The initial recorded arrivals of Puerto Ricans occurred around 1953, when a few families were brought to Chicago through an organized program, males as factory workers and wives for domestic service. They were settled in the Back of Yards, where there is not today a recognizable Puerto Rican neighborhood. When large groups started arriving, they settled on the Near North Side, but were displaced in the early '60s by the federal urban renewal program that erected Sandburg Village in what had been a tenement-type neighborhood with many Puerto Ricans. They moved toward Humboldt Park and West Town, where they remain.

• Initially, Puerto Rican migration into the Chicago area (subsequent to the major movement to New York) can be traced as a geographical westbound continuum that included Ohio and Michigan. The Commonwealth of Puerto Rico sought to protect these migrants, first farmworkers and then urban residents, by the creation of a Migration Division Office, part of Puerto Rico's Department of Labor. Puerto Ricans in Chicago have created over the years a series of social and political groups. In the early '70s, para-political activism was most important in the press, with the Young Lords, a radical organization, constituting the first national movement, expanding from Chicago to New York.

Current migration patterns:

The arrival of Puerto Ricans to Chicago has slowed in the '80s and '90s. From data about Puerto Ricans born on the continent, it can be assumed there has been a small return movement to the Island. It is not unusual for Puerto Ricans to move several times between the Island and mainland, in a circular pattern.

Language:

Spanish. The Island, after a long history of fluctuations in official policy, has declared Spanish the official language of Puerto Rico. Implications for continuing internal migration of Puerto Ricans, and for educational policies that may want to teach English and Spanish, affect not only this group but the U.S. as well.

Religion:

Accepted wisdom has it that Puerto Ricans, like other Latinos, are Roman Catholic. In the case of Puerto Ricans in Chicago, there are other very significant religious practices. Protestant denominations, Adventists and Jehovah's Witnesses have significant Puerto Rican followings. Protestant ministers, now and in the past, have taken a leading social and political role in the Puerto Rican community. *Santeria,* a religion with African roots that includes folk healing, also is practiced by many Puerto Ricans. Traditionally, Santeria's mysteries have been carefully kept among the initiated, so it is hard to ascertain the number of adherents. Santeria's practices coexist with conventional Christian observances.

Important traditions:

Baptisms and weddings are an occasion for gathering of extended families. The *quinceañera* (15th birthday) celebrates the coming out of young girls, and may include both a religious ceremony and a lavish party. Less frequent today in Chicago, old custom dictated that young couples be accompanied by a chaperone when going out.

Holidays and special events:

Christmas is very important, including the **Fiesta de Reyes** (Epiphany) (Jan. 6), when children receive their presents from the Three Wisemen. The **Feast of San Juan** (June 24), honoring the Patron Saint of the Island, includes both religious and social celebrations. **Constitution Day** (July 25) observes the compact between the Island and the United States, and the first constitution for the Commonwealth. In Chicago, the **Puerto Rican Parade**, in early June, and the accompanying festival in Humboldt Park, present the largest mass gathering of Puerto Ricans in the city.

Foods for special occasions:

A delicacy in Puerto Rican cuisine is the *lechon asado* (suckling pig). *Arroz con grandules* (rice with pigeon peas) is very tasty and frequently served. *Pasteles* are made with ground green plantains, *guineos* (bananas) and other ingredients and offer a passing similarity to *tamales*. *Tostones* (fried slices of plantain), often accompany the meal; *alcapurrias* (a type of fritter) are not as frequently served in Chicago as they are on the Island.

Names:

The most common names are of Spanish origin, and refer to saints, such as José, Manuel, Pedro, or to the many titles of the Virgin Mary, such as María, Dolores and Socorro. Last names include Dávila, Martínez, Barceló and Rivera, names common for Spanish-speaking people.

Major issues for community:

Puerto Ricans in Chicago share concern for the future of the Island and whether its current commonwealth status will change to that of either a state or an independent country. There is a division of opinion about that here, with no overwhelming majority for any position. People who live here can vote absentee only if they are registered in Puerto Rico and have a domicile there. Education, particularly bilingual education, is particularly important both here and there.

Political participation:

Within the past 15 years, political organizations have matured and lean toward the Democratic Party. Political action took substantive steps during the tenure of Mayor Harold Washington, for whom the election of a Puerto Rican alderman, Luis Gutiérrez, provided the necessary majority to break the backlog of opposition to his policies. Previously, in 1982, there was only one Puerto Rican holding elective office in Chicago, and he had been appointed by the Mayor. Today Chicago has sent to Washington its first Puerto Rican congressman, Gutiérrez (out of a district heavily inclusive of both Puerto Ricans and Mexicans), and Puerto Ricans also represent Chicago in Springfield and the Chicago City Council. Puerto Ricans, who arrive here as American citizens, tend to register and vote more than the average, and significantly more than other Latinos, who arrive as immigrants. Puerto Rican politicians in Chicago forge strong coalitions with other Latinos on issues concerning them. They support, for instance, legislation protecting (or at least not penalizing) immigration, an issue of concern to Mexicans and Mexican Americans.

Links to homeland:

Puerto Ricans continue to be the "airborne migration" with relations and contacts with the Island limited only by the cost of the airfare. The status of the Island is of great political concern, and many Puerto Ricans in Chicago feel an obligation to influence Washington's decisions about Puerto Rico from here. If they live on the Island Puerto Ricans cannot vote in U.S. elections. Puerto Rico sends a representative to the U.S. House of Representatives, but his or her vote is non-binding.

Myths & misconceptions:

Myth: Puerto Ricans are immigrants.

Fact: Puerto Ricans have been American citizens since 1917.

Myth: Puerto Ricans are Latinos. (Most statistics and data offered by governmental units are given for "Latinos" or "Hispanics.")

Fact: The grouping of Puerto Ricans, Mexicans and others into a common denomination is purely artificial. Puerto Ricans are a distinct and characteristic population, not generic "Latinos." This identity does not prevent them from coalescing with other Latinos for common purposes.

Myth: You can tell a Puerto Rican from looking at him (her).

Fact: Puerto Ricans come in all shades and colors, even siblings of the same parents. They are not a racial group, but an ethnic one. And the concept and experience of race is substantially different on the Island from that in the continental United States.

Etc.:

Puerto Ricans prefer the term Puerto Rican to either "Hispanic" or "Latino." Given a choice between the two more generic terms, Hispanic is preferred by those who are part of government leadership because the word was created by the federal government. Grassroots leaders prefer Latino, but see it as an artificial word. The overwhelming choice is Puerto Rican.

— By Dr. Isidro Lucas, Assistant Dean for Continuing Education and Director of the Office for Hispanic Programs at Chicago State University

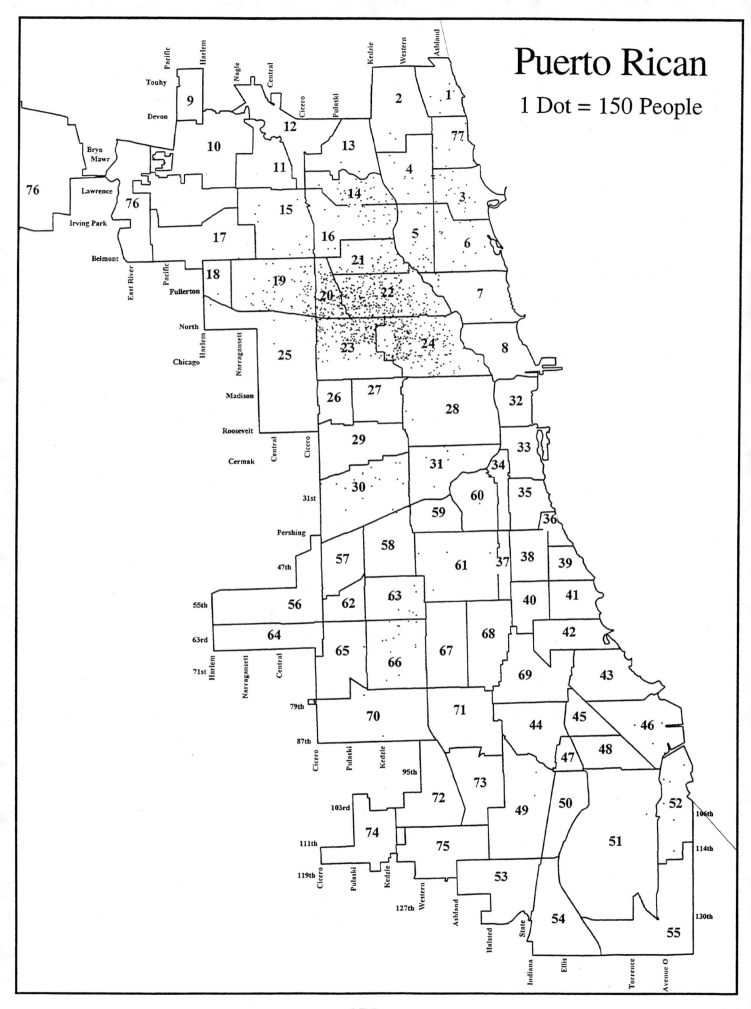

Puerto Rican

1 Dot = 150 People

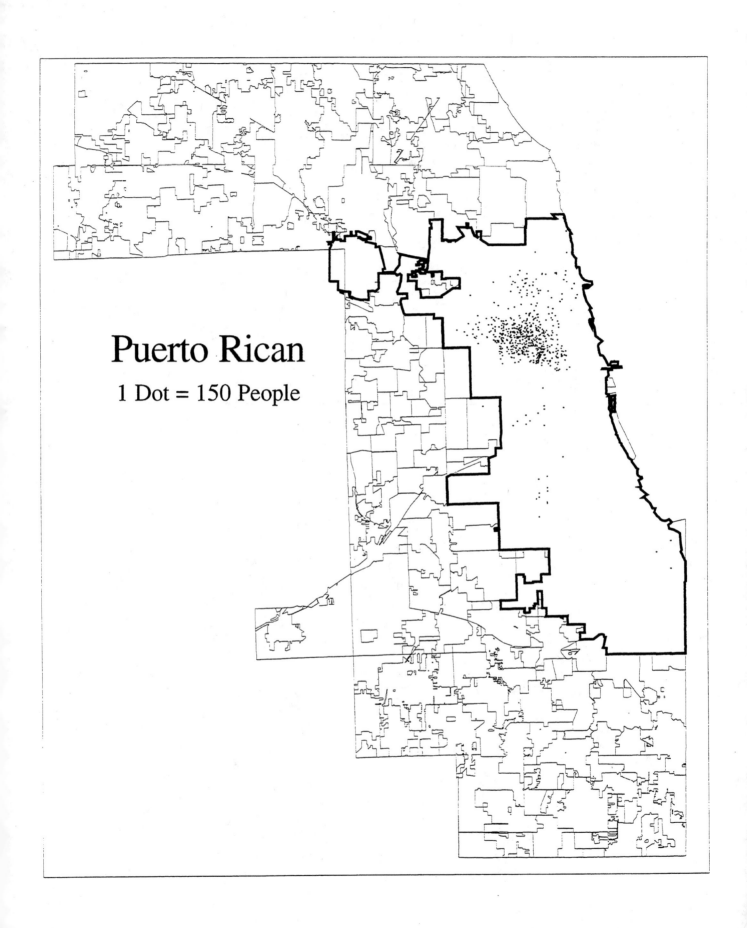

Puerto Rican

1 Dot = 150 People

Romanian Americans

Chicago population:
7,205 (1990 Census, first ancestry)
1,342 (Census, second ancestry)
45,000 (1996 community estimate).

Metro area population:
15,038 (1990 Census, first ancestry)
5,888 (Census, second ancestry)
65,000 (1996 community estimate)

Foreign-born:
75% in city, 58% in metro area

Demographics:
Romanians in Chicago are mainly spread across the North and Northwest Sides, bounded by Lake Michigan, Harlem Avenue, Belmont Avenue and Howard Street. Heaviest concentrations are in Albany Park, West Ridge, Rogers Park, Edgewater, Uptown, Lake View, Irving Park and Lincoln Square. A smaller number live on the South and Southwest Sides, where there are two Romanian churches, compared with 12 such churches on the North and Northwest Sides. An estimated one-third of the Romanian population lives in the suburbs, primarily to the north. It is estimated that Romanians generally have a good standard of living, with about 15% living in poverty. A very small number do not speak English.

Historical background:
The first immigrants came to the U.S. at the end of the last century from Transylvania, because the occupying Austro-Hungarian Empire wanted to convert the Romanian population into Hungarians by changing their names and imposing the Hungarian language. In 1900 the first Romanian immigrants settled in Chicago. The majority were peasants and lived in the Devon-Clark area, where they worked for the vegetable industry "greenhouses" and Weber-Krantz. Around 1910 Romanians started to work in the construction of roads and public works for the city, so the center of the community moved to Clybourn/Fullerton/Southport. The number of Romanians in Chicago in 1911 is said to have exceeded 5,000. The first known Romanian organization in Chicago was established on Dec. 29, 1907, under the name *Speranta*, and on July 15, 1911, the first Romanian Orthodox church was inaugurated.

Romanians immigrated to U.S. in four phases:

• From the end of 19th century to the end of WWI. They came mainly from Transylvania because of Hungarian oppression. More than 10,000 Romanians came to Chicago.

• Between the two World Wars. They came mainly for economic and family reasons. About 5,000 Romanians came to Chicago.

• During communist era (1945-1989). Escaping from communism, about 20,000 Romanians settled in Chicago.

• Since 1989. A lack of confidence in the neo-communist government sent about 8,000 Romanian immigrants to Chicago. It is estimated that another 1,000 or so immigrated illegally.

The '90s immigrants are those who wanted to emigrate during communism but were not allowed to by the Romanian government.

Romanians arriving in the U.S. were confronted with culture shock. Their expectation of America differs from the reality and most do not comprehend the freedom that exists here.

The solution adopted by Romanians is a rapid integration into American society, where they do not keep close ties with the ethnic community.

Current migration patterns:

The '90s immigrants represent those who wanted to emigrate during communism but were not allowed to by the Romanian government. Another category is those who come to reunite with family members. Many young Romanians entered Chicago after 1990 with work, student or fiancée visas and hope to remain here. Only a tiny percentage returns to Romania.

Language:

Descendants of Romanians speak mostly English, the second generation having abandoned the Romanian language. Newcomers speak both Romanian and English.

Religion:

In Romania, the religion is Christian Orthodox. Because of the communists' dislike of neo-Protestants, many were permitted to emigrate. Therefore, the Orthodox percentage of Romanians in Chicago dropped to about half the population here. There are two large Romanian Orthodox churches and 12 small neo-Protestant churches in the Chicago area.

Important traditions:

Romanians put great emphasis on family and maintain close contacts with extended family. Children's education is severe and rigid in order to secure a good future.

Holidays and special events:

National Day is observed Dec. 1, usually by a community gathering. Two important Christian-Orthodox holidays are traditionally observed: *Christmas* and *Easter*. Romanians also celebrate their *Name Day,* according to the Orthodox calendar. For example: St. Maria (Aug. 15), St. Ion (Jan. 7), and St. Gheorghe (April 23). *The Children's Day* (June 1) is a time for candy and gifts for the children. *Women's Day* (March 8), *The Day of the Harvest* (Oct. 1) and *Martisorul* (Spring Day, March 1) are lay holidays observed in the family. Martisorul is a typical Romanian holiday, celebrating the coming of spring. It resembles Valentine's Day. Flowers and a small token (hung from a red and white thread) are given to women and worn on blouses for about 10 days.

Foods for special occasions:

Every important holiday has a specific dish that is prepared at home. At Christmas a piglet is cooked, along with traditional *sarmale* (ground meat stuffed in cabbage rolls). New Year's Day, turkey is prepared. At Easter, lamb dishes and red eggs are served. On Harvest Day, there is pastrami and fresh-squeezed grape juice. Two typical Romanian dishes are *mamaliga* (polenta with dairy products) and *mititei* (spicy skinless sausage).

Dietary restrictions:

None, except for the periods of religious Orthodox fast when there is no meat. But this is usually observed only by the older generation.

Names:

Family names are generally derived from villages, rivers, provinces or trades. Most can be recognized by the "escu" or "anu" termination — for example, Ionescu, Popescu, Munteanu and Olteanu. Birth names are usually biblical: Ion, Nicolaie, Vasile, Gheorghe; or old Roman: Remus, Adrian, Cornel, Claudiu, Octavian, or specific Romanian: Mircea, Calin, Bogdan, Razvan.

Major issues for community:

Romanians arriving in the U.S. are confronted with culture shock. Their expectation of America differs from the reality and most do not comprehend the freedom that exists here — a departure from their rigid past. As a result, a large number of Romanian couples who immigrate get divorced. Another concern is the low level of the education that their children are subjected to in the U.S. They want the best for their children, and Chicago schools have too many problems, such as drugs and violence. The solution adopted by Romanians is a rapid integration into American society, where they do not keep close ties with the ethnic community.

Political participation:

The new generation of immigrants is not preoccupied with political or civic issues. American citizens of Romanian origin typically join the Republican Party. This is in part because of an unconscious association between the Democratic Party and the word "democracy," a term abused by the communists. Generally, the U.S. government is regarded favorably.

Links to homeland:

Almost all Romanians aspire to American citizenship. Few want to return home, though they visit frequently. Money and valuables are sent to family in Romania. Romanians from Chicago are displeased by the position of the U.S. government on economic ties with Romania and the issue of Romanian borders. The Soviet Union in 1940 occupied a good part of Romanian territory that still has not been returned. Furthermore, the U.S. does not have a clear and firm stand on the issues regarding Hungarian pretensions to Transylvania.

Myths & misconceptions:

Myth: Film and mass media created Dracula and the vampirism myth, which casts an unfavorable light on the Romanian region of Transylvania.

Fact: Vlad Tepes, the one portrayed as Dracula, was an important leader and a man of great honor from Muntenia, a different region of Romania, and had no connection with the subject of vampirism.

Myth: Romanians are all gypsies.

Fact: This confusion comes by a phonetic association between the word "Romany," which means gypsy, and the word "Romanian." In the Romanian Census of 1992, gypsies in Romania accounted for 1.8% of the population.

Etc.:

The Romanian community in Chicago is negatively affected by the American mass media view of Romania. Romania is portrayed as a country only of gypsies, beggars, desolation, poverty and AIDS victims. In fact, Romania is a civilized country with an old culture that faces the same problems as any other European country.

— *By Carol Olteanu, Founder of the Romanian Cultural Center*

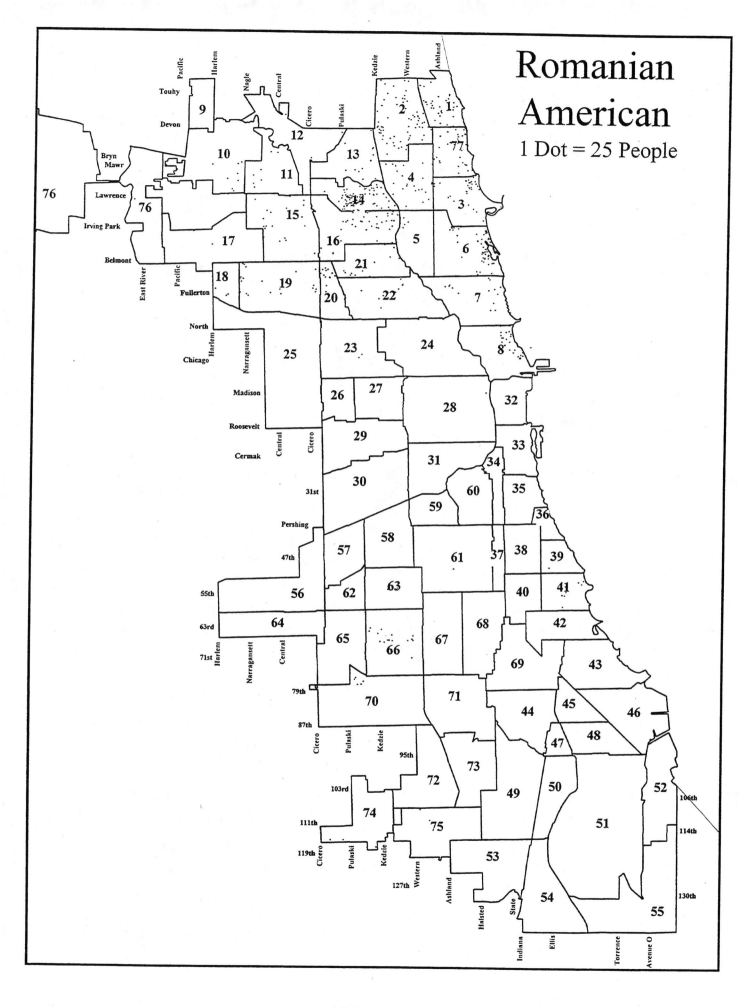

Romanian
American

1 Dot = 25 People

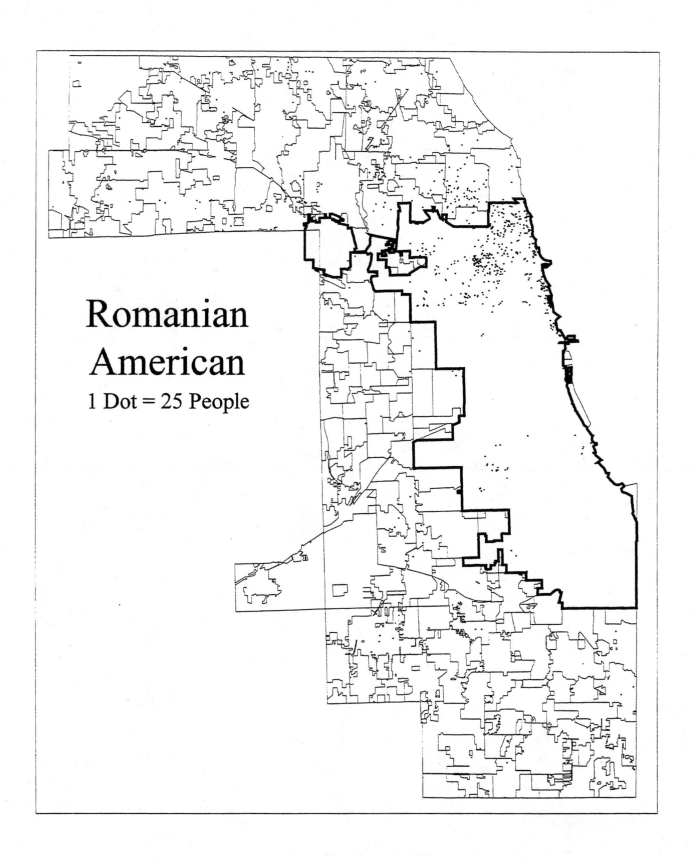

Romanian
American

1 Dot = 25 People

Serbian Americans

Chicago population:
4,692 (1990 Census, first ancestry)
523 (Census, second ancestry)
10,000 (1996 community estimate)

Metro population:
11,914 (1990 Census, first ancestry)
2,356 (Census, second ancestry)
30,000-50,000 (1996 community estimate)

Foreign-born:
NA

Note: In addition to those who reported their ancestry as Serb, another 4,630 in Chicago reported Yugoslavian as their first ancestry and 937 listed it as second ancestry. In the total metro area, 12,672 listed Yugoslavian first and 3,548 listed it second. It is impossible to tell how many of these are Serbs.

Demographics:
Generally, Serbs used to live — and some still do — in the proximity of their churches and businesses. In the past 30 years, however, many prosperous Serbs and professional young couples of first, second and third generations have moved to the suburbs. To the north and northwest, there are Serbs in Lincolnwood, Evanston, Skokie, Glenview, Wilmette, Winnetka, Lake Forest, Barrington, DesPlaines, Mt. Prospect, Arlington Heights and Niles. To the south, besides the old settlement in South Chicago, Serbs live in Lansing, where there is a large Serbian Cultural Hall, and in the adjacent towns. There also are many Serbian homes and businesses in Bellwood, LaGrange, Downers Grove, Oak Park, Burr Ridge, Riverside, Lyons, Naperville and Joliet.

Historical background:
Several immigration waves brought the Serbs to the U.S. They came as citizens of a variety of countries. Before 1918 they were from the Austro-Hungarian Empire, Turkey, Montenegro and Serbia; after that date they came from the Kingdom of Serbs, Croatians and Slovenians, which changed its name to Yugoslavia.

• The first Serbian immigration to the Midwest began in the 1880s and lasted until WWII. Most of the early immigrants (before WWI) came here to make a better living for themselves and the families they left behind. Others came to avoid serving in the Austro-Hungarian army. Most had very little education and did not speak English. They worked in the steel mills and slaughterhouses. They were considered honest, hard-working and family-oriented people who did not cause trouble and whose lives revolved around their churches and social organizations. They knew the value of education and encouraged their children to get it, sacrificing their own pleasures and standard of living for the sake of their children's advancement.

• The second surge of immigrants began after WWII and lasted until around 1960. These Serbs were predominantly political immigrants

The first Serbian immigration to the U.S. began in the 1890s. Most had very little education and did not speak English.

Immigration since the 1960s has brought relatively young, ambitious professionals who emigrated both for political and economic reasons. Most know English.

The Serbs in America are very religious and many are active members in their churches, which also serve as the focal points of cultural and social life.

and other displaced persons, who came to the U.S. in the late '40s and early '50s, and eventually were joined by their families under the War Refugee Act of 1954. These people were generally well-educated or had professional skills, but a large number did not speak English and had a hard time adjusting here to low-paying jobs. Once they learned English, they were able to compete for better-paying positions in their professional fields. When their families came, they too made sure their children got the best possible education. These post-WWII immigrants strengthened the Chicago Serbian community both numerically and financially.

• The third immigration of Serbs began in the early 1960s. It lasted until the disintegration of the former Yugoslavia (around 1990) and brought relatively young, ambitious professionals who emigrated for both political and economic reasons. Among them were physicians, engineers, architects, scientists, scholars, artists and graduate students, most of whom came with a reasonably good knowledge of English. They were relatively quickly integrated into Chicago life and have been very prosperous.

Current migration patterns:

The disintegration of Yugoslavia and the wars in Croatia and Bosnia that followed in the '90s are bringing a new group of Serbian immigrants. Some are Serb refugees from Croatia and Bosnia; others are young people from Serbia and Montenegro who did not approve of the wars and did not want to be drafted and forced to fight. There is no way to estimate how many are coming legally and how many are undocumented. Some early immigrants, mostly from South Chicago and adjacent towns, eventually returned to "the old country," but most have remained here.

Language:

Serbian, a South Slavic language. Serbs officially use the Serbian Cyrillic alphabet, but also know the Latin alphabet. Immigrants speak Serbian, but generations born here are more comfortable with English.

Religion:

Serbian Orthodox. The Serbs in America are very religious and many are active members of their churches, which also serve as the focal points of cultural and social life of the Serbian American community. In Libertyville, St. Sava Monastery and Church house the Serbian Orthodox Theological Seminary, where future Serbian priests in the U.S. are being educated. In Third Lake, Ill., the newest Serbian Orthodox Church and Monastery, Grachanitsa, was consecrated in 1984. There are Serbian Orthodox Churches in Chicago, South Chicago and Bellwood.

Important traditions:

Kissing, hugging and touching are normal for Serbs. Common greetings among men and women alike are to embrace and kiss on the cheek three times, first one cheek and then the other. When together, Serbs can be loud, because they are temperamental and speak all at once. In interpersonal relationships, they are open, sincere and loyal. If they are not provoked, they are very pleasant and polite, but they also are proud and strong-willed and if offended or provoked, can easily explode and be fierce opponents. Traditionally, Serbian men take off their hat or cap when entering an enclosed space. To sit in a room or classroom with a baseball cap on is considered rude and disrespectful. Serbs tend to be easy-going and may be late for appointments or parties. They are very protective of their families and close-knit with their relatives. Grandparents and older relatives are respected and children are taught to help old people and be kind to them. Adult sons and daughters consider it their sacred duty to take care of their elderly parents. The ideal is for children to marry other Serbian Americans but this is getting more and more difficult to achieve. Active efforts of the Serbian American communities in the Chicago area to preserve their traditions include: church schools, children's camps, sport clubs, and the establishment of the Serbian Studies program at the University of Illinois at Chicago.

Holidays and special events:

The major non-religious holidays are **Serbian New Year** (Jan. 13) and **Vidovdan** (June 28). The latter is a celebration commemorating heroic Serbian warriors who perished in a battle against the Ottoman Turks in the Field of Kossovo in 1389. The Kossovo battle marks the beginning of the end of Serbian Medieval prosperity. Religious holidays are **Christmas, Easter, Slava** and **St. Sava Day.** Christmas is celebrated Jan. 7 (which is Dec. 25 according to the old Julian Calendar). Serbian Christmas encompasses many traditional, pre-Christian folklore elements dealing with prosperity and health for the family and fertility of the land. On Christmas Eve day, traditionally, the men of the house would go to the forest to bring the *badnjak* (Yule log) home. The cutting of the badnjak was a ritual, performed with gloves and with careful cutting, so that the tree fell to the east. The log was cleared of side branches and dragged home by oxen. At the entrance of the house, wheat and wine were poured over the log and it was welcomed as if it were a guest, because it was believed to represent the earthly abode of an ancestral soul whose visit would protect the home and bring prosperity in the year to come. After the ceremonial greeting, the log was put on the hearth, where it slowly burned until Christmas morning. In modern times, especially in the U.S., the custom is reduced to bringing home a symbolic Yule "log," a twig of the oak tree blessed in church. **Easter** is called *Uskrs.* It is the most holy of holidays celebrated by the Serbs. It falls on a different date from the Protestant and Catholic Easter, because of a different way of calculating its date. Serbian custom is to color eggs for Easter. Some decorate them with wax designs and let them stand in water boiled with onion skins for reddish-brown color; others prefer to color them bright red, by boiling them in natural red dye called *varzilo.* The custom of *tucanje jajima,* an egg-breaking game, is fun for the children. **Slava** celebrates the Patron Saint of the Serbian Family and is lavishly celebrated in the U.S. The most frequently celebrated patron saints are: St. Archangel Michael (Nov. 21), St. Nicholas (Dec. 19), St. Steven (Jan. 9), St. John the Baptist (Jan. 20) and St. George (May 6). On this day people open their homes to guests. The custom goes back to the time the Serbs adopted Christianity (9th-10th centuries) and with it a patron saint of the family, who replaced the pagan home-protecting spirit. On the morning of the Slava, traditional food items are taken to the church to be blessed. **St. Sava's Day** (Jan. 27) is celebrated for the most important Serbian saint, the Patron Saint of Serbian Schools and Education. The day is celebrated the same way as family Slava, in all churches and schools.

Foods for special occasions:

The traditional Christmas roast is a very young suckling pig, roasted in the oven by city dwellers, or a bigger one cooked on a spit above a pit full of red coals. In Chicago, whole roasted suckling pigs can be ordered for holidays in several Serbian delicatessens. *Sarma od kiselog kupusa* (sour cabbage leaves stuffed with ground meat and rice and cooked with smoked pork ribs in a lightly thickened juice) is served before the roast and after the clear soup and the boiled meat and vegetables from the soup. Many Serbs, even in America, prepare their own sour cabbage for winter by putting whole heads of cabbage, well salted and covered with water, to marinate in wooden barrels for a month or two, until the cabbage becomes sour and its leaves are soft. For Christmas Eve, Lenten food is served: smoked fish, boiled beans, figs and dates, and a sweet noodle dessert with sugar and ground nuts. The traditional Easter roast is a very young whole lamb, which is difficult to buy in the U.S., or a leg of lamb as a substitute. For the Slava, Serbs prepare a sweet dish called *žito* (wheat) or *koljivo,* and a *slavski kolač* (a round, specially decorated egg-bread).

Dietary restrictions:

Lent is observed for six weeks before Christmas and six weeks before Easter. Some religious Serbs fast every Friday and some fast twice a week, on Wednesdays and Fridays.

Names:

Children are usually given the names of their grandparents, deceased or alive, but rarely their parents' names. The name is decided by the parents and the godfather. Common Serbian last names end in "ić", such as Dimitrijević, Ilić, Jovanović and Petrović. In the Vojvodina region, the names also often end in "ov," such as Popov, or in "in," as in Beleslin or Pupin. Common male names are Aleksàndar, Bránko, Ivan, Jovan (John) Milan, Nikola, Petar (Peter) Vladimir and Zoran. Names ending in "slav" are also common, like Branislav and Borislav. Common female names are Aleksandra, Danica, Jelisaveta (Elizabeth) Jelena (Helen), Natalija, Vera and Nada. Also popular are names ending in "slava," like Branislava, Miroslava, Stanislava.

Major issues for community:

These include preserving the traditions, religion and customs; raising children to have decent social skills; providing the best (affordable) education possible for their children; and whatever political issue is the topic of the day. Currently they are concerned about U.S. policies toward Serbia and Yugoslavia, particularly propaganda against Bosnian Serbs and Serbs in general. Serbs feel that, as a nation, they were always "on the right side," as allies of Great Britain and the U.S. in both WWI and WWII. They feel that their loyalty to America has been poorly rewarded, and that the U.S. government today supports the allies of the Nazi Germany and Hitler. They believe Yugoslavia should not have been dismantled in a hurry, and that Western Europe and the U.S. have unwisely succumbed to the pressure of Germany, whose politics toward the Balkans they see as self-serving. Helping Serbian refugees from Bosnia, here and in Serbia, is another concern.

Political participation:

Most Serbs consider it their duty to vote. At this time they have no clout, but now that Rod Blagojevich has won election as 5th District Congressman, they believe they will have some voice in Washington. Among younger Serbian Americans, there are now ambitious lawyers and successful businessmen who are genuinely interested in civic and political life in Chicago and may soon emerge on the political scene.

Links to homeland:

Few maintain their original citizenship or plan to return, though they visit their "old country" as often as they can. Even during the very difficult years of the embargo on Yugoslavia and the war in Bosnia, many braved difficult travel conditions to visit and help their relatives and fellow Serbs in distress. Many send money to parents and relatives regularly. For the past three or four years, almost every dollar made in charitable and fund-raising activities was used to buy medical supplies, food and clothes for Serbian refugees from Croatia and Bosnia, those who came to the U.S. as well as those who are in Yugoslavia. Some lobbying has been done in Washington for the Serbian cause in the current Balkan conflict, but without much success.

Myths & misconceptions:

Myth: The Serbs caused WWI by assassinating the heir to the Austro-Hungarian throne, Prince Ferdinand Hapsburg, in Sarajevo in 1914.

Fact: Austria-Hungary was ready to attack Serbia and was looking for a pretext to do so, when the assassination of Prince Ferdinand came about and provided a perfect pretext for Austro-Hungarians to launch the war and enlarge their empire, which already included Croatia, Slovenia, and parts of Bosnia and Hercegovina.

Myth: The Serbs are the only aggressors in the former Yugoslav territories and the only guilty party in the recent Balkan conflicts.

Fact: All parties involved in the conflict are equally guilty of atrocities and misrepresentation of facts. Unbiased foreign journalists and travelers have confirmed that many photos taken in Bosnia illustrate atrocities committed against the Bosnian Serbs, though they were shown on television as misdeeds committed by the Serbs. Serbs have never been very good diplomats, and in recent years they paid for that dearly.

Myth: The Serbs unlawfully "occupied" Bosnian territories that did not belong to them.

Fact: The Serbian Orthodox population lived in the countryside of Eastern Bosnia for centuries and owned the lands around their villages. The Bosnian Serbs have as much right to inhabit Bosnia as the Bosnian Moslems and Bosnian Croatians do, and as much right as the others in Bosnia to protect the lands that have belonged to them since time immemorial.

— Compiled by Dr. Biljana Sljivic-Simsic, Professor and Chair of the Department of Slavic and Baltic Languages and Literatures, University of Illinois at Chicago

Slovak Americans

Chicago population:

11,662 (1990 Census, first ancestry)
5,744 (Census, second ancestry)
20,000 (1996 community estimate)

Metro area population:

56,180 (1990 Census, first ancestry)
36,906 (Census, second ancestry
110,000 (1996 community estimate)

Foreign-born:

NA

Note: In addition to those reporting Slovak ancestry, an undetermined number of Slovaks were among the 2,527 in Chicago and 16,000 in the metro area listing Czechoslovakian as their first ancestry.

Demographics:

Illinois has the third largest Slovak population in the United States, the bulk of whom reside in Chicago and its collar counties. The largest number live in suburban Cook County, about 38,000 of those listing first or second ancestry as Slovak, followed by about 15,000 in DuPage, 11,000 in Will and 6,000 in Lake. Most Slovak Americans are assimilated into mainstream middle-class communities, but some concentrations remain around 52nd and California and in Berwyn, Westchester, Streator and Joliet. In Chicago, there are concentrations of Slovaks in the Gage Park, Garfield Ridge and West Lawn neighborhoods. Census information is sketchy and it is difficult to tell how many Slovak Americans here were born abroad. In 1990, about 1,300 in Chicago and 6,500 in the metro area reported they were born in Czechoslovakia. There is no way to tell how many of those were Slovaks. Czechoslovakia was split into the Czech Republic and Slovak Republic in 1993.

Historical background:

Some Slovaks were in America at the time of the Civil War. A Slovak American military officer, Col. Gejza Mihalotzy-Michalovsky, formed a corps known as the Lincoln Riflemen of Slavic Origin. Most Slovak immigrants came later, however.

• Massive immigration to the United States began around 1880. The first settlers came prompted by the oppressive policies of Slovakia's foreign rulers and a desire for improved living conditions. The majority of the forebears of Slovaks arrived in Illinois at that time. In the late 1880s and early 1900s, vibrant Slovak settlements were established both in Chicago and in Berwyn, Blue Island, Chicago Heights, Cicero, Joliet, Riverside and Westchester. At one time, the Chicago area had 10 Slovak Roman Catholic Churches. The first Lutheran church in Chicago for Slovak immigrants, Trinity Lutheran, was established in 1893 at May and Huron streets on the North Side. Five years later, the first Roman Catholic church for Slovaks, dedicated to St. Michael the Archangel, was established on the South Side at 48th and Damen. Trinity Lutheran, now at 5106 N. LaCrosse, still has a Slovak congregation. Sts. Cyril &

Methodius Slovak Roman Catholic Church, founded in 1900, still serves the needs of the Slovak Roman Catholics of Joliet and Will County, while the Slovak Roman Catholic Church of St. Simon the Apostle, established in 1926 at 52nd and California, is the only remaining Roman Catholic church for Slovaks in Chicago. Many Slovaks in the area known as the Back of the Yards worked in the slaughterhouses of the Chicago Stockyards, while others labored on railroads or in steel mills. Henry Ford employed a number of Slovak *drotari* (wireworkers) in the manufacture of wire wheels for his Model A automobile, while others were employed by Pullman. American author Upton Sinclair immortalized the Slovak stockyard workers of Chicago in his novel, *The Jungle*.

 • Some additional immigrants came after WWI and again after WWII.

 • The final surge came when the Russians invaded Czechoslovakia in 1968. Border guards unofficially opened the borders to allow people to escape.

Current migration patterns:

Very few Slovaks have emigrated since the start of democracy in 1993. Most of those who come are tourists and return to their homeland.

Language:

Slovak. Most of the 1968 immigrants and second-generation Slovak Americans (the first U.S.-born generation) are bilingual.

Religion:

Slovaks are about 75% Roman Catholic, 15% Lutheran, 5% Greek Catholic, with 5% Jewish, Orthodox, and other Protestants.

Important traditions:

Among Catholic, Lutheran and Orthodox Slovak Christians, the most universally preserved Slovak tradition is that of the family dinner on Christmas Eve, most commonly referred to as *Stedry Vecer* (The Bountiful Evening) or *Vilija* (The Vigil). Among Catholic and Orthodox Christians, the special foods for Easter are an equally cherished custom that involves taking those foods in baskets to church to be blessed by the priest. For Slovaks of the Jewish faith, the celebration of Passover likewise decrees the preparation and serving of specifically designated foods for the Passover seder. Traditions of birth, coming of age, courtship, marriage and death are for the most part governed by religious laws and customs.

Holidays and special events:

The major Christian holidays are **Stedry Vecer** or Christmas Eve (Dec. 24) **Vianoce** or Christmas Day (Dec. 25) and **Vel'ka noc** or Easter (spring). Jewish holidays are **Passover** (spring), and **Rosh Hashanah**, the Jewish New Year (autumn). **Slovak Fest Midwest** (a Sunday in late August), rotates from one suburb to another. Sponsored by the Slovak American Cultural Society of the Midwest, it celebrates Slovak American heritage and culture.

Foods for special occasions:

Christmas Eve dinner is likely to include *oblatky* (a flat wafer spread with honey, to which garlic is sometimes added); *hribova kapustnica* (a mushroom or mushroom/sauerkraut soup); farina with honey and cinnamon; fried fish; peas; mashed potatoes or *pirohy* (a potato-filled dough, boiled or fried and served with butter and onions); and a dish called *opekance* or *bobalky* made of small yeast dough balls, scalded milk, sugar or honey and fresh-ground poppy seeds. The meal is usually followed by servings of unshelled mixed nuts and various fruits such as apples, oranges, dates and figs, as well as servings of horn- or crescent-shaped pastries called *rozky* filled with a walnut, prune or other fruit filling, and walnut and poppy seed-filled pastries rolled up like jelly rolls and called *orechovy kolac* and *makovnik*. Also served is a braided, sweet Christmas bread called *Vianocka* and wine. On Easter, there are hard-boiled eggs, smoked *sunka* (ham), *klobasy* (smoked sausage), *slanina* (smoked bacon), *cvikla s krenom* (a mixture of grated beets, horseradish root, salt and vinegar), rye bread, *syrek* (a custard-like cheese made of eggs milk, salt, sugar and vanilla) and a baked stuffing called *plnka* or *nadievka*, made from white bread rolls, diced ham, eggs, onions, broth and various seasonings. Easter breads called *paska* and *babka*, as well as *Vel'konocny Baranok* (a special Easter cake in the shape of a lamb), also are served. As on Christmas Eve, *rozky*, walnut and poppy-seed rolls, and wine round out the meal.

Names:

In former days, when large families were the norm and infant mortality high, newborn Christian children often were given the first name of the same-gender sibling whose death had preceded their birth. Today, common first names for boys include Jan, Jozef, Pavol (Paul), Peter and Juraj (George). For girls, popular names are Maria, Anna, Katarina, Magdalena and Helena. Male surnames are likely to end in "ek," "ik," "ak," "ka," "ko," "ec" or "sky". Surnames for females contain the suffix "ova," except for those with a "sky" ending, which changes to 'ska."

Political participation:

American Slovaks are strong believers in the power of the ballot box. They are estimated to be evenly distributed between the Republican and Democratic parties.

Major issues for community:

U.S. government support for the Slovak Republic joining NATO is the main issue for Slovaks here.

Links to homeland:

There is considerable travel back and forth for immigrants and the first two generations born here, especially since Slovakia became a free and democratic country. The Slovak World Youth Congress draws from all over the world to the Slovak Republic. Slovaks come to Chicago to visit relatives. For younger tourists, who grew up behind the Iron Curtain, America is a magnet, like a fairy tale. In August 1995, President Michal Kovac of the Slovak Republic was in Chicago to accept the American Bar Association's prestigious 1995 CEELI Award for his efforts to establish democracy in the Slovak Republic. While here, he visited St. Simon the Apostle Church.

Myths & misconceptions:

Myth: "Slovak" and "Slavic" mean the same thing.
Fact: "Slovak" is a particular nationality within the "Slavic" group of nations. "Slavic" denotes a group or branch of nationalities that includes Bielorussians, Bulgarians, Croatians, Czechs, Lusatian Serbs, Kasubians, Macedonians, Montenegrins, Poles, Rusins, Russians, Serbians, Slovaks, Slovenians and Ukrainians.

Etc.:

Bratislava, the capital of the Slovak Republic, is a highly musical city with fine classical music and world-famous opera. There also are many old castles, some of which have been restored, as well as historic churches and synagogues. The beautiful Tatra Mountains with their high peaks provide excellent skiing, and Slovakia's wines are among the world's best.

— By Thomas Klimek Ward, Honorary Consul of the Slovak Republic, and Founder and Chairman of the Slovak American Cultural Society of the Midwest

(Mr. Ward would like to express his gratitude to the following, who provided information: Msgr. Peter E. Bolerasky, Bonnie Clark, Rev. Ivon P. Harris, Rev. Francis Q. Kub, Jeffrey H. Marker, Dr. Susan Mikula, Yvonne M. Mikutis, Rev. Edward A. Slosarcik, Anthony X. Sutherland, Sister Mercedes Voytko and Rosemary Macko Wisnosky.)

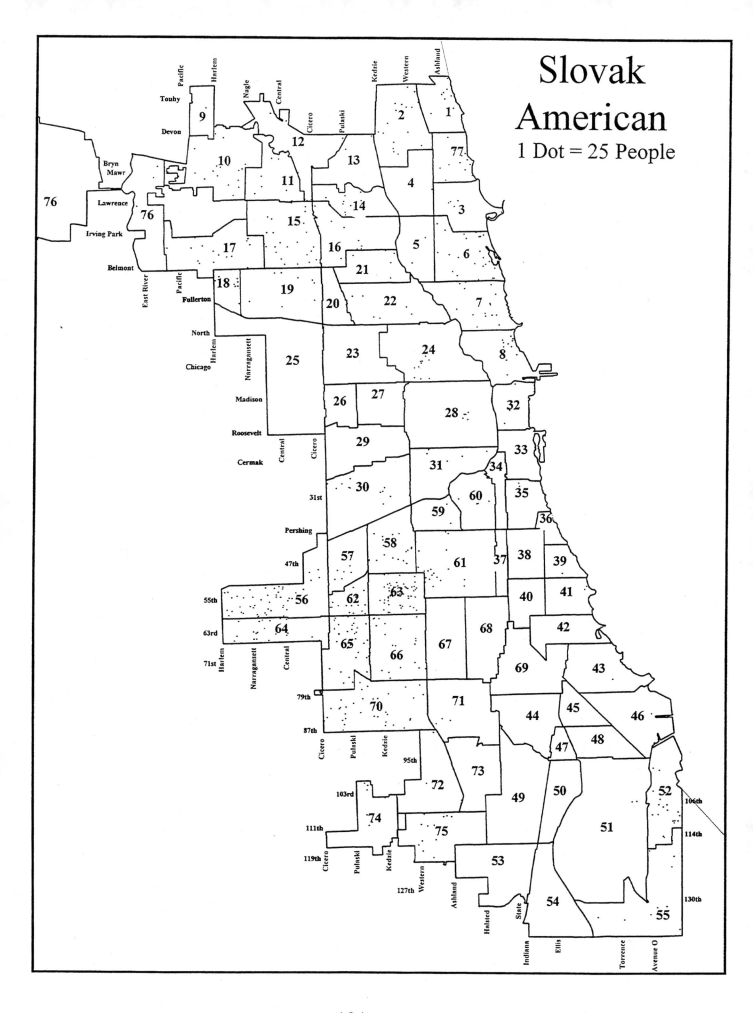

Slovak
American
1 Dot = 25 People

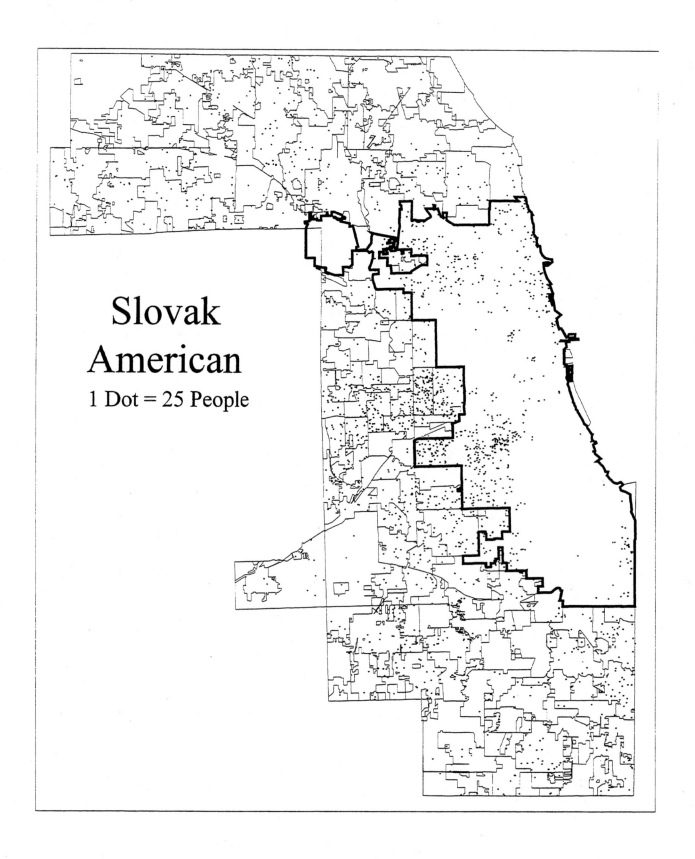

Slovak
American

1 Dot = 25 People

Swedish Americans

Chicago population:

19,814 (1990 Census, first ancestry)
12,941 (Census, second ancestry)
1996 community estimate similar to Census

Metro area population:

131,226 (1990 Census, first ancestry)
87,524 (Census, second ancestry)
1996 community estimate similar to Census

Foreign-born:

5% in Chicago, 3% in metro area

Demographics:

The overwhelming majority of the Swedish population in the metro area is suburban, widely scattered but living primarily in the north and west suburbs. Cook, DuPage and Lake counties have the highest numbers of people with Swedish ancestry. In the city, Swedes are mostly on the North Side, with Andersonville and North Park remaining the predominant enclaves. There is very little Census breakdown for people of Swedish ancestry.

Historical background:

Approximately 1.3 million Swedes came to North America between 1850 and 1930.

• Most came between 1870-90. In 1880, Chicago had 12,982 Swedish residents born in Sweden, and another 5,112 Swedish Americans born in the U.S., totaling 3.6% of the city's population at the time. The original Swedish enclave, "Swede Town," was bordered by Erie Street, Wells Street and the Chicago River. Emigration was heaviest from southern Sweden. In 1880, 64% of the Chicago Swedes were occupied in handicrafts and industry, 17% in trade and communications, 2% in public service and liberal professions, and 17% in domestic work. At that time, 66% of Swedish workers were male, 24% female. The majority of the Swedish population in Chicago was under the age of 35. In the trades there was an emphasis on carpentry and bricklaying. Swedes and other Scandinavians did much of the work to rebuild after the Great Chicago Fire.

• In 1900, a reported 48,836 Chicagoans born in Sweden and 157,236 claiming some Swedish ancestry lived in the city of Chicago. Only the Swedish capital, Stockholm, had more Swedish residents. Economic crises, notably in timber, iron and agriculture, as well as labor, temperance and religious upheavals, brought many of the Swedes to Chicago. The immigrant community was complex, often dividing along religious and secular lines, as well as by class. Older immigrants had a rural background. New arrivals after 1900 tended to come from urban and industrial situations. Swedish movement to the suburbs occurred between 1880 and 1920. By 1920 Swedes were the largest single ethnic group in city neighborhoods of Albany Park, North Park, Andersonville, Belmont-Cragin, Lake View, Englewood, West Englewood, Austin, Armour Square, Hyde Park, Woodlawn, South Shore, Greater Grand Crossing,

Swedes did much of the work to rebuild after the Chicago Fire.

In 1900 there were more Swedes in Chicago than anywhere but Stockholm.

A major split occurred between Sweden and the United States during the Vietnam War, when Sweden was critical of the U.S. involvement.

East Side, Morgan Park and Roseland. Swedes related most closely socially and occupationally with Danes, Norwegians and Germans. Intermarriage in 1900 was most common with Norwegians, followed by Danes, Germans, English, Irish, English Canadians and Scots. Swedish Americans numbered about 140,000 in 1930, as some residents moved out from the city.

Current migration patterns:

Current immigration is minuscule. Most visits by Swedes to the United States are short-term and temporary, primarily for business or education.

Language:

Third- and fourth-generation descendants are more likely to speak English than Swedish in the home. Those remaining from the first and second generations speak either language, depending on the setting. Swedish is spoken in the home primarily by recent arrivals, most likely those here for business or education.

Religion:

The State Church of Sweden is Lutheran, as is the predominant religion. Those not from a Lutheran tradition are most likely from another Protestant free church tradition, including: Evangelical Covenant, Free Church, Methodist, Baptist, Pentecostal or Salvation Army.

Important traditions:

These revolve around the major religious and secular holidays of Advent, Christmas, Easter, Midsummer, Walpurgis Night, Flag Day, and St. Lucia Day. Swedish Americans value education and public service. They believe good citizenship means being loyal, honest and industrious.

Holidays and special events:

St. Lucia Day (Dec. 13) and *Midsummer* (June 23) are related as celebrations of light. St. Lucia, the Catholic Saint who represents light, comes in the darkest of winter to bring light as a reminder of longer days and more light to come; Midsummer celebrates the longest days of the year with a big festival in Chicago's parks that includes cultural events such as the Maypole dance, folk music and food. A *Lucia Fest* has been held at the Daley Center for a number of years. Midsummer is celebrated in the Andersonville neighborhood and at several parks along the Fox River Valley near Geneva and Elgin. *Julotta* is an early morning Christmas service, held in a number of area churches, with at least part of the service often conducted in Swedish. *Flag Day* (June 6) is like Swedish National Day and celebrates Sweden and the Swedish people. Activities, including a parade and speeches by community leaders, are coordinated by the Central Swedish Committee, an umbrella organization for Swedish groups in Chicago. Swedish flags are hung from homes.

Foods for special occasions:

St. Lucia Day is celebrated with the eating of *lussekatter* (saffron buns) and drinking coffee, most often in bed during the early morning. Other foods that are part of traditional celebrations include *glogg, pepparkakor* (ginger cookies), *risgrynsgrot* (rice pudding), hardtack, herring, salmon, ham, and *semlor* (round, unsugared buns).

Names:

Common last names include Johnson, Peterson, Olson, Nelson, and Carlson, all ending in "son." That is because traditionally each generation was given the father's first name with "son" added. The last name kept changing until the late 19th century, when surnames started to be carried from generation to generation. At that time, those in the military often were given names referring to places and nature, ending in "strom" (stream) or "dahl" (valley) for example, because there were too many Johnsons and Petersons in the military to keep them all straight.

Major issues for community:

Preservation of ethnic heritage is a major concern of the community and is carried out by the Swedish American Museum Center, the Central Swedish Committee and its member organizations, the Swedish-American Historical Society (an international organization headquartered in Chicago) and by the Center for Scandinavian Studies at North Park College through programs, concerts, exhibits, classes, conferences, workshops, and other activities.

Political participation:

Swedish Americans traditionally have identified more with the Republican Party, though the trend may be reversed for those living in the city. This is a reflection, somewhat, of the rural/urban dichotomy of Swedish settlement in the U.S. There is a history of active and conscientious involvement in voting and community activity, often through churches, fraternal lodges and other organizations. While they do not necessarily have "clout," Swedish Americans have influenced reform movements to route out corruption in political and labor organizations.

Links to homeland:

Most links to Sweden are through business, travel and education. A major split occurred between Sweden and the United States during the Vietnam War, when Sweden was critical of U.S. involvement. Sweden became a refuge for those avoiding the draft. That rift has healed, however, and contacts between the two countries are positive. Major businesses like Volvo and SAS are active in Chicago. In addition, a very active Swedish-American Chamber of Commerce promotes business between the two countries. The community lost a major link with the dissolution of the consular office (there are now honorary consulates). All major Swedish government functions are now funneled through New York and Washington.

— By Tim Johnson, Director of Archives at North Park College and Theological Seminary, and Treasurer of the Swedish American Historical Society

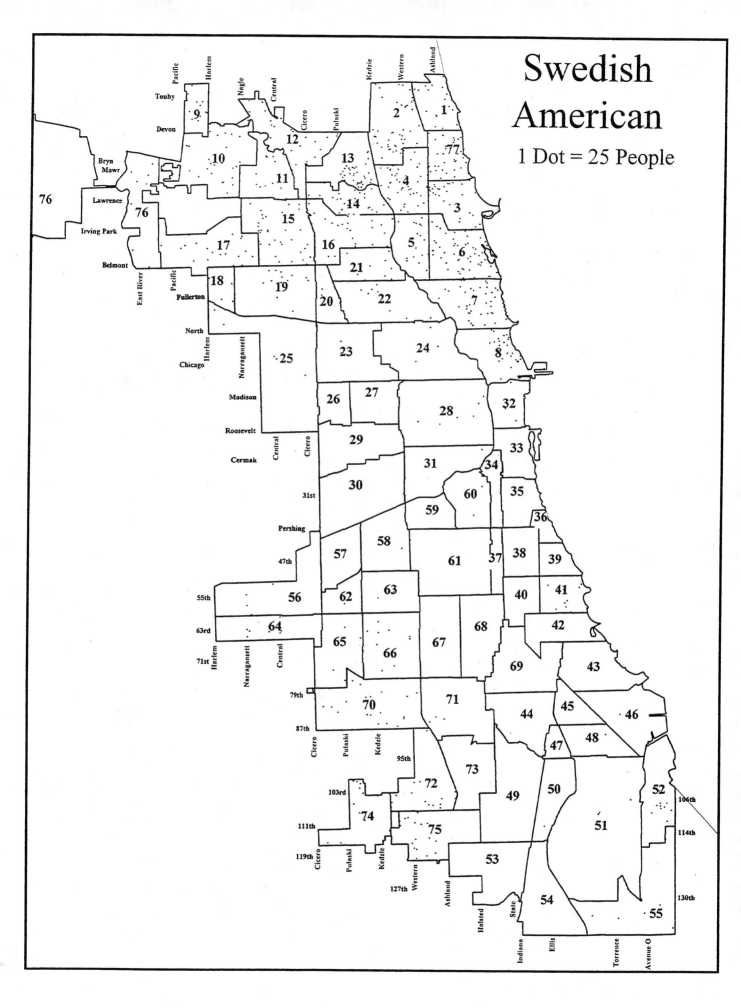

Swedish American

1 Dot = 25 People

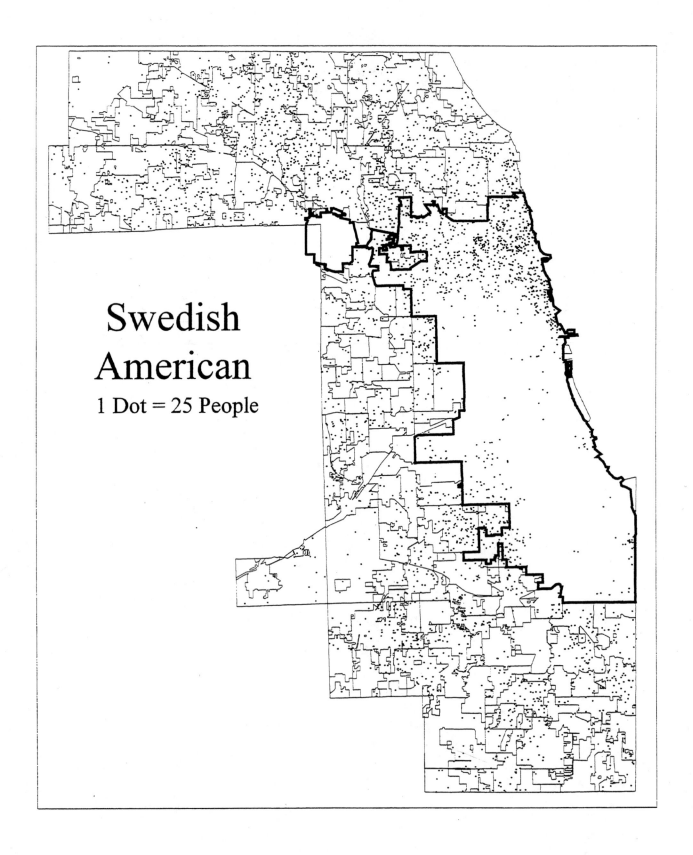

Swedish
American

1 Dot = 25 People

Ukrainian Americans

Chicago population:
9,321 (1990 Census, first ancestry)
2,540 (Census, second ancestry)
40,000 (1996 community estimate)

Metro area population:
24,908 (1990 Census, first ancestry)
9,954 (Census, second ancestry)
60,000 (1996 community estimate)

Foreign-born:
NA

Demographics:
Census breakdown for is almost non-existent for Ukrainians in the Chicago area. Ukrainians in Chicago are known to be concentrated in Ukrainian Village, bounded by Division, Mozart, Huron and Damen. Those living in the suburbs are scattered.

Historical background:
The United States has had three mass immigrations from what is today Ukraine:

• The first immigration began in the 1880s and ended in 1914, at the start of WWI. Dominated for centuries by foreign powers, Ukraine did not exist as a separate nation-state at the time of the first mass immigration. Most early immigrants from Ukraine were poor, illiterate and unskilled peasants, seeking a better life in America. Many were unaware of their ethno-national heritage, calling themselves by their ancient name, "Rusyns." Few early emigres returned to Ukraine. It was during these early times that the community established its churches and fraternal benefit societies. Most were from the Transcarpathian region. With financial help from the Czarist government, they built the Holy Trinity Russian Orthodox-Greek Catholic Church at Leavitt and Haddon in 1903. A second group built St. Mary's Greek Catholic Church at 50th and Seeley in 1905. Immigrants from the Galician region also were arriving during this period, settling in an area bounded by Division, Racine, Orleans and what is now Roosevelt Road, where a parish was established in 1905. They bought a church and renamed it St. Nicholas Greek Catholic Church. Land later was purchased at Rice and Oakley and a new St. Nicholas was completed in 1913. A Byzantine-Slavonic masterpiece, it is now a cathedral. Another community of Ukrainian immigrants settled in the Burnside area, where Sts. Peter and Paul was completed in 1909. At about the same time, a group of Ukrainians moved into the Back of the Yards, where a church was completed in 1912.

• Ukraine declared its independence in 1918, only to be divided among its neighbors at the end of WWI. Most members of the second immigration (1920-39) were ethno-nationally conscious, literate and semi-skilled. They came looking for work and committed themselves to Ukraine's resurrection as a nation-state. Their reasons for emigrating were both economic and political. They gave new life to the existing community here.

Dominated for centuries by foreign powers, Ukraine did not exist as a separate nation-state at the time of the first mass immigration (1880s-1914).

Ukraine declared its independence in 1918, only to be divided among its neighbors after WWI.

After Ukraine became an independent nation-state in 1991, a new immigration to Chicago began.

Ukrainians are thrifty. They run four banks in Chicago.

• The third mass immigration (1948-55) was composed largely of skilled and professional people, permitted to enter the U.S. following passage of the Displaced Persons Act of 1948. They too were committed to Ukraine's freedom crusade. Forced to leave Ukraine on the eve of the Soviet onslaught, this immigration was largely political.

Current migration patterns:

After Ukraine became an independent nation-state in 1991, a new immigration to Chicago has begun. An estimated 2,000 Ukrainians arrived legally in the '90s, and another 500-1,000 probably arrived legally but remained illegally, overstaying their visas. The INS, which did not separate out Ukrainians, counted nearly 12,000 legal immigrants from the former Soviet Union from 1990-94. Many were from Ukraine.

Language:

Ukrainian. Most immigrants from western Ukraine also speak Polish, while those arriving in the 1990s speak Russian. Saturday schools are used to preserve the Ukrainian language. There are two in Chicago and one in Palatine.

Religion:

Most Ukrainians (about 65%) in the metro area belong to the Eastern-rite (Byzantine) Catholic Church; some 30% are Ukrainian Orthodox; 5% are Baptist. Many of the recent immigrants from Ukraine are Jews.

Holidays and special events:

The most important religious holidays are **Easter** and **Christmas**. The most significant political holidays are **Independence Day** (Jan. 22), proclaimed in 1918 and still celebrated by some; **Independence Day** (Aug. 24), proclaimed in 1991; and the birthday of **Taras Shevchenko** (March), Ukraine's poet laureate.

Foods for special occasions:

The most sacred day of the religious calendar is Christmas Eve, when a 12-course meatless, dairyless family dinner is served. Traditional dishes include *prosphora*, a specially baked bread that the head of the family gives each member with honey and wishes for the New Year; *borscht* (clear beet soup) with *vooshka*, a triangle of dough filled with mushrooms; *varennyky* (dough filled with potato and sauerkraut); *holoptsi* (cabbage rolls made with rice and mushrooms or buckwheat); and *komput* (dried fruit cooked together in a juice). *Kutia* (a very sweet dessert make from baked wheat, poppy seeds, honey, raisins and nuts) traditionally is thrown against the ceiling and if it sticks it is a favorable omen for a good agricultural year.

Important traditions:

Language maintenance, church attendance and organizational membership are important traditions for Ukrainian Americans. Assimilation is eroding these customs, however. Marriage to non-Ukrainians is running extremely high. Church and organizational membership are dwindling. The 1990s immigration is either indifferent to organized Ukrainian life or still too unsettled to consider membership. Ukrainians are thrifty. They run four banks in Chicago and the Ukrainian Self Reliance Credit Union is one of the largest in the United States.

Names:

Common names are Michael, Stephen, Nicholas, Volodymyr (Walter), Gregory, Oksana, Alexandra (Lesia), Laryssa, Martha and Mariana. Many Ukrainian surnames end in "ko," "sky" or "wycz."

Major issues for community:

Issues of concern are assimilation and its effect upon Ukrainian American institutions, Western media defamation, and the future of Ukraine as an independent nation-state.

Political participation:

Although Ukrainians can boast of having a state senator, participation in American political and civic affairs is minimal. The major political focus was and remains on Ukraine. Most Ukrainian Americans do vote, however. In Chicago, in local politics, most are Democrats. In national elections they tend to vote Republican because they view the GOP as more aware of the Russian threat. This has been the case since President Franklin D. Roosevelt recognized the Soviet Union.

Links to homeland:

Ties are very strong. Now that Ukraine is independent once again, travel is far more frequent. Money is constantly being sent to relatives in Ukraine. Attendance is high at events featuring cultural, political and intellectual groups and individuals from Ukraine. Donations to such groups as the Children of Chernobyl are generous. Ukrainians remain informed about events in Ukraine by reading *Svoboda*, a Ukrainian-language daily, and *The Ukrainian Weekly*, an English-language publication, both of which have reporters in Ukraine.

Myths & misconceptions:

Myth: Ukrainians are "Little Russians" who speak a Russian dialect.
Fact: Ukrainians have their own unique history, culture and language.
Myth: During WWII, Ukrainians welcomed Hitler and were his most willing collaborators.
Fact: Ukrainians living under Stalinist terror initially welcomed the German army, believing they were being liberated. But once they learned of Hitler's real plans for Ukraine, many organized the Ukrainian Partisan Army (UPA), the largest nationalist, underground anti-Nazi force in Europe. In addition, Ukrainians constituted 60% of the Soviet partisan forces fighting the Nazis. Millions of Ukrainians fought in the Soviet army or as members of the American and Canadian armies, while some fought for the Germans. During the course of the conflict, some 6.8 million Ukrainians perished. They included 3.9 million civilians and slave laborers (including some 800,000 Jews), and 1.3 million military dead. Some 700 Ukrainians cities and towns were destroyed, along with 28,000 villages. "No single European country," wrote journalist Edgar Snow in 1945, "suffered deeper wounds to its cities, its industries, its farmlands, and its humanity."

—By Dr. Myron Kuropas, Adjunct Professor at Northern Illinois University and National Co-chairman of the Ukrainian American Justice Committee

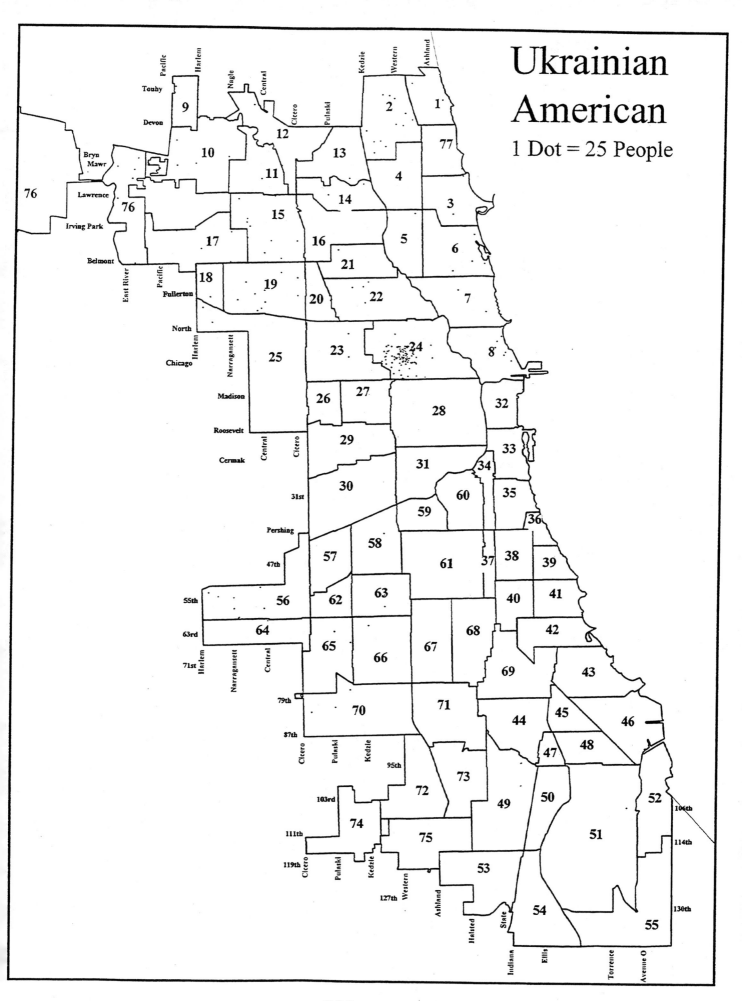

Ukrainian American

1 Dot = 25 People

Ukrainian
American

1 Dot = 25 People

Vietnamese Americans

Chicago population:
4,640 (1990 Census)
10,000 (1996 community estimate)

Metro area population:
8,053 (1990 Census)
18,000 (1996 community estimate)

Foreign-born:
Approximately 82%

Note: Community estimate comes from Illinois Bureau of Refugee & Immigrant Services.

Demographics:

The majority of Vietnamese in Chicago live in Uptown, Edgewater, Rogers Park, Albany Park and West Ridge. Outside the city, Vietnamese can be found in some concentration in Wheaton, Joliet and Lombard. Median household income for Vietnamese is $24,033 in Chicago and $31,724 in the metro area. Nearly one-third in Chicago are below poverty level, about one-quarter in the metro area. About 37% of Vietnamese adults in the U.S., over the age of 25, do not have a high school degree. Occupational distribution in the labor force is as follows: Executive/administrative/professional 16%, technical 7%, service 38%, blue collar 31%. About 34% of Vietnamese found work in manufacturing industries, 21% in the retail and trade, and 16% in the professional or public-service sector. Nationwide, about 48% of Vietnamese households are considered "linguistically isolated." In 1990, no one 14 or older reported speaking English "very well." Close to 80% of Vietnamese households nationwide still speak Vietnamese at home. More than half of Vietnamese Americans are U.S. citizens. There are virtually no undocumented Vietnamese because they have been able to enter the U.S. legally, either as refugees or through family reunification.

Historical background:

The presence of a Vietnamese community in Chicago is a fairly recent phenomenon. About a dozen Vietnamese families were here prior to 1975.

• The fall of Saigon in April 1975 resulted in an unprecedented exodus of Vietnamese fleeing South Vietnam for fear of persecution by the new communist government. Under the Indochina Refugee Assistance Program, in 1975 alone 128,250 Vietnamese were admitted to the U.S. as refugees. A large percentage of those arriving in the first wave of refugees in 1975 were former South Vietnamese government officials, religious leaders, writers, journalists, businessmen and military commanders. Today, it is estimated there are more than a million Vietnamese in America.

• The Refugee Act of 1980 for the first time allowed the U.S. to establish a framework for federal refugee assistance. Many Vietnamese

Amerasians and former political prinsoners are the most recent arrivals.

A traditional family expects the woman to defer to the wishes of her father, husband and sons. Many of the younger generation no longer practice these values.

There is still an unwritten community rule that any actions that could be construed as helpful to the communist government in power will be condemned.

escaped by boat across the South China Sea or walked through Cambodia into Thailand to seek political asylum in several countries. A number of special programs were instituted to assist Vietnamese seeking resettlement in the U.S. The Vietnamese population in the U.S. represents widely diverse socio-economic strata. Among the latter arrivals were fishermen, farmers and urban dwellers. Amerasians (children of American men and Vietnamese women) and former political prisoners are the most recent arrivals. The majority of Vietnamese now living in the Chicago area survived many traumas. Prolonged armed conflicts and the perilous escapes from Vietnam left many without intact families. Former political prisoners were isolated from their families and tortured. Many require extensive counseling and assistance to rebuild their lives. Amerasians abandoned by their fathers and discriminated against in their homeland are still looking for their place in the U.S.

The first group of Vietnamese arrivals in the Chicago area was resettled in Uptown because of a few key voluntary agencies working there and affordable housing. This first group established a social and economic foundation on the North Side, through the creation of religious and community-based organizations and the development of a vibrant small-business strip on and around Argyle Street, between Broadway and Sheridan. The area then became a magnet for later arrivals, who spread farther north and west to Edgewater, Rogers Park and Albany Park. These all were communities with affordable housing and an ethnically diverse population, where Vietnamese found themselves more welcome. Vietnamese community leaders have worked closely with leaders of other refugee communities, such as Cambodians, Chinese, Laotians and Ethiopians, on joint projects to find jobs for new arrivals and to provide necessary adjustment services. Joint efforts also have resulted in an economic development program, helping to create and expand small businesses and build new homes.

Current migration patterns:

Each year since 1990, approximately 55,000 Vietnamese entered the U.S. as refugees or legal immigrants reuniting with family members. It is anticipated that the number of Vietnamese arrivals in the U.S. as refugees will be reduced significantly. The Chicago area has received an average of 755 legal Vietnamese immigrants each year from 1990-94. A number of Vietnamese have left the area for one of two key reasons: to reunite with family and friends living elsewhere or because they have difficulty adjusting to Chicago's cold winters. Not many Vietnamese have returned to Vietnam, though a few have gone back seeking business opportunities. Many more are still petitioning to leave Vietnam to rejoin families in the Chicago area. A small number has migrated to the suburbs where jobs are more plentiful, or to seek better educational opportunities for their children.

Language:

Vietnamese. There are minimal differences in vocabularies and intonations among people who are from the North, Central and South Vietnam.

Religion:

The majority of Vietnamese practice what could be considered a combination of Buddhism, Confucianism and Taoism. Catholicism also claims a significant following. There is also a growth of Vietnamese Protestants, partially due to the active participation and assistance provided to Vietnamese refugees by many churches. A smaller number practice Cao Daism. There are five Vietnamese Buddhist temples in the Chicago area. Two Catholic churches have significant Vietnamese congregations (St. Thomas of Canterbury in Chicago and Trinity in Lombard). The Uptown Baptist Church is a gathering place for Vietnamese Baptists living in the city.

Important traditions:

Vietnamese culture has adapted to many other cultures as the result of colonization and survival needs. Traditional values, heavily influenced by Confucian teaching include: Reverence for education and learned individuals, respect for the elderly and people in positions of authority, and pursuit of harmony rather than confrontation. Men are assumed to hold a superior social position. A traditional family expects the woman to defer to the wishes of her father, husband and sons. Among the younger generation, many no longer practice these traditional values because they conflict with the common values in the U.S. Many younger people have had to play the role of decision-maker in the household because of their fluency in English and understanding of U.S. customs and practices. This reversal of the leadership role, normally held by the parents or the elders, has created much social displacement and tension in some households. Many women also are working, which presents new challenges in traditional households. Other traditions include:

 • For the newborn child, there are special celebrations the first full month after birth and the first full year.

 • For marriage, contrary to U.S. practices, Vietnamese tradition dictates that the groom's family assume the cost of both the engagement and wedding ceremonies. The wedding usually includes a ceremony at the home of the bride, where the groom's family pays respect to the bride's family and formally asks to take her away to become a member of their family. Another ceremony is held at the home of the groom to formally welcome the bride to her new family.

 • At death, for a Buddhist, a monk often prays for the soul of the departed to reach Nirvana. Vietnamese Catholics observe what is practiced by Catholics worldwide. White is the color of mourning.

Holidays and special events:

Most holidays and special events are based on the lunar calendar. **TET/Lunar New Year** (first day of the first month, in late January or February) is the biggest Vietnamese holiday of the year and is celebrated, traditionally, for at least three days. It is seen as an opportunity for renewal and the beginning of all good things and is usually a time for family reunion and a welcoming of spring (Vietnam is a tropical country and spring usually arrives in January or February). **The Trung Sisters' Anniversary** (sixth day of the second month, from late February to late March) is observed as a national holiday to pay respect to these heroines, who in 39 A.D. succeeded in driving the Chinese out of Vietnam after 247 years of domination. This is a day to pay respect for the talents and contributions made by Vietnamese women in history and culture. **Ancestor Day** (March or April) observes the anniversary of the death of King Hung Vuong, founder of the Vietnamese nation. The elderly organize this observation each year. **Mid-Autumn Festival** (September) is primarily a children's festival, normally held in the evening when the full moon can be seen. The children have special lanterns made in beautiful images of flowers, birds, stars and other shapes that are candle-lit for processions through the streets. These traditional holidays have been modified to adjust to the conditions in the U.S. The celebrations are usually held on weekends, when the majority of Vietnamese are not working, instead of on the actual holidays. Celebrations that traditionally were observed in a family setting are now community-wide events.

Foods for special occasions:

Banh chung (sticky rice "cake") is made for the Lunar New Year, usually in the shape of a square or cylinder, with sweet rice on the outside and meat with mung bean in the center. The "cake" is wrapped in banana leaves and steamed. Sometimes the meat is replaced with banana when the cake is served as dessert. Banh trung thu or moon cake (made of mung bean and flour with berries, nuts, fruits and egg yolk inside) is made for Mid-Autumn Festival and is usually consumed with tea.

Dietary restrictions:

Vietnamese Buddhists avoid eating meat on special Buddhist holidays. Many faithful followers are vegetarians year 'round.

Names:

There are only about 100 family names for the whole population of some 70 million Vietnamese. Most common are Nguyen, Le, Tran, Pham, Phan, Vo and Huynh. People with the same family name are not always related to each other and Vietnamese rarely address each other by the family name. Contrary to the U.S. practice, in Vietnam, the family name comes first and the given name comes last. Living in the U.S., many reverse the order. Some have chosen not to do so. Vietnamese women do not change their last name when they marry. In formal settings women may be addressed by their husband's name, but their legal name is never changed. Given names generally have a meaning selected with great care by the parents to reflect their aspirations. Names normally express a quality or virtue. For men, Hung (courage), Liem (integrity) and

Trung (fidelity) are examples. Women's names can also be of beautiful things; for example Hong (rose), Lan (orchid) or Van (cloud).

Major issues for community:

Newly arrived refugees need to achieve economic independence as soon as possible, as well as make social adjustments and overcome language barriers. An equally important issue is the need for resettlement of people still in refugee camps today and those in Vietnam seeking to leave.

Political participation:

Being political refugees, many Vietnamese understand the need to comprehend and participate in the civic and political life of their new country. The Vietnamese Association of Illinois, a key community-based organization founded in 1976, has an active program to teach citizenship classes and help prepare Vietnamese to become naturalized citizens. Voter registration drives have been held in the community. A number of community leaders are active in local elections and serve in various capacities that bring them into contact with political leaders.

Links to homeland:

Many Vietnamese refugees, especially the older generation and former political prisoners, think of themselves as exiles awaiting the opportunity to return to the homeland (if the communist regime should fall). And, because so many families are not intact, community leadership is preoccupied with political and economic developments inside Vietnam, as well as with the ability to maintain communication with people there. Many Vietnamese Americans communicate by mail and telephone with family in Vietnam. They also send packages home, including basic living necessities such as over-the-counter medicine and clothes. The normalization of diplomatic relations between Vietnam and the U.S. has encouraged a number of Vietnamese individuals and organizations here to establish links with Vietnam for business or humanitarian assistance reasons. This issue, however, is still very sensitive with the Vietnamese community. A number of Vietnamese Americans in leadership positions believe that until the government of Vietnam is changed from communist to democratic, any contact with that government will be seen as aiding the "enemy." This belief is the source of community tension for many reasons. The younger generation, which has little or no knowledge of Vietnam, wants to explore and learn more about its roots. Those who have succeeded want to help alleviate poverty and the multiple problems in Vietnam that prevent the country from moving forward. Businessmen want to participate in the emerging Vietnamese market. In fact, the internal debate on whether or not Vietnamese Americans should have any contact with Vietnam has gone through some evolution. During the early 1980s there was a clearer consensus in the community that any contact with "the other side" was unacceptable. There was even a militant element that wanted to organize the community to topple the government in Vietnam. With the collapse of communism in the Soviet Union and Eastern Europe, there is greater hope that political change is possible and therefore communication through family visits or humanitarian actions are more accepted. Yet, there is still an unwritten community rule that any actions that could be construed as helpful to the communist government in power will be condemned.

Myths & misconceptions:

Myth: All Vietnamese children are smart, hard-working, and do well in school.

Fact: While a number of Vietnamese children have done remarkably well in school, many are struggling to catch up with their peers. Some were out of school several years while in refugee camps. Others still must master English before they can learn the subjects taught in school. A small number have dropped out of school.

Myth: All Vietnamese live in poverty and use public assistance extensively.

Fact: While most Vietnamese arrived with few or no possessions and have had to learn new skills and a new language, after 20 years of resettlement in the U.S., 73% have made significant economic progress and earn enough to live above poverty level. The majority of those receiving public assistance are recent arrivals who need help in the initial stage of resettlement.

— By Ngoan Le, formerly Executive Director of the Vietnamese Association of Illinois, now a Deputy Administrator with the Illinois Department of Public Aid

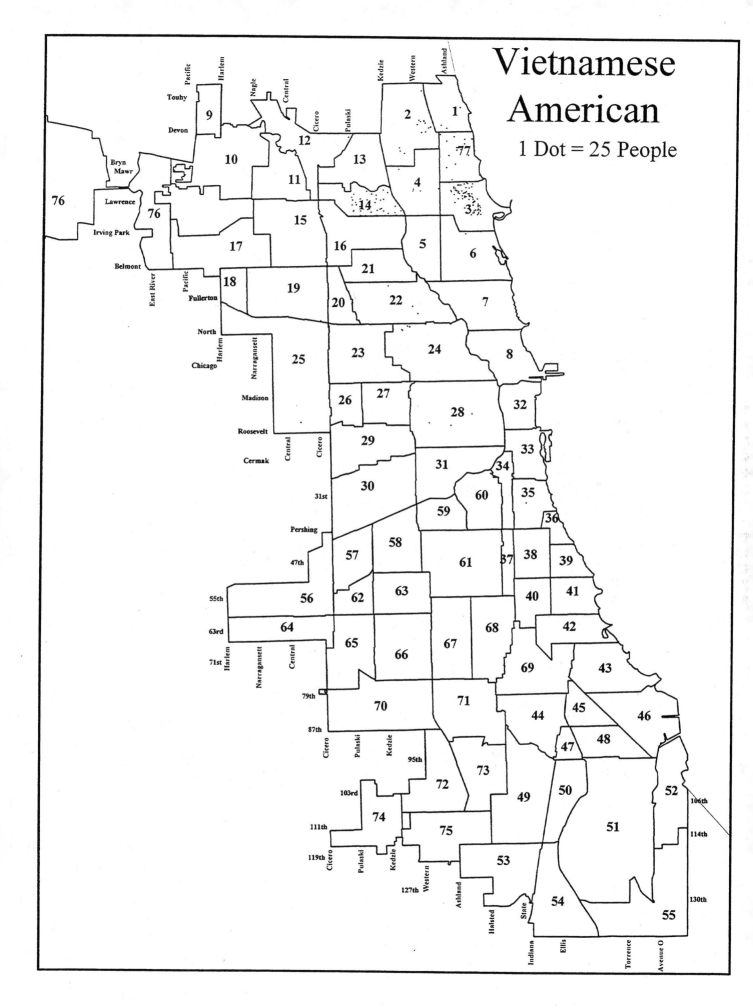

Vietnamese
American

1 Dot = 25 People

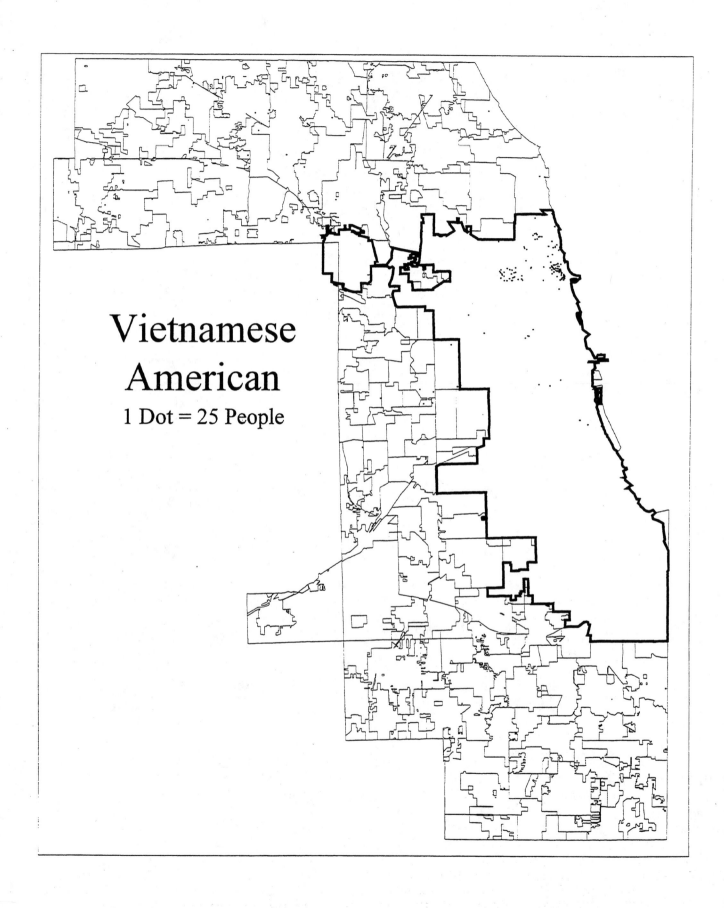

Vietnamese
American

1 Dot = 25 People

METAMORPHOSIS

By Ngoan Le

I was born in South Vietnam after my family fled from the North, following the installation of the communist government in Hanoi. As a child growing up in an extended family, comprising my grandmother (the matriarch), aunts, uncles and many cousins in addition to my own immediate family of six, I did not know we stayed together and shared cramped quarters because we were refugees with limited resources.

Our family spoke with a Northern accent, so the neighbors understood we were not "native." Dalat, where we settled, however, was a resort town where people came from everywhere, so we didn't stand out.

The adults in my family often talked about their past in the North and the relatives who still lived there. I read books about the North and dreamed of the time I could travel there to visit places where the history of Vietnam and my family began.

Unlike the adults in my family, I was a native of the South, because Dalat was my birthplace and where I grew into a teenager. I have many fond memories of my walk to school every morning in the fog and strolls with my friends around the lake in the middle of the town. I also have sad memories, living in a war-torn country where the sounds of bullets, fighter jets and artillery were everpresent. There were times we went to bed not knowing if we would be alive the next morning. We went to many funerals, of friends who were drafted in the military.

As I was ending my first year at the University of Saigon, the communist government of Hanoi gained control of South Vietnam. Dalat already had fallen in March 1975, and by April 29, my family once again found ourselves refugees. We fled from Dalat and then again from Saigon, leaving behind everything we owned and all the people we knew. We didn't even have a chance to say good-bye.

We left Saigon on a barge, on the chaotic final day before the takeover. Hundreds of refugees crowded on the floating platform, not knowing how we would be rescued. A ship picked us up and took us to a refugee camp in the Philippines. After a few short days, we were transferred to Wake Island, where we spent two months before being taken to a third camp at Ft. Chaffee, Ark., for a short stay. In the refugee camps, we learned to live with the humiliation of having to stand in line for food. When there was not enough, we simply went hungry. Not knowing what the future would hold for us, we spent our days trying to be productive. I volunteered to teach a class of small children. Our family also searched through the camps and talked to new arrivals, to see if anyone knew what happened to the family members we left behind.

We were resettled in Normal, Ill., where a very kind American family helped us get started, with clothing and furniture donated from local churches. Our rebirth in the United States was marked by the generosity of strangers who did not know us.

Normal is a college town with students coming from everywhere, including far-flung countries in Asia, Europe, the Middle East and Africa. For my four years of college, I thought of myself as a foreigner trying to make my way in this new world like all the other foreign students. The only difference was that their stay was temporary. They had a place to return to.

Once in Chicago, working for a Vietnamese organization helping new refugees resettle, I realized that a transformation had taken place. In the eyes of these refugees who arrived a few years after me, I had been "Americanized." While my English was accented and far from fluent, I could converse, socialize and conduct my work in the English-speaking world. I was no longer the quiet, shy person expected of Vietnamese women in Vietnam. I had become too assertive, by Vietnamese standards!

I now have lived in the United States 21 years and have become an American citizen. I also am identified as a Vietnamese American and an Asian American. In Vietnam, I was in the majority; here, I have had to learn about being the minority.

What I have become is far from what I began as on the other side of the globe. Life would have been much simpler if I could be just an American or just a Vietnamese. But I consider myself fortunate to have been given one identity and then had the opportunity to expand my human experience. I have become a multicultural, multilingual American.

Living in such diverse communities as first Uptown and then Rogers Park, I treasure the access to people and experiences of different cultures and national origins. I can function comfortably in both the Vietnamese- and English-speaking worlds. I also could survive in the Spanish-speaking world with my limited Spanish.

Naturally, I am still very much Vietnamese. I care deeply about the progress of the Vietnamese community in the U.S. and of Vietnam itself. I feel a great sense of guilt when I am unable to help the many refugees still living in camps in Southeast Asia. It pains me to know of the distressful poverty in Vietnam and lack of progress there.

The rift in the American Vietnamese community, created by differences of opinion about whether to work with the current government in Vietnam is disconcerting for me to witness. The wounds of the war and its aftermath are perhaps much too deep to heal easily.

I also am very much an American. I care deeply for the well-being of my neighborhood, city, state and nation. It saddens me to see the rise in violence and deterioration of living conditions in so many communities. I want to remind people who have given up on themselves, their children and their communities that here we have the resources many countries can only dream of.

I worry about the growing gap between the haves and have-nots in our society. I am angry about what seems to be an increasing trend of scapegoating immigrants as the source of many of our country's problems. Like other immigrants and refugees who have come before and after me, I have faith in the potential of America to be a great nation, as the direct consequence of the collective wisdom and energy of generations of immigrants who have come here to better their lives and communities.

If you see me walking down the street, the color of my skin gives me away as Asian. But if you stop and talk to me, you will soon learn that I was born in Vietnam and am now an American. The term "Vietnamese American" is a statement of fact acknowledging the experiences that have shaped my life.

Those who worry that such a description divides people of different racial and ethnic identities need to think about it as no different from my other identities as a woman and a professional in the field of human services. All of us are multi-dimensional.

In the end, the best description of me may be a "lucky survivor who has yet to explore all the possibilities of the human experience."

Ngoan Le is Deputy Administrator for Planning and Community Services at the Illinois Department of Public Aid.

Appendix

Appendix 1

Key for Chicago Maps

1	Rogers Park
2	West Ridge
3	Uptown
4	Lincoln Square
5	North Center
6	Lake View
7	Lincoln Park
8	Near North Side
9	Edison Park
10	Norwood Park
11	Jefferson Park
12	Forest Glen
13	North Park
14	Albany Park
15	Portage Park
16	Irving Park
17	Dunning
18	Montclare
19	Belmont Cragin
20	Hermosa
21	Avondale
22	Logan Square
23	Humboldt Park
24	West Town
25	Austin
26	West Garfield Park
27	East Garfield Park
28	Near West Side
29	North Lawndale
30	South Lawndale
31	Lower West Side
32	Loop
33	Near South Side
34	Armour Square
35	Douglas
36	Oakland
37	Fuller Park
38	Grand Boulevard
39	Kenwood
40	Washington Park
41	Hyde Park
42	Woodlawn
43	South Shore
44	Chatham
45	Avalon Park
46	South Chicago
47	Burnside
48	Calumet Heights
49	Roseland
50	Pullman
51	South Deering
52	East Side
53	West Pullman
54	Riverdale
55	Hegewisch
56	Garfield Ridge
57	Archer Heights
58	Brighton Park
59	McKinley Park
60	Bridgeport
61	New City
62	West Elsdon
63	Gage Park
64	Clearing
65	West Lawn
66	Chicago Lawn
67	West Englewood
68	Englewood
69	Greater Grand Crossing
70	Ashburn
71	Auburn Gresham
72	Beverly
73	Washington Heights
74	Mt. Greenwood
75	Morgan Park
76	O'Hare
77	Edgewater

Some often-used community names are not the same as the official community names. To find Chinatown, look for Armour Square (34). Pilsen and Little Village are Lower West Side and South Lawndale (31 and 30).

Major Immigration Laws

Naturalization Act of 1790. Limited citizenship to "free white persons" who had been in the U.S. two years. Allowed unrestricted entry of Europeans.

Alien and Sedition Acts (1798). President could expel alien enemy males suspected of treason.

Chinese Exclusion Act (1882). Denied entry to Chinese laborers; those already here were denied citizenship.

Quota Law of 1921. Limited any nationality to 3% of foreign-born living in U.S. in 1920 (about 350,000/year, mostly from Northern and Western Europe). Professionals and domestic servants exempt.

National Origins Law (1924). For five years 2% could come based on nationalities here in 1890. Greeks, Italians and Eastern Europeans, who had come later, were severely restricted. Also denied entry to those unable to become citizens, such as Chinese. Repealed in 1960s.

Act of April 1943. Permitted temporary agricultural workers from Western Hemisphere during WWII. Later extended to 1947, became basis for Mexican *bracero* program, which lasted to 1965.

Act of December 1943. Repealed Chinese Exclusion Act and set quota of 105 per year.

Act of 1944. Permitted temporary alien workers to help in war-effort industries and services, leading to agreements with British Honduras, Jamaica, Barbados and British West Indies.

Act of June 1946. Allowed Indians and Filipinos to come under quotas and made them eligible for citizenship.

Displaced Persons Act (1948). First U.S. policy admitting people fleeing persecution. Allowed up to 205,000 people, during two-year period, who were displaced by WWII in Europe.

Agricultural Act of 1949. Facilitated entry of seasonal farm workers to meet labor shortage. Extended bracero program.

Act of 1951. Provided framework for bracero program, setting up reception centers to provide transportation, sustenance and medical care, guaranteeing employers would pay prevailing wage and provide free housing.

Immigration & Naturalization Act of 1952 (McCarran-Walter). Held immigration to 1920 levels. Made all races eligible for citizenship and eliminated gender discrimination for immigrants. Gave preference to skilled workers needed here and relatives of U.S. citizens and aliens. Allowed 100 minimum from each country and set ceiling of 2,000 for total Asian-Pacific triangle.

Refugee Relief Act of 1953. Established new category, people persecuted for political beliefs. Helped those fleeing communism, like Cubans and Hungarians.

Act of 1961. Eliminated 2,000 quota for Asian-Pacific triangle. Ensured minimum quota.

Act of 1962. Granted non-quota visas to brothers, sisters and children of citizens and to those with special occupational skills.

Immigration Act of 1965. Stopped use of 1890 Census as basis for entry. Set 20,000 annual limit from any nation, eliminating nationality, race or ancestry as basis for immigration. Families of U.S. citizens had priority. Professionals and skilled workers, most of whom came from Asia, also had preference. Spouses, children and parents of U.S. citizens were exempt from quota, as were some clergy, some medical graduates and some of those who had worked for U.S. government abroad. Set limit of 170,000 for East Hemisphere; for first time West Hemisphere was not exempt from quotas (120,000 limit), but preference categories and 20,000/country quota didn't apply to West. The bracero program that let migrants go back and forth to Mexico was ended, but hiring of undocumented without penalty was allowed. Said immigrant workers should not replace U.S. workers or adversely affect wages and working conditions.

Indochina Migration and Refugee Assistance Act (1975). Established resettlement program for Cambodians and Vietnamese. (Laotians added in 1976.)

Immigration and Naturalization Act Amendments of 1976. Applied 20,000-per-country limit and preference system to Western Hemisphere. Exempted Cubans already in U.S. from quota.

Act of 1978. Combined quotas for East and West Hemispheres into one worldwide limit of 290,000.

Refugee Act of 1980. Set worldwide ceiling of 270,000, exclusive of refugees. Established comprehensive program for resettling refugees.

Immigration Reform and Control Act of 1986. (Simpson-Mazzoli) Gave amnesty to undocumented who had come before 1982. Set sanctions for employees knowingly hiring illegal aliens. Increased border enforcement.

Immigration Act of 1990. Increased total immigration, to 675,000 annually, consisting of 480,000 family-sponsored and 140,000 employee-based immigrants, plus another 55,000 from a new "diversity lottery." The latter was for those not able to come in large numbers under other quotas and preferences. About one-third went to Europeans, largely Irish already here but undocumented. Allowed for 4,800 people who would invest $1 million each in the U.S.

Welfare Overhaul Act of 1996. Denied benefits such as food stamps, welfare and Supplemental Security Income to legal immigrants who are not U.S. citizens.

Further Reading

African Americans:

Billingsley, Andrew. *Climbing Jacob's Ladder: The Enduring Legacy of African-American Families.* New York: Simon & Schuster, 1992.

Bell, Derrick. *Faces at the Bottom of the Well: The Permanence of Racism.* New York: Basic Books, 1992.

Berman, Paul, ed. *Blacks and Jews: Alliances and Arguments.* New York: Delacorte Press,1994.

Chideya, Farai. *Don't Believe the Hype.* New York: Penguin Books, 1995.

Cose, Ellis. *The Rage of the Privileged Class.* New York: HarperCollins, 1993.

Drake, St. Clair and Horace R. Cayton. *Black Metropolis: A Study of Negro Life in a Northern City.* Chicago: University of Chicago Press, 1993.

Dunier, Mitchell. *Slim's Table: Race, Respectability, and Masculinity.* Chicago: University of Chicago Press, 1992.

Grimshaw, William. *Bitter Fruit: Black Politics and the Chicago Machine, 1931-1991.* Chicago: University of Chicago Press, 1992.

Grossman, James R. *Land of Hope: Chicago, Black Southerners, and the Great Migration.* Chicago: University of Chicago Press, 1989.

Holli, Melvin and Paul M. Green, *The Making of a Mayor, Chicago, 1983.* Grand Rapids: William B. Eerdsman Publishing Co., 1984.

Kotlowitz, Alex. *There Are No Children Here.* New York: Doubleday, 1991.

Lemann, Nicholas. *The Promised Land: The Great Black Migration and How it Changed America.* New York: A.A. Knopf, 1991.

Levinsohn, Florence. *Harold Washington: A Political Biography.* Chicago: Review Press, 1983.

McClain, Leanita. *A Foot in Each World.* Evanston: Northwestern University Press, 1992.

Page, Clarence. *Showing My Colors.* New York: HarperCollins, 1996.

Ralph, James R. *Northern Protest: Martin Luther King, Jr., Chicago, and the Civil Rights Movement.* Cambridge: Harvard University Press. 1983.

Rivlin, Gary. *Fire on the Prairie: Chicago's Harold Washington and the Politics of Race.* New York: H. Holt, 1992.

Spears, Allan H. *Black Chicago: The Making of a Negro Ghetto, 1980-1920.* Chicago: University of Chicago Press.

Terkel, Studs. *Race: How Blacks and Whites Think and Feel about the American Obsession.* New York: New Press, 1992.

Travis, Dempsey. *An Autobiography of Black Chicago.* Chicago: Urban Research Institute, 1981.

Travis, Dempsey. *An Autobiography of Black Politics* Chicago: Urban Research Institute, 1987.

Tuttle, William M. *Race Riot: Chicago in the Red Summer of 1919.* New York: Atheneum, 1970.

Wells-Barnett, Ida B. *Crusade for Justice: The Autobiography of Ida B. Wells.* Chicago: University of Chicago Press, 1970.

Wilson, William Julius. *The Truly Disadvantaged: The Inner City, the Underclass, and Public Policy.* Chicago: University of Chicago Press, 1987.

Wilson, William Julius. *When Work Disappears: The World of the New Urban Poor.* New York: A.A. Knopf, 1996

Assyrians:

Assyrian Universal Alliance. *Census of Assyrians in the United States and the World.* Chicago, 1996.

Malech, George David. *History of Syrian Nation and the Old Evangelical-Apostolic Church of the East.* Ed. and trans. Nestorius George Malech. Trans. Ingeborg Rasmussen. Minneapolis: Privately Printed by Nestorius George Malech, 1910.

Joseph, John. *The Nestorians and Their Muslim Neighbors: A Study of Western Influences on Their Relations.* Princeton: Princeton University Press, 1961.

Mar Shimun, Surma d'Bait. *Assyrian Church Customs and the Murder of Mar Shimun.* Burlingame, CA and New York: Mar Shimun Memorial Fund;Vehicle Editions, 1983 (1920).

Cambodians:

Hansen, Marty. *Behind the Golden Door: Refugees in Uptown.* Chicago: 1991.

Ouk, Mory, Franklin E. Huffman, and Judy Lewis. *Handbook for Teaching Khmer-Speaking Students.* California: Folsom Cordova Unified School District and Southeast Asia Community Resource Center, 1988.

Chinese:

Asian American Institute. *Asian American Political Empowerment in Illinois.* Chicago: 1994.

Asian American Institute. *Profile of Asian Americans in Illinois.* Chicago: 1996.

Chan, Sucheng, ed. *Entry Denied: Exclusion and the Chinese Community in America 1882-1943.* Philadelphia: Temple University Press, 1991.

Chinese Historical Society of Southern California. *Origins and Destinations.* Los Angeles: UCLA Asian American Studies Center, 1994.

Hing, Bill and Ronald Lee. *Reframing the Immigration Debate.* UCLA: LEAP, 1996

Moy, Susan, "The Chinese in Chicago," in *Ethnic Chicago: A Multicultural Portrait,* edited by Melvin Holli and Peter d'A. Jones. Grand Rapids: Eerdmans Publishing Co., 1995.

Siu, Paul. *The Chinese Laundryman.* New York: New York University Press, 1987.

Takaki, Ronald T. *Strangers from a Different Shore: A History of Asian Americans.* Boston: Little Brown and Co., 1989.

Croatians:

Eterovich, Francis and Christopher Spalatin, editors. *Croatia: Land, People, Culture.* 2 Vols. Toronto: University of Toronto Press, 1964(1), 1970(2).

Prpic, George J. *The Croatian Immigrants in America.* New York: Philosophical Library, 1980.

Preveden, Francis R. *A History of the Croatian People.* 2 Vols. New York: Philosophical Library, 1955, 1962.

Cubans:

Boswell, Thomas D. and James R. Curtis. *The Cuban-American Experience, Culture, Images, and Perspectives.* Totowa, NJ: Rowman & Allanheld Publishers, 1984.

Casuso, Jorge. *Hispanics in Chicago.* Chicago: The Community Renewal Society, 1985.

Diaz-Briquets, Sergio. *The Health Revolution in Cuba.* Austin: University of Texas Press, 1983.

García, María Cristina. *Havana USA.* Berkeley: University of California Press, 1996.

Jaffe A. J., Ruth M. Cullen, and Thomas D. Boswell. *The Changing Demography of Spanish Americans.* New York: Academic Press, 1980.

Llanes, José. *Cuban Americans. Masters of Survival.* Cambridge, MA.: Abt Books, 1984.

Lluriá de O'Higgins, Maria Josefa. *A Taste of Old Cuba.* New York: Harper Collins, 1994.

Massud-Piloto, Felix Roberto. *With Open Arms: Cuban Migration to the United States.* Totowa, NJ: Rowman & Littlefield, 1988.

Massud-Piloto, Felix Roberto. *From Welcomed Exiles to Illegal Immigrants:* Cuban Migration to the U.S. 1959-1995. Lanham, MD: Rowman & Littlefield, Inc. 1996.

Olson, James S. and Judith E. Olson. *Cuban Americans. From Trauma to Triumph.* New York: Twayne Publishers, 1995.

Czechs

Blei, Norbert and Jennifer Gaudial. *Neighborhood.* Peoria: Ellis Press, 1987.

Ethiopians:

Levine, D.L. *Greater Ethiopia.* Chicago: University of Chicago Press, 1974.
Pankhurst, S. *Ethiopia: A Cultural History.* Lalibela House, London, 1955.
Ullendorff, E. *The Ethiopians: An Introduction to Country and People.* London: Oxford University Press, 1965.

Filipinos:

Cordova, Fred. *Filipinos: Forgotten Asian-Americans — A Pictorial Essay 1763 - Circa 1963.* Dubuque, IA: Kendall/Hunt Publishing Company, 1983.
Guyotte, Roland L. and Barbara M. Posadas. "Celebrating Rizal Day: The Emergence of a Filipino Tradition in Twentieth-Century Chicago." In *Feasts and Celebrations in North American Ethnic Communities.* Edited by Ramon A. Gutierrez and Genevieve Fabre. Albuquerque: University of New Mexico Press, 1995.
Karnow, Stanley. *In Our Image: America's Empire in the Philippines.* New York: Random House, 1989.
Kitano, Harry H.L. and Roger Daniels. *Asian Americans: Emerging Minorities.* Englewood Cliffs, NJ: Prentice Hall, 2nd ed., 1995.
Melendy, H. Brett. *Asians in America: Filipinos, Koreans, and East Indians.* Boston: Twayne Publishers, 1977.
Pido, Antonio J.A., *The Pilipinos in America: Macro/Micro Dimensions of Immigration.* New York: Center for Migration Studies, 1986.
Posadas, Barbara M. and Roland L. Guyotte. "Aspiration and Reality: Occupational and Educational Choice Among Filipino Migrants to Chicago, 1900-1935." *Illinois Historical Journal* 85:2 (Summer 1992).
Posadas, Barbara M. "At a Crossroad: Filipino American History and the Old-Timers' Generation." *Amerasia Journal* 13:1 (1986).
Posadas, Barbara M. "Crossed Boundaries in Interracial Chicago: Pilipino American Families since 1925." *Amerasia Journal* 8 (Fall/Winter 1981). Reprinted in *Unequal Sisters: A Multi-Cultural Reader in U.S. Women's History.* Edited by Ellen Carol DuBois and Vicki L. Ruiz. 2nd ed. New York: Routledge, 1994.
Posadas, Barbara M. "The Hierarchy of Color and Psychological Adjustment in an Industrial Environment: Filipinos, The Pullman Company, and the Brotherhood of Sleeping Car Porters." *Labor History.* 23 (Summer 1982).
Posadas, Barbara M. "Ethnic Life and Labor in Chicago's Pre-World War II Filipino Community." In *Labor Divided: Race and Ethnicity in United States Labor Struggles, 1840-1970.* Edited by Robert Asher and Charles Stephenson. Albany: SUNY Press, 1988.
Posadas, Barbara M. "Mestiza Girlhood: Interracial Families in Chicago's Filipino American Community Since 1930." In *Making Waves: Writing By and About Asian American Women.* Edited by Judy Young. Boston: Beacon Press. 1989.
Posadas, Barbara M. and Roland L. Guyotte. "Unintentional Immigrants: Chicago's Filipino Foreign Students Become Settlers, 1900-1941." *Journal of American Ethnic History.* (Spring 1990).

Germans:

German American National Congress. *Chicagoland: A World Class Metropolis.* Glen Ellyn: Bert Lachner & Associates, Inc., 1994
Holli, Melvin G. "German American Ethnic and Cultural Identity from 1890 Onward." In *Ethnic Chicago.* Edited by Melvin Holli and Peter d'A. Jones. (4th Ed.) Grand Rapids: Eerdmans Publishing Co., 1995.

Greeks

Diacou, Stacy, ed. *Hellenism in Chicago.* Chicago: United Hellenic American Congress, 1982.

Cutler, Irving. *Chicago: Metropolis of the Mid-Continent,* 3rd ed. Chicago: Kendall/Hunt Publishing Company, 1982.

Kopan, Andrew T. *Education and Greek Immigrants in Chicago, 1892-1973: A Study in Ethnic Survival.* New York: Garland Publishing Company, 1990.

Kopan, Andrew T., "Greek Survival in Chicago," in *Ethnic Chicago,* edited by Melvi G. Holli and Peter d'A. Jones 4th ed., Grand Rapid: William B. Eerdmans Publishing Company, 1995.

Moskos, Charles C. *Greek Americans: Struggle and Success.* Englewood Cliff, NJ: Prentice-Hall, Inc., 1980.

Pacyga, Dominic A. and Ellen Skerrett. *Chicago, City of Neighborhoods.* Chicago: Loyola University Press, 1986.

Guatemalans:

Hansen, Marty. *Behind the Golden Door: Refugees in Uptown.* Chicago: 1991.

Immerman, Richard H. *The CIA in Guatemala,* Vol. 2: *The Foreign Policy of Intervention.* Austin: University of Texas Press, 1982.

McClintock, Michael. *The American Connection Volume Two: State Terror and Popular Resistance in Guatemala.* London: Zed Books, 1985.

Riding, Alan. "Guatemala Revolution and Reaction in Central America." *New York Times Magazine,* Aug. 24, 1980.

Simon, Jean-Marie. *Guatemala: Eternal Spring, Eternal Tyranny.* New York: W.W. Norton & Co., 1987.

Haitians

Laguerre, Michel S. *American Odyssey: Haitians in New York City.* Ithaca and London: Cornell University Press, 1984.

Hungarians:

Bognar, Desi K. and Katalin Szentpaly, eds. *Hungarians in America: A Biographical Directory.* (East European Biographies and Studies Series), Vol. 3, Mt. Vernon, NY: Alpha Publications, 1971.

Chicago Department of Development and Planning. *Historic City, The Settlement of Chicago.* Chicago: 1976.

Gale Encyclopedia of Multicultural America. Vol 1., Galens et. al., eds. Gale Research Inc., 1995.

Lengyel, Emil. *Americans from Hungary.* Philadelphia and New York: J.B. Lippincott, 1948; reprinted, Westport, CN: Greenwood, 1974.

Puskas, Julianna. *From Hungary to the United States, 1880-1914.* Budapest: Akademiai Kiado, 1982.

Tezla, Albert. *The Hazardous Quest: Hungarian Immigrants in the United States, 1895-1920.* Budapest: Corvina, 1993.

Indians:

Bhardwaj, Surinder M. and N. Maddhusudana Rao. "Asian Indians in the United States." In *South Asians Overseas, Migration and Ethnicity,* edited by Colin Clarke, Ceri Peach and Steven Vertovec. Cambridge: Cambridge University Press, 1990.

Brown, Richard Harvey and George V. Coelho, eds. *Tradition and Transformation: Asian Indians in America. Societies* 38. Williamsburg: College of William and Mary, 1986.

Fisher, Maxine P. *The Indians of New York City. A Study of Immigrants from India.* Columbia: South Asia Books, 1980.

Helwig, Arthur W. and Usha M. *An Immigrant Success Story. East Indians in America.* Philadelphia: University of Pennsylvania Press, 1991.

Leonard, Karen B. and Chandra S. Tibrewal. "Asian Indians in Southern California:

Occupations and Ethnicity." In *Immigration and Entrepreneurship. Culture, Capital and Ethnic Networks,* edited by Ivan Light and Parminder Bhachu. New Brunswick: Transaction Publisher, 1993.

Rangaswamy, Padma. "Asian Indians in Chicago. Growth and Change in a Model Minority" in *Ethnic Chicago,* edited by Melvin J. Holli and Peter d'A. Jones. Grand Rapids: William B. Eerdmans Publishing, 1995.

Williams, Raymond B. *Religions of Immigrants from India and Pakistan, New Threads in the American Tapestry.* Cambridge: Cambridge University Press, 1988.

Irish:

Biles, Roger. *Big City Boss in Depression and War: Mayor Edward J. Kelly of Chicago.* DeKalb: Northern Illinois University Press, 1984.

Fanning, Charles. *Finley Peter Dune and Mr. Dooley: The Chicago Years.* Lexington: University Press of Kentucky, 1978.

Farrell, James T. *Studs Lonigan: A Trilogy.* New York: Modern Library, 1935.

Farrell, James T. *A World I Never Made.* Cleveland: World Publishing Company, 1947.

Farrell, James T. *Father and Son.* New York: Vanguard Press, 1940.

Farrell, James T. *My Days of Anger.* New York: Vanguard Press, 1943.

Funchion, Michael F. *Chicago's Irish Nationalists, 1881-1890.* New York: Arno Press, 1976.

Gleason, William F. *Daley of Chicago.* New York: Simon and Schuster, 1970.

Green, Paul Michael. "Irish in Chicago: The Multiethnic Road to Machine Success." In *Ethnic Chicago,* ed. by Melvin Holli and Peter D'A. Jones. Grand Rapids: William B. Eerdmans Publishing Co., 1981.

McCaffery, Lawrence J., Ellen Skerrett, Michael F. Funchion, Charles Fanning. *The Irish in Chicago.* University of Illinois Press, 1987.

McMahon, Eileen. "What Parish Are You From?" *The Chicago Irish Parish Community and Race Relations, 1916-1970.* Lexington, KY: University Press of Kentucky, 1995.

Shanabruch, Charles. *Chicago's Catholics: The Evolution of an American Identity.* South Bend, IN: University of Notre Dame Press, 1981.

Italians:

Candeloro, Dominic. "Chicago's Italians: A Survey of the Ethnic Factor." In *Ethnic Chicago,* ed. by Melvin Holli and Peter d'A. Jones. 4th ed. Grand Rapids: Eerdmans, 1995.

Gambino, Richard. *Blood of My Blood: The Dilemma of Italian Americans.* Garden City, NY: Doubleday, 1974 and 1996.

Giordano, Joseph, ed. *The Italian-American Catalog.* Garden City, NY: Doubleday, 1986.

Agnelli, Fondazione Giovanni. *The Italian Americans: Who They Are, Where They Live, How Many They Are.* Turin, 1980.

Gardaphe, Fred L. *Italian Signs, American Streets,* Durham: Duke University Press, 1996.

Gardaphe, Fred L. *Dagoes Read: Tradition and the Italian-American Writer,* Toronto: Guernica Editions, 1996.

Mangione, Jerre Gerlando and Ben Morreale. *La Storia: Five Centuries of the Italian American Experience.* New York: Harper Collins, 1992.

Japanese:

Daniels, Roger, Sandra C. Taylor and Harry H.L. Kitano, eds. *Japanese Americans: From Relocation to Redress.* Salt Lake City: University of Utah Press, 1986.

Kessler, Lauren. *Stubborn Twig: Three Generations in the Life of a Japanese American Family.* New York: Random House, 1993.

Osaka, Masako. "Japanese Americans: Melting into the All-American Melting Pot" in *Ethnic Chicago: A Multicultural Portrait.* Edited by Holli and Jones. 4th Ed. Grand Rapids: Eerdmans, 1995.

Weglyn, Michi, *Years of Infamy.* New York: William Morrow and Company, 1976.

Jews:

Baum, Charlotte, Paula Hyman and Sonya Michel. *The Jewish Woman in America.* New York: Plume Books, 1975, 1976.

Cutler, Irving H. *The Jews of Chicago: From Shtetl to Suburb.* Urbana: University of Illinois Press, 1995.

Jewish Federation. *JUF Guide to Jewish Living in Chicago, 1995-96.*

Flannery, Edward H. *The Anguish of the Jews: Twenty-Three Centuries of Antisemitism.* New York: Stimulus Books.

Lerner, Michael and Cornel West. *Jews & Blacks: Let the Healing Begin.* New York: G.P. Putnam's Sons, 1995.

Singer, David and Ruth Seldin, eds. *American Jewish Year Book* Vol. 96. New York: American Jewish Committee, 1996.

Koreans:

Kim, Elaine and Eui-Young Yu. *Korean American Life Stories from East to West,* New York: New Press, 1996.

Lee, Helie. *Still Life with Rice.* New York: Scribner, 1996.

Lithuanians:

Van Reenan, Antanas J. *Lithuanian Diaspora: Königsberg to Chicago.* University Press of America, 1990.

Mexicans:

de la Garza, Rodolfo O. et al. *Latino Voices: Mexican, Puerto Rican & Cuban Perspectives on American Politics.* Boulder, CO: Westview Press, 1992.

Novas, Himilce. *Everything You Need to Know About Latino History.* New York: Penguin Books, 1994.

Padilla, Felix M. *Latino Ethnic Consciousness: The Case of Mexican Americans and Puerto Ricans in Chicago.* South Bend, IN: University of Notre Dame Press, 1985.

Native Americans:

American Indian Economic Development Association. *Chicago Native American Demographic Profile.* Chicago, 1994.

Beck, David, *The Chicago American Indian Community, 1893-1988: Annotated Bibliography and Guide to Sources in Chicago.* Chicago: NAES College Press, 1988.

Strauss, Terry, ed. *Indians of the Chicago Area.* 2nd ed. Chicago: NAES College Press, 1990.

Palestinians:

Abraham and Abraham. *Arabs in the New World,* Wayne State University Press, 1983.

Cainkar, Dr. Louise. *Palestinian Immigration in the U.S.* (forthcoming from Temple University Press).

Hanania, Ray. *I'm Glad I Look Like a Terrorist: Growing up Arab in America.* Tinley Park, IL: USG Publishing Inc., 1996

Lamb, David. *The Arabs: Journeys Beyond the Mirage.* New York: First Vintage Books, 1987.

Naff, Alixa, *Becoming Americans,* Southern Illinois University Press, 1985.

Poles:

Grammich, Clifford A. *The Chicago Area Polish Community: An MCIC Special Survey Report.* Chicago: Metro Chicago Information Center, 1992.

Kantowicz, Edward R. *Polish-American Politics in Chicago, 1888-1940.* Chicago: University of Chicago Press, 1975.

Lopata, Helena Znaniecka. *Polish Americans: Status Competition in an Ethnic Community.* Englewood Cliffs, NJ: Prentice Hall, 1976.

Lopata, Helena Znaniecka with Mary Patrice Erdmans. *Polish Americans* (2nd ed.). New Brunswick, NJ: Transaction, 1994.

Pacyga, Dominic. *Polish Immigrants and Industrial Chicago: Workers on the South Side, 1880-1922.* Columbus: Ohio State University Press, 1991.

Pacyga, Dominic and Ellen Skerrett. *Chicago, City of Neighborhoods.* Chicago: Loyola University Press, 1986.

Thomas, W.I. and Florian W. Znaniecki. *The Polish Peasant in Europe and America.* New York: Dover, 1918-1920/1958.

Puerto Ricans:

de la Garza, Rodolpho O. et al. *Latino Voices: Mexican, Puerto Rican, & Cuban Perspectives on American Politics.* Boulder, CO: Westview Press, 1992.

Jennings, James and Monte Rivera, eds. *Puerto Rican Politics in Urban America.* Westport, CN: Greenwood Press, 1984.

Novas, Himilce. *Everything You Need to Know About Latino History.* New York: Penguin Books, 1994.

Padilla, Felix M. *Latino Ethnic Consciousness: The Case of Mexican-Americans and Puerto Ricans in Chicago.* South Bend: Notre Dame Press, 1985.

Padilla, Felix M. *Puerto Rican Chicago.* South Bend: Notre Dame Press, 1985.

Serbians:

Blesich, Mirko and Danica, compilers and editors. *The Serbian Who's Who: Biographic Directory of Americans and Canadians of Serbian Descent.* Park Ridge, IL.: A Serb World Magazine Publication, 1983.

Colakovich, Branko M. *Yugoslav Migrations to America.* San Francisco: R. & E. Research Associates, 1973.

Gakovich, R.P. and M.M. Radovich. *Serbs in the U.S. and Canada: A Comprehensive Bibliography.* Minneapolis: University of Minnesota, Immigration History Research Center, 1976.

Halpern, Joel. *A Serbian Village.* New York: Columbia University Press, 1958. Revised ed. New York: Harper and Row, 1967.

Halpern, Joel and Barbara Kerewski-Halpern. *A Serbian Village in Historical Perspective.* New York: Holt, Rinehart and Winston, 1972.

Pavlovich, Paul. *The Serbians: The Story of a People.* Don Mills, Ontario: Serbian Heritage Books, 1983.

Petrovich, Micheal Boro and Joel Halpern. "Serbs" in the *Harvard Encyclopedia of American Ethnic Groups.* Cambridge: Belknap Press, 1980.

Slovaks:

Beliansky, J. *The Unconquerable Slovaks.* Slovak Research Institute of America. Lakewood,1988.

Dola, G. *A History of the Slovak Evangelical Lutheran Church in the United States of America, 1902-1927.* St. Louis: Concordia Publishing House, 1955.

First Catholic Slovak Union. *Slovak Catholic Parishes and Institutions in the U.S. and Canada.* Cleveland: First Catholic Slovak Union Printery, 1955.

Swedes:

Anderson, Philip J. and Dag Blanck, eds. *Swedish American Life in Chicago: Cultural and Urban Aspects of an Immigrant People 1850-1930.* Urbana and Chicago: University of Illinois Press, 1992.

Beijorn, Ulf. *Swedes in Chicago: A Demographic and Social Study of 1846-1880.* Chicago: Chicago Historical Society, 1971.

Ukrainians:

Kuropas, Myron. "Ukrainian Chicago: The Making of a Nationality Group in America," in *Ethnic Chicago.*, ed. by Melvin Holli and Peter d'A. Jones. Grand Rapids: Eerdmans Publishing Co., 1995.

Kuropas, Myron, *The Ukrainian Americans: Roots and Aspiriations, 1884-1954.* Toronto: University of Toronto Press, 1991.

Subtelny, Orest. *Ukraine: A History.* Toronto: University of Toronto Press, 1988.

Vietnamese:

Huynh Dinh Te, *Introduction to Vietnamese Culture,* San Diego: San Diego University Multicultural Resource Center, 1989.

Multi-ethnic:

Borjas, George J. and Stephen J. Trejo. "Immigrant Participation in the Welfare System." *Industrial and Labor Relations Review* 44 No. 2 (1991).

Chan, Sucheng. *Asian Americans: An Interpretive History.* Boston: Twayne Publishers, 1991.

Cutler, Irving. *Chicago: Metropolis of the Mid-Continent.* 3rd ed. Chicago: Kendell/Hunt Publishing Co., 1982.

Chicago Department of Development and Planning. *Historic City: The Settlement of Chicago.* Chicago, 1976.

Cornelius, Wayne A., Philip L. Martin and James F. Hollifield. *Controlling Immigration: A Global Perspective.* Stanford: Stanford University Press, 1994.

Dalton. Harlon L. *Racial Healing: Confronting the Fear Between Blacks and Whites.* New York: Doubleday, 1995.

Glazer, Nathan. *Ethnic Dilemmas 1964-1982.* Cambridge, MA: Harvard University Press, 1983.

Glazer, Nathan and Daniel P. Moynihan. *Beyond the Melting Pot.* Cambridge, MA: MIT Press, 1963

Heer, David. *Immigration in America's Future: Social Science Findings and the Policy Debate.* University of Southern California: Westview Press, 1996.

Holli, Melvin G. and Peter d'A. Jones, eds. *Ethnic Chicago: A Multicultural Portrait.* 4th ed. Grand Rapids: Eerdmans Publishing Co., 1995.

Jencks, Christopher. *Rethinking Social Policy.* New York: HarperCollins, 1992.

Kessner, Thomas and Betty Boyd Caroli, *Today's Immigrants, Their Stories: A New Look at the Newest Americans.* London: Oxford University Press, 1982.

Krickus, Richard. *Pursuing the American Dream: White Ethnics and the New Populism.* New York: Doubleday, 1975.

Kull, Andrew. *The Color-Blind Constitution.* Cambridge, MA.: The Harvard University Press, 1992.

Latino Institute. *Latinos Face to Face / Latinos Cara a Cara.* Chicago: October 1994.

Latino Institute and Office for Social Policy Research, Northern Illinois University. *Indicators for Understanding: A Profile of Metro Chicago's Immigrant Community.* Chicago: 1995.

Latino Institute. *A Profile of Nine Latino Groups in Chicago.* Chicago: October 1994.

Latino Institute. *Latino Statistics and Data. Latino-Origin Groups.* No. 5. Chicago: August 1995.

Lee, Joann Faung Jean, *Asian Americans.* New York: New Press, 1991.

Lindberg, Richard. *Passport's Guide to Ethnic Chicago: A Complete Guide to the Many Faces & Cultures of Chicago.* Lincolnwood, IL: Passport Books, 1993.

McClain, Paula D. and Joseph Stewart, Jr. *Can We All Get Along? Racial and Ethnic Minorities in American Politics.* Boulder: Westview Press, 1995.

Pachon, Harry and Louis DeSipio. *New Americans by Choice: Political Perspectives of Latino Immigrants.* Boulder: Westview Press, 1994.

Reimers, David M. *Still the Golden Door: The Third World Comes to America.* New York: Columbia University Press, 1985.

Sowell, Thomas. *The Economics and Politics of Race: An International Perspective.* New York: William Morrow and Co., 1983.

Stavans, Ilan. *The Hispanic Condition: Refections on Culture and Identity.* New York: HarperCollins Publishing, 1996.

Steinberg, Stephen. *The Ethnic Myth. Race, Ethnicity & Class in America.* Boston: Beacon Press, 1981, 1989.

Takaki, Ronald. *Strangers from a Different Shore: A History of Asian Americans.* Boston: Little, Brown and Company, 1989.

Ungar, Sanford J. *Fresh Blood: The New American Immigrants.* New York: Simon and Schuster, 1995.

U.S. Commission on Civil Rights. *Civil Rights Issues Facing Asian Americans in Metropolitan Chicago.* Washington, D.C., 1995.

Zorbaugh, Harvey. *The Gold Coast and the Slums.* Chicago: University of Chicago Press, 1929.

RICHARD M. DALEY
MAYOR

PROCLAMATION

WHEREAS, the Illinois Ethnic Coalition was founded in 1971, and is Chicago's oldest multi-ethnic, multi-racial coalition; and

WHEREAS, the Illinois Ethnic Coalition is a network of civic-minded individuals who represent Chicago's diverse communities while promoting intergroup understanding and cooperation; and

WHEREAS, the Illinois Ethnic Coalition has published the *Ethnic Handbook: A Guide to the Cultures and Traditions of Chicago's Diverse Communities*, which profiles 33 of our city's prominent ethnic communities, supplying information on demographics, historical backgrounds, immigration and migration patterns, languages, religions, traditions, holidays and special events, common names, major issues political participation and myths and misconceptions; and

WHEREAS, the *Ethnic Handbook* also contains personal essays, ethnic maps for Chicago and Cook County, an appendix of important immigrant laws and a recommended reading list; and

WHEREAS, this user-friendly guide will help not-for-profit organizations, the business community, educators, journalists, government agencies and anyone wanting information about Chicago's diverse ethnic and racial groups; and

WHEREAS, the *Ethnic Handbook* is the third in a series of resources that the Illinois Ethnic Coalition has published this year to improve intergroup understanding; and

WHEREAS, the *Ethnic Handbook* is an affirmation and celebration of pluralism--a tribute to the many communities that make Chicago a vibrant, world-class city:

NOW, THEREFORE, I, RICHARD M. DALEY, MAYOR OF THE CITY OF CHICAGO, do hereby proclaim December 9, 1996, to be ETHNIC HANDBOOK DAY IN CHICAGO, in honor of the publication of the Ethnic Handbook.

Dated this 5th day of December, 1996.

Mayor